KILL THE INDIAN, SAVE THE MAN

Other Books by Ward Churchill

Authored: *On the Justice of Roosting Chickens:*
Reflections on the Consequences of U.S. Imperial Arrogance
And Criminality (2003)

Perversions of Justice:
Indigenous Peoples and Angloamerican Law (2003)

Acts of Rebellion:
The Ward Churchill Reader (2003)

Fantasies of the Master Race:
Literature, Cinema and the Colonization of American Indians (1992, 1998)

Struggle for the Land:
Native North American Resistance to Genocide, Ecocide and Colonization (1993, 1999)

Indians Are Us?
Culture and Genocide in Native North America (1994)

From a Native Son:
Selected Essays in Indigenism, 1985-1995 (1996)

Que Sont les Indiens Devenus? (1994)

Since Predator Came:
Notes from the Struggle for American Indian Liberation (1995)

A Little Matter of Genocide:
Holocaust and Denial in the Americas, 1492 to the Present (1997)

Coauthored: *Culture versus Economism:*
Essays on Marxism in the Multicultural Arena (1984)
with Elisabeth R. Lloyd

Agents of Repression:
The FBI's Secret Wars Against the Black Panther Party and the American Indian
Movement (1988)
with Jim Vander Wall

The COINTELPRO Papers:
Documents from the FBI's Secret Wars Against Dissent in the United States (1990)
with Jim Vander Wall

Pacifism as Pathology:
Reflections on the Role of Armed Struggle in North America (1998)
with Mike Ryan

Edited: *Marxism and Native Americans* (1983)

Critical Issues in Native North America, 2 vols. (1989–90)

Das indigene Amerika und die marxistiche Tradition:
Eine kontroverse Debatte über Kultur, Industrialismus und Eurozentrismus (1993)

Coedited: *Cages of Steel:*
The Politics of Imprisonment in the United States (1992)
with J.J. Vander Wall

Islands in Captivity:
The Record of the International Tribunal on the Rights of Indigenous Hawaiians,
    2 vols. (2004)
with Sharon H. Venne

KILL THE INDIAN, SAVE THE MAN

The Genocidal Impact of
American Indian Residential Schools

BY WARD CHURCHILL

CITY LIGHTS BOOKS
SAN FRANCISCO

Cover design by Rex Ray
Book design by Elaine Katzenberger
Typography by Harvest Graphics

Library of Congress Cataloging-in-Publication Data

Churchill, Ward.
    Kill the Indian, save the man : the genocidal impact of American Indian residential
schools / by Ward Churchill.
        p.   cm.
    Includes bibliographical references and index.
    ISBN 0-87286-434-0
    1. Off-reservation boarding schools—History.   2. Indian children—Relocation—
United States—History.   3. Indian children—Education.   4. Indian children—Social
conditions.   5. Indians of North America—Government policy.   6. United States—
Social policy.   7. United States—Race relations.   I. Title.
    E97.C57 2005
    371.829'97—dc22

                                                                            2004008941

Visit our web site: www.citylights.com

CITY LIGHTS BOOKS are edited by Lawrence Ferlinghetti and Nancy J. Peters and published
at the City Lights Bookstore, 261 Columbus Avenue, San Francisco, CA 94133

ACKNOWLEDGMENTS

Thanks are due to Shiinindio (John Peter Kelly) for his counsel and encouragement in my preparation of this book, inspired as it was by the fate of his late daughter-and my own much beloved wife-Kizhiibaabinisek (Leah Renae Kelly), one of the myriad victims still being claimed by the genocide embodied in Canada's Indian residential schools. Thanks also to the many others who have shared their stories and the immensity of their pain as I've tried to come to grips with the sheer magnitude of what has happened, and continues to happen, to my people. My deepest appreciation extends as well to my sisters and brothers in Colorado AIM, who have over the past quarter-century allowed me to draw quite steadily upon the strength of their resolve to fight back. Too, there is Elaine Katzenberger, my friend and editor at City Lights, who has not only believed in this project from its beginning, but the calmness and quiet consistency of whose support has done more than I can say to ensure its completion. Finally, my eternal gratitude goes to Natsu Taylor Saito, who not only read, absorbed, and often improved upon every word as it was put to paper, but who has routinely displayed the extraordinary humanity of understanding what must have seemed an endless stream of often tearful silences that attended my writing of them. To all of you, I owe debts I can only I can only hope this book in some measure repays.

for little Charlie Wenjack,
and all the other youngsters, then and now,
lost to the residential schools

CONTENTS

FORWARD

Charlie Wenjack

(Who died in 1966, aged twelve, running away from an Indian residential
school near Kenora, Ontario, trying to get back to his father and his people)

> Walk on, little Charlie
> Walk on through the snow.
> Heading down the railway line,
> Trying to make it home.
> Well, he's made it forty miles,
> Six hundred left to go.
> It's a long old lonesome journey,
> Shufflin' through the snow.
>
> He's lonesome and he's hungry,
> It's been a time since last he ate,
> And as the night grows bolder,
> He wonders at his fate.
> For his legs are wracked with pain
> As he staggers through the night.
> And sees through his troubled eyes,
> That his hands are turning white.
>
> Lonely as a single star,
> In the skies above,
> His father in a mining camp,
> His mother in the ground,
> And he's looking for his dad,
> And he's looking out for love,
> Just a lost little boy by the railroad track
> Heading homeward bound.

Is that the great Wendigo
Come to look upon my face?
And are the skies exploding
Down the misty aisles of space?
Who's that coming down the track,
Walking up to me?
Walk on, little Charlie,
Walk on through the snow.
Moving down the railway line,
Try to make it home.
And he's made it forty miles,
Six hundred left to go.
It's a long old lonesome journey,
Shufflin' through the snow.

—Willie Dunn

Tracing a Contour of Colonialism
American Indians and the Trajectory of Educational Imperialism
by George E. Tinker

> There are neither good nor bad colonists: there are colonists.
>
> —Jean-Paul Sartre
> 1957

Who can quarrel with education? That much, at least, should be an unmitigated good deriving from the last five hundred years of eurowestern colonialism. And the Indian residential schools, created by church denominations and the federal governments of the United States and Canada, were the best attempt of the liberal colonizer to advance the state of Indian peoples in North America.[1] Such is the colonizer's apologetic for colonization and rationalization of conquest. In this volume, however, Ward Churchill lays to rest any misapprehensions we may still harbor that the residential education of American Indian children has in any way functioned as a good in native communities over the past couple of centuries. Again and again, with incisive argumentation and lucid citation of evidence, Churchill demonstrates that the Indian schools were consciously designed as part of the colonizers' imperial project.

In 1835, in his "Minute on Education," T.B. Macaulay had already understood the role of schooling for the colonized as a principal tool of empire. Living on the subcontinent as a member of the British "Supreme Council of India," and signaling the beginning of what became known in colonial hierarchies as "indirect rule," Macaulay held that the task of empire in India called for educating "a class who may be interpreters between us and the millions we govern, a class of persons, Indian in blood and colour, but English in taste, in opinions, in morals, and in intellect."[2] Serious efforts to accomplish similar results had commenced in the United States shortly after the War of 1812 under the leadership of Thomas L. McKenney, who served four presidents, first as Superintendent of Indian Trade and then, beginning in 1824, as head of the newly created Office of Indian Affairs.[3] Close to missionaries and intellectually/politically liberal, McKenney won federal support through the so-called Civilization Fund for early mission schools and introduced rhetoric concerning euroamerica's supposed "civilizing project" that remained largely unchanged for the next century-and-a-half.

Unlike the model developed by British imperialism in India and much of the rest of the world, however, the colonization of North America took the form of settler-state colonialism (that is, of literally supplanting indigenous peoples within their own territories).[4] This meant that in North America, as was also true in Australia and New Zealand, the colonizer had to undertake measures very different—and far more drastic—than merely training a new entrepreneurial "broker class" among the colonized.[5] To legitimate an ever-increasing occupancy of the land by whites, the U.S. and Canada were compelled to reduce the native population to a state of subjugation so complete that they might "willingly" concede the whole of their territorial entitlement to the settler society.

"Education" of the colonized became a central and conscious technique for attaining this end. Verbiage concerning the "betterment" of "savage" natives was regularly voiced by policymakers, their missionary supporters, and those whose job was implementation of schools for native children.[6] The larger goal was always not only the control of native peoples, but the "consensual"—i.e., "legal"—theft of their properties. It was *this* intended outcome which dictated that a particular mode of schooling, quite distinct from that envisioned by Macaulay for use in India, be visited upon American Indian children.

In India, with its huge population, imperial strategists deemed it most cost-effective to rely upon manipulation rather than sheer coercion in the extraction of labor and other resources from the colonized mass. Hence, a relative few of the latter were indoctrinated from childhood to assist the British in maximizing the efficiency of their exploitative endeavor.[7] In more sparsely populated North America, by contrast—given the settlers' oft-stated ambition to expropriate *everything* possessed by the natives—only the most comprehensive sort of assimilation posed a viable alternative to the campaigns of physical extermination by which indigenous resistance was quelled until the final decade of the nineteenth century.[8]

The type of schooling necessary to attainment of so sweeping an assimilationist agenda devolved upon the inculcation of subservience among those forced to undergo it. Thus, as Churchill demonstrates, the curriculum imposed on American Indian youngsters in what were openly described as "industrial schools" focused mostly upon "training" rather than education in any real sense.[9] Training meant teaching young Indian women to become maids and household servants—or to toil in commercial laundries—while young men were expected to master the skills needed to place them in the cheap hire of ranchers and farmers—and sometimes factory, mine or mill operators—throughout the western U.S.[10] Most importantly, as Secretary of the Interior Carl Schurz expressed it, the object was to impart the eurowestern concept of *work* upon every pupil. This, in order to "wean" them from their traditional ways of life and drive them into the vortex of euroamerica's emerging capital-driven wage labor economy. [11]

Churchill presses the point even further, demonstrating that in the course of providing "vocational" training, the schools functioned as no more than factories—or labor camps—producing goods and generating profits. This was a predictable result and even mandated by Washington, since Congress insisted from the outset that the process of Indian residential education be rendered self-supporting.[12] Coupling forceful argumentation to the evidence accruing from his meticulous research, Churchill relates the toll taken among the supposed beneficiaries of the system and thereby shatters any honest misperception that the boarding schools were spawned of white benevolence.

For the most part, the Indian schools were a product of nineteenth-century liberal inclinations born of roughly four centuries of evolution in eurowestern theology and philosophy. One could seek on this basis to make the case that schools and education embodied the best attempt of liberal politicians and protestant church officials to soften the blow upon native peoples already pushed to the brink of extinction by the ravages of conquest. Indeed, one could try and claim that the whole effort was aimed at genuinely improving the lot of those most heavily victimized by the acquisition and consolidation of the North American settler states. Such, however, is merely the substance of standard apologist contentions that whatever was done, no matter how egregiously "in error," was motivated, and thus presumably redeemed, by "the best of intentions."[13]

More accurately, as now countless authors engaged in the discourse of "postcolonialism" have observed, even the best European thinking during this period called "The Enlightenment" was *always* dedicated to the eurosu-premacist task of rationalizing and legitimating empire.[14] Here, it matters lit-tle whether one considers the thought of Hobbes or Hume, Locke or Hegel, Jefferson or Mill. Nor, somewhat ironically, should Karl Marx be excluded from the line-up, no more than Descartes, Kant or Montesquieu. All were hopelessly mired in the intellectual/moral morass of trying to frame Europe's blood-drenched reality in terms of an "unparalleled advancement" in actual-izing the loftiest of ideals.[15] Far from offsetting or countering the vulgarities of Europe's imperial pretension, Enlightenment philosophy served as the intellectual engine powering its expansion to global proportions.[16]

While the rhetoric and policies that would lead to the residential schools were being articulated as early as 1816, McKenney's vision began to find programmatic traction only towards the end of the century, a time when the military capacity of North America's indigenous nations to resist dispos-session was thought to have been largely exhausted, the overall native popu-lation reduced by privation, disease and attritional warfare to a "manageable" number.[17] The shift in emphasis from annihilating to assimilating the residue of surviving Indians commenced in earnest following the end of a very uncivilized civil war in the U.S. when newly installed President Ulysses S. Grant, responding to the concerted lobbying of church reformers and liberal politicians, enunciated what was referred to as his "Peace Policy" in 1869.[18] From there on, an ever-increasing weight was placed upon perfection of the means by which the remains of Native North America might be most expe-ditiously digested. And, in this connection, "education" constituted a—per-haps *the*—key ingredient.[19]

The early stages of the reform movement resulted in a long series of annual meetings held at Lake Mohonk, New York, beginning in 1883.[20] Calling themselves "Friends of the Indian," these conferences initially brought together much the same cast of characters who had successfully swayed Grant during his two terms in office (1869-1877). The growing extent of their influence is revealed, however, in the fact that a range of high government officials, including three presidents, could soon be numbered among the participants.[21] Also involved was Massachusetts Senator Henry M. Dawes, engineer of the 1887 General Allotment Act, under which indi-vidual rather than communal ownership of land was imposed on Indian reservations throughout the U.S., thereby undermining the integrity/cohe-sion of indigenous societies while providing a legal pretext for divesting native people of approximately two-thirds of the property still in their possession.[22]

Three principle themes emerged early on in the Lake Mohonk conferences and were thereafter regularly deployed as rationales guiding the formulation of federal Indian policies: 1) the "need" for inculcation of individualism among native people, 2) that to achieve this end Indians should be universally "educated" to hold eurowestern beliefs, and that, 3) all Indians, duly educated and thus individualized, should be absorbed as citizens into the U.S. body politic. Individualism, of course — as was very concretely reflected in the rationale advanced in support of the Allotment Act — represented the very antithesis of the traditional communal values upon which all American Indian societies are based.[23] As U.S. Indian Commissioner George Manypenny put it as early as 1856, for assimilation to occur, it was necessary that Indians learn to say "I" instead of "we," "me" instead of "us," "mine" instead of "ours."[24]

The imposition of U.S. citizenship, which is also covered in part by the Allotment Act,[25] meant first and foremost that Indians would no longer be citizens of their own nations in any genuine sense — indeed, the term subsequently employed, even by most Indians, has been "tribal members"[26] — but would henceforth be held accountable to the internal laws of the United States. To that end, the reformers put an end to federal treatymaking with Indians through a rider attached to the 1871 Appropriations Act,[27] thereby abolishing the last vestige of the nation-to-nation negotiations between the U.S. and indigenous peoples that had previously prevailed. With formal acknowledgment of native sovereignty thus nullified,[28] congressional reformers moved through the 1885 Major Crimes Act to assert U.S. jurisdiction over all that was left of the Indians' reserved territories.[29] Incorporating each Indian as a citizen directly into the U.S. polity, thereby finalizing her/his subordination to the settler state's "rule of law," was simply the culmination of the whole thrust. At that point, the internal colonization of Native North America was effectively complete.[30]

The only remaining task was, when- and wherever possible, to condition native people to be not only accepting but embracing of their circumstance. Where this was not possible, the goal was to render them to all intents and purposes dysfunctional (i.e., psychologically/intellectually incapable of coherent resistance). Failing that, the literal rather than figurative deaths of genuine "recalcitrants," all too frequently inflicted by their own hands, was still considered an "acceptable cost" attending fulfillment of settler policy objectives.[31] At all three levels, what Churchill calls "the residential mode of schooling" was found to be an ideal mechanism with which to wreak the desired havoc. Hence, the longterm emphasis placed by assimilationists upon the "education" of American Indian children.

Taken, often by force, from their homes at ages as young as four, transported to facilities remote from their families and communities,[32] confined there for a decade or more, relentlessly stripped of their cultural identities while being just as methodically indoctrinated to see their traditions — and thus themselves — through the eyes of their colonizers, chronically malnourished and overworked, drilled to regimental order and subjected to the harshest forms of corporal punishment, this was the lot of one in every two native youngsters in North America for five successive generations. Of those ushered into the steadily expanding system of residential schools during its first forty years or more, about half did not survive the experience. In other words, roughly one-quarter of the American Indian population during the early twentieth century was physically destroyed by the process of schooling.[33]

It is well to reiterate that this protracted horror was for the most part perpetrated by self-styled progressive politicians and liberal churchmen, not the ostensibly less sensitive "conservatives" among their peers. Worth noting, too, is the fact that, for all their humanitarian veneer, the "enlightened" settler élite which advocated, implemented and maintained the system suffered no discernible qualms in hiring the very dregs of their society — sadists, pedophiles and the like — to preside over the indigenous youngsters consigned to residential institutions. Thus, as Churchill recounts in brief but agonizing detail, the "discipline" visited upon native children often assumed the form of outright torture.[34] As well, sexual predation was common in most, if not all the schools. At some, it appears that every student, without exception, was raped, many of them regularly, over periods of years.[35]

Such things did not happen to all children who passed through the system, of course. Equally true, however, is the fact that virtually every child knew another — or several — to whom it *did* happen, or *was happening*. Thus were they forced to face on a daily basis the nature of their own/their parents'/their people's powerlessness to prevent it, and thereby to confront continuously the grim truth of their own vulnerability. The knowledge that the same thing(s) *could* happen to any — or each — of them, at any moment, and that the choice of whether or not it happened was entirely in the hands of the predators who served as their overseers, was unavoidable. This awful reality, taken in combination with the "normal" techniques employed by school authorities to achieve the desired deculturation/reculturation of their charges, all but guaranteed that *every* student would suffer the effects of severe emotional trauma.[36]

Hence, the ubiquitous "residential school syndrome"—a complex and intractable blend of devastated self-concept and self-esteem, psychic numbing, chronic anxiety, insecurity and depression—to which Churchill devotes an entire section of his essay. It must be understood, moreover, that such results embody the *best case* scenario. For those who *were* directly assailed with serious physical violence, sexual abuse, or both—and they were/are legion—the psychoemotional desolation was—or remains—worse still. Usually.[37] And this goes far towards accounting for the endemic alcoholism, catastrophic suicide rates, pervasive domestic violence and a host of related maladies with which Native North America has been afflicted, in some ways increasingly so, for the past century or more.[38]

I must say at this point that the issues raised here are for me, as they are for all native people, exceedingly personal. This is so in a way that both underpins and transcends the intellectual understandings embodied in our common experience of and resistance to racial/colonial oppression. Every American Indian knows and will always know in the depths of his or her gut the pain with and of which Churchill writes. We know it, moreover, irrespective of whether we ourselves, personally, ever spent so much as an instant in a residential school (or a prison, a concentration camp, a psychiatric ward, or some comparable facility). The truth of this is bound up in the fact that each of us has felt the disemboweling anguish attending emotional intimacy with one or more of those who *did* suffer the schools and/or was raised by someone ravaged by them.[39] Thus, through those we love most deeply do we incur knowledge firsthand of the ongoing carnage wrought therein.

For me, attainment of this excruciating insight devolved upon the nature of the life and death of my close friend and adopted brother, Donnie. Endowed with undeniable intellectual gifts, he was never able to bring his natural brilliance to bear in any sustained way. Instead, by the time of his suicide at the age of fifty-two, he had been living out an only slightly more figurative form of self-nullification for decades. Indeed, the whole of his adulthood had been consumed by an unending stream of nightmares and resulting periods of insomnia, the relentlessness of the depression which engulfed him punctuated mainly, if sporadically, by moments of screaming rage. At times, he was reduced to helpless tears. At others, we'd lose him for months on end to the oblivion of drunken despair.[40] In the end, a combination of alcohol and antidepressant medication became the instrument through which he obtained a final release from the misery which was perhaps the most constant theme of his existence.[41]

While the stories Donnie sometimes confided to those of us closest to him were seldom offered in chronological order, the sequence can be reconstructed. Among his earliest and most searing memories was when, as a small child—he was five at the time—he'd been taken off to boarding school. As he recalled, always with the sort of vividness that only serious trauma can induce, a Bureau of Indian Affairs police officer—Donnie usually described him as a "huge white man"—had forcibly removed him from his home in Kyle, on the Pine Ridge Reservation, quite literally stripping him from the arms of his weeping mother. He was then handcuffed to the dashboard of a patrol car while other children were collected. One by one, the youngsters were handcuffed together in a "daisy chain," until finally, his day's mission complete, the cop drove them to the town of St. Francis, South Dakota, about a hundred miles away. There, he delivered his carload of terrified captives to a Jesuit-run mission school.[42]

From that point on, things took a turn for the worse. Much worse. By the time he was six, the little boy was suffering sexual abuse at the hands of another huge white man at the school, an authority figure, a priest, who would steal into his room in the dead of night, force his submission to the act of sodomy, then threaten him with eternal damnation should he dare ever to speak of what had been done. This horror was repeated again and again— exactly how often is anybody's guess—and not just to Donnie. His roommate, Conrad, a child of the same age, was also and regularly raped by the same predator, who sometimes defiled both youngsters during a single evening.[43] In the mornings after, they'd often share their shame and humiliation, unspeakable as such things were to anyone but themselves, each whispering to the other of their hurt. In effect, they'd been fused by the mutuality of their helpless degradation in ways and to an extent unknowable to all who have not themselves experienced some comparable rape of the soul.[44]

With Conrad, the end came early. He committed suicide during his mid-teens.[45] For his part, Donnie seems as a consequence to have acquired an additional and incalculable burden, an enduring and intractable sense of guilt arising from the fact that he'd been unable somehow to protect his friend from the pattern of molestation that precipitated the hideously premature termination of his life.[46] There is much more that might be said with respect to Donnie's formative experiences in the school, and much of it he eventually did say to those of us near enough to hear, but what has been mentioned herein should be sufficient—indeed, *more* than sufficient—to explain the overpowering feelings of inadequacy against which he would have always, as best he could, to struggle. Given the malignancy of the self-concept with which he was saddled from the outset, and the near-absolute void of self-esteem this inevitably engendered, there can be little mystery in why Donnie was ultimately unsuccessful in reclaiming the man he might have been.[47]

The real wonder is that he fought so long and hard to do so. His ability to sustain himself at all can only have derived from an innate strength of character that is and was always staggering in its dimensions. Thus can we begin to assess the magnitude of what was taken by/lost to the residential schools. For, although I am compelled to write of Donnie in particular because of who he was and will always be to me, quite personally and uniquely, the truth of his life must be measured by standards other than my own heartfelt embrace of its particularity and uniqueness. His story is, after all, Conrad's as well. No less, is it that of all the other Conrads, in their hundreds, their thousands, each of them particular, each of them unique, each of them, like Donnie himself, endowed with talents thwarted long before they might have ripened or been constructively engaged.

What was lost in Donnie was lost not to him alone. Or to those of us who loved him. It was lost to and by us all. And, as it was with him, so it was with all the others claimed by the schools, each of them, child by child, generation after generation, for an entire century. He was/they were our future, the future of Native North America. As their prospects for living their lives as functional human beings were systematically demolished, so too were the prospects open to Native America as a whole by design foreclosed.[48] Understanding the situation of this continent's native people for what it is thus requires that the acuity with which each individual lost was/is experienced by those closest to him or her be extrapolated in such a way as to calibrate the impact of losing *all* such individuals, collectively, upon our communities, our societies, our cultures, and thus the possibilities inherent to our future.[49]

Put another way, there is a symmetry involved: as I was/am traumatized by the permanently traumatic effects of the residential school experience upon Donnie, so too is every American Indian who loves someone who suffered that experience. At this point in our history, that is, as I noted earlier, *all* of us. *Every* native person in North America is, figuratively speaking, either "a Donnie," or one who mourns him. The sorrow with which I write is thus a sorrow shared in common, lodged so deeply within the marrow of our lives that it has become definitive of our very identity as native people. In the collectivity of our grief, we are left with a yearning so powerful that it defies even the best effort at description. One either knows the feeling or one does not. Suffice it here to observe that what we crave is to recapture not only that which was but, more importantly, that which should have been.[50]

Without denying that there may well be an element of wistfulness at issue here — such would be an entirely natural reaction, given our circumstances — the matter nowhere reduces to mere self-indulgence or abstraction. The basis of our longing displays itself quite readily in terms of the most concrete possible need. This devolves upon the fact that native people are now living the future imposed upon us in the residential schools a generation and more ago. The reality we've thereby inherited is — as it was *meant* to be by those who imposed it — one of catastrophic dysfunction. Indian country is today a genuinely Fanonesque panorama marked not only by such earlier-mentioned factors as endemic alcoholism and suicide, but by the most grinding sort of destitution and ubiquitous forms of social violence (which were by all credible accounts completely absent from our own traditions).[51] The punch line, if one is needed, is the fact that the average life expectancy for an American Indian in either the U.S. or Canada is presently about fifty years, or one-third less than that evidenced by the settler population.[52] Such is the legacy of the schools.

At its best, the collective yearning of native people translates into an active effort at reclamation. It takes the form of an insistence — indeed, an assertion — that that which was will not be forever lost. It follows that, despite all that has happened, that which might/should have been can still and therefore *will* be. Much more than what is customarily referred to as a "culture of resistance" is involved. Although acts and postures of resistance are certainly integral to it, the process in which we are of both right and necessity engaged might more aptly be described as that of cultural revitalization and resurgence.[53] The evidence will be found on numerous fronts, from the ever-growing number of our young people choosing once again to speak their own languages to the reemergence and proliferation of such cardinal ceremonies as Sun Dances and Potlatches in areas/among peoples where such practices and the beliefs/values attending them were supposedly eradicated a century or more ago.[54]

Likewise, considerable evidence of revitalization will be found in an increasing willingness on the part of younger American Indians to directly confront those who would presume to continue the usurpation of our rights, politically, materially, or otherwise. Here again, examples abound, among the best-known being the armed clashes between U.S. authorities and the American Indian Movement at Wounded Knee in 1973,[55] and between Canadian forces and the Mohawk Warrior Society at the town of Oka, outside Montréal, in 1990.[56] Augmenting such in-your-face tactics has been a sustained initiative at the United Nations pursued over the past quarter-century by a range of native organizations, much of it geared to ensuring promulgation of a Universal Declaration of the Rights of Indigenous Peoples in international law.[57] Meanwhile, efforts to explicitly link the political and spiritual spheres of activity — that is, to reaffirm the traditional unity of the two — have been undertaken through forums such as the Indian Ecumenical Conferences organized by the late Robert K. Thomas.[58]

There is to be sure an intellectual component guiding the resurgence for which we yearn. It may in fact be likened both to the glue with which each of the dynamics just mentioned is bound to the others and the fuel by which they are each and equally propelled. While there are many facets to this indigenous intellectuality, some of them explored quite ably in books like Linda Tuhiwai Smith's *Decolonizing Methodologies* and Ngugi wa Thiong'o's *Decolonising the Mind*,[59] all of them hinge upon the procedure, fundamental to all native traditions with which I am in the least aware, of apprehending one's location in the present through the most rigorous scrutiny of the past which has led up to it. Such firmness of analytical grounding in turn allows for precision in determining what it is that must be done in the present if desired outcomes are to be attained in the years ahead. As Lakota elder Noble Red Man (Mathew King) used to put it: "You can't know how to get to where you want to go unless you know where you are now, and you can't know where you are now unless you can see clearly where it is that you've been."[60]

Few scholars have excelled Ward Churchill in applying Matthew's prescription for "seeing things clearly." Or of helping—sometimes forcing—others do so. The key to his approach in this regard, as he himself has elsewhere remarked, has always been his insistence upon "calling things by their right names."[61] By this, far more is meant than a simple rejection of euphemism. On the contrary, the scope of demystification Churchill has pursued over the past twenty years or more has evolved to include nearly the full inventory of "interpretive techniques"—from cinema to literature to historiography to political and legal theory—with which North America's settler intelligentsia has sought to expunge from the accuracy of memory certain actualities attending its forebears' initial "encounters" and subsequent "interactions" with the continent's indigenous peoples.[62] His overall project has thus been counterhegemonic in the truest sense.

It follows that in *Kill the Indian, Save the Man*, as in others of his books, Churchill takes as his first task a seizure of the vocabulary necessary to impart clarity of context and consequent implication. In this essay, as in others, the pivotal word is "genocide."[63] Restoring to the term the dignity of its proper meaning (i.e., its explanatory power), and in the process dispensing with the pretensions of those who have sought to constrain or dilute it as a means of fostering the comfortable illusion that it never "really" happened here, he positions himself—and readers as well—to explore with exactitude the topic upon which he has elected to focus.[64] As a result, like no other analyst to date, he has been able to segregate shadow from substance with regard to the form, function, and impacts of the systems of residential schooling imposed upon American Indians by both the U.S. and Canada.[65] So too, are the intentions of those who created and maintained those systems revealed for what they were.

Viewing the schools through the lens provided herein eliminates any possibility of ambiguity in assignment of their meaning. The death rates among children confined in such facilities was, after all, as high or higher than that prevailing in some of the nazis' more notorious concentration camps.[66] This was so not for a single decade, as in the camps like Dachau and Buchenwald, but for four decades, or five. Those in charge, both north of the border and south, determined not only such a toll to be "acceptable" but steadily increased the rate at which native youngsters were fed into the death mills. Nor can any significant proportion of these deaths be legitimately dismissed as "accidental." They for the most part resulted from a combination of malnutrition, overcrowding, forced labor and deficient medical care, the lethal effects of which were, as Churchill conclusively demonstrates, were well known to the bureaucrats who continued to pack the schools with victims. Needless to say, the abuses suffered by those like Donnie who survived, at least in an immediate sense, were entirely in keeping with this broader setting.[67]

Faced with this data, no honest observer can do other than conclude that the residential schools were mechanisms of genocide, purely, simply, and "by any other name." From there, the dominoes begin to fall rather naturally, precipitating an unambiguously radical reappraisal of the social matrix from which the genocide emerged. The Lake Mohonk Conference, for example, loses the benign complexion bestowed upon it through conventional settler scholarship. Far from being a well-intentioned assembly motivated, however arrogantly or erroneously, by a desire to "do good" for American Indians, it finds a more appropriate parallel in the infamous Wannsee Conference during which the nazis crafted their "Final Solution."[68] The liberal claim that they posed an "enlightened" and "humanitarian" alternative to the openly exterminationist policies embraced by their more conservative counterparts finds its echo in the instruction of Heinrich Himmler that European Jewry be eradicated in the most "humane" manner possible. Those, like Richard Henry Pratt in the U.S. and Duncan Campbell Scot in Canada, who implemented the scheme devised at Lake Mohonk find their peers, not among the Paolo Frieres of this world but among the Adolf Eichmanns.[69]

Tracing this line of reasoning to its logical conclusion, we find the supposed virtues of the Enlightenment tradition itself drawn squarely into question, its oft-asserted superiority to all other traditions swept away by the utter depravity of its practice, if not the values lodged at its core. So much for the incessantly extolled tenets of Eurosupremacism and the purported legitimacy of its adherents' "civilizing mission" vis-à-vis American Indians (or any other peoples, for that matter).[70] So much as well for the overweening sense of entitlement manifested by Eurosupremacists of every stripe—liberal and conservative, marxist and nazi alike—to possess or benefit from that which rightly belongs to others, or the proposition that there might be anything at all benevolent about their recently-professed inclination to "compensate" their victims (that is, to "share" some tidbit or another of what they've stolen with those from whom they've stolen it). As Russell Means has put it, "American Indians neither need nor want 'charity.' Instead, we demand justice, and justice itself demands that we receive it."[71]

For the members of any victim group, perhaps especially the members of a group which has been or is on the receiving end of genocide, hearing (or reading) such things said (or written) is of immense and undeniably therapeutic value.[72] Simply to hear the nature of one's victimization called by its right name affords immeasurable psychic relief. The more so when the correct name is put to one's perpetrators in such a way as to make it difficult or impossible for them to wriggle off the hook of their deeds.[73] Still more so when those who have benefited from or been otherwise complicit in the perpetration are called at least figuratively to account for what they've done/are doing.[74] Hearing it said, forcefully, coherently, as a matter of *fact* rather than "opinion," is often an empowering experience, enabling victims to internalize what has been said (or read) and say it themselves. As is all but axiomatic in the literature, such "recovery of voice" is a sure indicator that a process of repairing the effects of severe trauma has begun.[75]

This brings up the issue of whether "truth commissions" of the sort established in South Africa and several other Third World countries might, in connection with the residential schools, be appropriate to the U.S./Canadian context.[76] More pointedly, it raises questions with regard to how "healing and reconciliation"—in Canada, this three-word phrase has come to be used as if it formed a single word, and the same tendency is presently gaining momentum in the U.S.[77]—might fit into such a procedure. The answers can be advanced without hesitation. In South Africa and the other countries in which truth commissions have been established (Chile, for example), the régimes whose crimes are documented thereby had been removed as a prerequisite.[78] For an offending government to sponsor—which is to say *control*—the very entity charged with investigating/chronicling/assessing the nature and extent of its misconduct constitutes so transparent a subterfuge as to be unworthy of further comment.

How the matter of "healing" must be understood relates quite directly to this conclusion. Here, it is important to state the obvious: What American Indians are in need of healing *from* is the range of extraordinarily vicious wounds inflicted upon us in the residential schools. These institutions were not imposed gratuitously. They were purposefully designed to serve as an essential ingredient in a process through which the disempowerment and dispossession of native people was systematized, thereby facilitating consolidation of the U.S. and Canadian settler states. Those states continue to exist by virtue of the ongoing disempowerment, dispossession and generalized dysfunction inculcated among native people in the schools. Our wounding reconfiguration of relations between those formerly defined as oppressor and oppressed will finally usher into being some variation or many of what Ché Guevara once, in a moment of extraordinary optimism, described as "the new man."[106] We can hope, as Ché did, and as Churchill does, that this is so. In any event, we are obliged, all of us, to try realize the potentials inherent to such worthy dreams. We owe it, as Churchill says, not only to ourselves, but to the ancestors who fought so hard to prevent that which has come to pass, to the Donnies who have borne by far the worst torment of its coming, and, most of all, to our future generations, those whose pain and degradation we can yet avert. To love, we must fight,[107] as Ché put it, and Ward Churchill is to be thanked for having once again reminded us in the most forceful way of why this is so.

George Tinker is an enrolled member of the Osage Nation and has been an activist in urban American Indian communities for many years. Tinker is the author of Missionary Conquest: The Gospel and Native American Cultural Genocide, *among other works.*

Notes

1. For a thoroughgoing apology for the Catholic mission schools, see Francis Paul Prucha, S.J., *The Churches and the Indian Schools, 1888-1912* (Lincoln: University of Nebraska Press, 1979).

2. Thomas Babington Macaulay, "Minute of 2 February 1835 on Indian Education," *Macaulay: Prose and Poetry* (Cambridge, MA: Harvard University Press, 1957) p. 729. A broad overview of how the principle was applied throughout the Empire will be found in Martin Carnoy, *Education as Cultural Imperialism* (New York: David McKay, 1974).

3. Herman J. Viola, *Thomas L. McKenney: Architect of America's Early Indian Policy, 1816-1830* (Chicago: Swallow Press, 1974). Francis Paul Prucha, S.J., *The Great Father: The United States Government and the American Indian* (Lincoln: University of Nebraska Press, 1995), *inter alia*, but esp. the section entitled "The Role of Thomas L. McKenney," pp. 148*ff*.

4. For a seminal delineation of the distinctions separating settler-state colonialism from the more classic "overseas" variety, see A. Grenfell Price, *White Settlers and Native Peoples: An Historical Study of Racial Contacts between English-speaking Whites and Aboriginal Peoples in the United States, Canada, Australia and New Zealand* (Cambridge, UK: Cambridge University Press, 1950).

5. The term "broker class" is borrowed from Rodolfo Acuña, *Occupied America: A History of the Chicanos* (New York: HarperCollins, [3rd ed.] 1988) pp. 377-86.

6. An excellent selection of such statements is offered in Francis Paul Prucha, S.J., *Americanizing the American Indian: Writings by the "Friends of the Indian," 1880-1900* (Lincoln: University of Nebraska Press, 1973).

7. See V.V. Oak, *England's Educational Policy in India* (Madras: B.G. Paul, 1925); Edward Thompson and Geoffrey T. Garratt, *The Rise and Fulfillment of British Rule in India* (Allahabad: Central Book Depot, 1962).

8. On the extermination campaigns, see Ward Churchill, *A Little Matter of Genocide: Holocaust and Denial in the Americas, 1492 to the Present* (San Francisco: City Lights, 1997) esp. pp. 209-45. On the assimilationist alternative, see Frederick E. Hoxie, *A Final Promise: The Campaign to Assimilate the Indians, 1880-1920* (Lincoln: University of Nebraska Press, 1985).

9. Consider, for example, the 6th resolution contained in the Second Annual Address to the Public of the Lake Mohonk Conference (1884); "Resolved, That…our conviction has been strengthened as to the importance of taking Indian youth from the reservations to be trained in industrial schools placed among communities of white citizens"; cited from William T. Hagan, *The Lake Mohonk Conference of Friends of the Indian*, on-line at ohonkConference.asp. An early volume on the merits of training in the "domestic arts" should not go unnoticed here; see Pearl Idelia Ellis, *Americanization Through Homemaking* (Los Angeles: Wetzel, 1929).

10. Alice Littlefield and Martha C. Knack, *Native Americans and Wage Labor: Ethnohistorical Perspectives* (Norman: University of Oklahoma Press, 1996).

11. Carl Schurz, "Present Aspects of the Indian Problem," *North American Review*, cxxxiii (July 1881); excerpted in Prucha, *Americanizing the American Indian*, pp. 13-26.

12. This was not, as is often claimed, a "transient problem" afflicting the system of Indian residential schools mainly in "the early years." Indeed, as was outlined in the so-called Meriam Report, the budgetary situation had actually *worsened* during the 1920s; see Lewis Meriam, et al., *The Problem of Indian Administration* (Baltimore: Johns Hopkins University Press, 1928). Further examples were subsequently provided by then-future Indian Commissioner John Collier in an article entitled "The Indian Bureau's Record," published in *The Nation* on Oct. 5, 1932.

13. See, e.g., Prucha, *Churches and the Indian*.

14. For what may be the best overview, see Bart Moore-Gilbert, *Postcolonial Theory: Contexts, Practices, Politics* (London: Verso, 1997). Also see Patrick Williams and Laura Chrisman, eds., *Colonial Discourse and Post-Colonial Theory: A Reader* (New York: Columbia University Press, 1994); Bill Ashcroft, Gareth Griffiths and Helen Tifflin, eds., *The Post-Colonial Studies Reader* (New York: Routledge, 1995); Padmini Mongia, *Contemporary Postcolonial Theory: A Reader* (London/New York: Arnold, 1997).

15. Ironic, if only because Marx and Marxists have disavowed the European Enlightenment as an élitist discourse. See George Tinker, "Spirituality, Native American Personhood, Sovereignty and Solidarity," in K.C. Abraham and B. Mbuy-Beya, eds., *Spirituality in the Third World: A Cry for Life: Papers*

and *Reflections from the Third Assembly of the Ecumenical Association of Third World Theologians, Nairobi, Kenya, January 1992* (Maryknoll, NY: Orbis Books, 1994) pp. 119-32. For further indigenist critique, see Ward Churchill, ed., *Marxism and Native Americans* (Boston: South End Press, 1983), esp. the essays by Russell Means and Vine Deloria, Jr., entitled, respectively, "The Same Old Song" (pp. 19-34) and "Circling the Same Old Rock" (pp. 113-36). To get some of the more relevant aspects Marx's thinking from the proverbial horse's mouth, see Shlomo Alvineri, ed., *Karl Marx on Colonialism and Modernization* (Garden City, NY: Doubleday, 1968).

16. This is no overstatement. By the early twentieth century some 85 percent of the earth's landmass was either claimed as a possession of the empires of Great Britain, France, Russia, Spain, Portugal, Belgium, Germany, Italy and the Netherlands, or, like the territory within the U.S., by one or another euroderivative settler state. Although it is somewhat dated, one of the best overviews remains Harry Magdoff's *The Age of Imperialism* (New York: Monthly Review Press, 1969).

17. The preinvasion size of the population indigenous to the U.S. portion of North America is rather speculative, with estimates running as high as 18 million or more. By 1890, the number had been reduced to fewer than a quarter-million; see generally, Russell Thornton, *American Indian Holocaust and Survival: A Population History Since 1492* (Norman: University of Oklahoma Press, 1987).

18. See Francis Paul Prucha, *American Indian Policy in Crisis: Christian Reformers and the Indian, 1865-1900* (Norman: University of Oklahoma Press, 1976).

19. It is instructive that what is to date the most comprehensive history of Indian residential schooling in the U.S. is titled "education for extinction"; see David Wallace Adams, *Education for Extinction: American Indians and the Boarding School Experience, 1875-1928* (Lawrence: University Press of Kansas, 1995).

20. See Prucha, *Americanizing the American Indian*.

21. Rutherford B. Hayes, Theodore Roosevelt and William Howard Taft.

22. General Allotment Act (ch. 119, 24 Stat. 388, now codified as amended at 25 U.S.C. 331 *et seq.*) For background, see D.S. Otis, *The Dawes Act and the Allotment of Indian Land* (Norman: University of Oklahoma Press, 1973); Janet A. McDonnell, *The Dispossession of the American Indian, 1887-1934* (Bloomington: Indiana University Press, 1991).

23. This is framed quite clearly in Wilcomb E. Washburn, *The Assault on Indian Tribalism: The General Allotment Dawes Act of 1887* (Philadelphia: J.B. Lippincott, 1975).

24. U.S. Dept. of Interior, Bureau of Indian Affairs, *Annual Report of the Commissioner of Indian Affairs* (Washington, D.C. 34th Cong., 1st Sess., 1856) p. 559.

25. "[E]very Indian born within the territorial limits of the United States to whom allotments shall have been made under provision of this act, or under any law or treaty…is hereby declared to be a citizen of the United States"; General Allotment Act § 6. In 1924, U.S. citizenship was unilaterally imposed upon all Indians—including those who had expressly refused it—who had not already been "naturalized" through the Allotment Act and other federal statutes; Indian Citizenship Act (ch. 233, 43 Stat. 25).

26. The implications of this terminology are explored elsewhere; see Ward Churchill, "Naming Our Destiny: Toward a Language of American Indian Liberation," in his *Indians Are Us? Culture and Genocide in Native North America* (Monroe, ME: Common Courage Press, 1994) pp. 291-357.

27. Ch. 120, 16 Stat. 544, 566, now codified at 25 U.S.C. 71.

28. As was argued by Attorney General A.H. Garland in *U.S. v. Kagama* (18 U.S. 375, 1886), the 1871 termination of treatymaking with Indians represented a "revolution in the policy of the government respecting Indian affairs," the result of which was that Indians were no longer viewed as sovereign nations; U.S. Supreme Court, *Records and Briefs*, "Brief of A.H. Garland," p. 10. Justice Edward D. White, writing for the majority, concurred. See generally, David E. Wilkins, *American Indian Sovereignty and the Supreme Court* (Austin: University of Texas Press, 1997) esp. pp. 64-117.

29. Major Crimes Act (ch. 341, 24 Stat. 362, 385, now codified 18 U.S.C. 153). For background, see Sidney L. Harring, *Crow Dog's Case: American Indian Sovereignty, Tribal Law, and United States Law in the Nineteenth Century* (Cambridge, UK: Cambridge University Press, 1994) esp. pp. 100-41.

30. The Gramscian concept of internal colonialism was developed during the 1920s to explain northern Italy's domination of the country's southern region; see Antonio Gramsci, "The Southern

Question," in his *The Modern Prince and Other Writings* (New York: International, 1957) pp. 24-51. The idea was first applied to analysis of the situation in which American Indians find themselves by Cherokee anthropologist Bob Thomas during the mid-60s; see Robert K. Thomas, "Colonialism: Classic and Internal," *New University Thought*, Vol. 4, No. 4, Winter 1966-67.

31. As Churchill observes at p. 70, quoting noted penologist Richard Korn, this same continuum of objectives remains in effect in U.S. "super-max" prisons to this day. Although such prisons are typically reserved for adults, official disdain for the lives of Others' children remains as evident now as it did a century ago. As but one example, consider UN Ambassador, later Secretary of State, Madeleine Albright's 1996 calculation, publicly announced, that the readily-preventable deaths of more than a half-million Iraqi children were "worth the price" in assuring the success of U.S. sanctions against their country. Albright's statement aired on the *60 Minutes* "television news magazine" on May 12, 1996, and appeared in the *New York Times* the following day; William Blum, *Rogue State: A Guide to the World's Only Superpower* (Monroe, ME: Common Courage Press, 2000) pp. 5-6.

32. A related technique involved the sending of siblings to widely separated facilities in order to undermine family cohesion. For an especially poignant account, see Don Talayesva with Leo W. Simmons, *Sun Chief: The Autobiography of a Hopi Indian* (New Haven, CT: Yale University Press, 1942).

33. It is commonly understood among military tacticians that the incurring of 25th percentile casualties—i.e., killed and wounded—will cause a well-trained infantry unit to lose the cohesion lending it "combat effectiveness." At the 30th percentile, the same unit will begin a process of outright disintegration; see, e.g., Dorothy K. Clark, *Casualties as a Measure of Effectiveness of an Infantry Battalion* (Baltimore: Operations Research Office, Johns Hopkins University, 1954). By comparison, American Indian peoples were suffering the equivalent of 25th percentile kill-rates throughout the entire period.

34. In this connection, it would be worth exploring the ways in which such "excesses" are integral to the European "enlightenment" from the moment of its inception. See, e.g., Michel Foucault, *Discipline and Punish: The Birth of the Prison* (New York: Vintage Books, 1979). For examination of an entirely relevant "spill-over effect," see Alice Miller, *For Your Own Good: Hidden Cruelty in Child-Rearing and the Roots of Violence* (New York: Farrar, Straus, Giroux, 1983).

35. Anyone inclined to dismiss this as an overstatement should consider the extent to which pedophilia have lately been documented as existing even in church-run facilities "serving" *mainstream* youngsters. See, as examples, Associated Press, "More Church Abuse Claims Likely: Several Dozen More People to Accuse Boston Archdiocese," *The Columbian*, May 24, 2004; Michelle Nicolosi, "'Code of Silence' Among Priests Shields Abusers: Hundreds of Clergy Victims as Children, Many Experts Believe," *Seattle Post Intelligencer*, Sept. 23, 2004; Associated Press, "Local Archdiocese to Settle Suits," *Bradenton Herald* (Miami), Sept. 23, 2004; Shirley Ragsdale, "Vatican Removes Accused Priest," *Des Moines Register*, Sept. 24, 2004; Don Lattin, "Judge Expected to Set Trial Date in Abuse Cases: Move Could Push Church Lawyers to Settle Out of Court," *San Francisco Chronicle*, Oct. 5, 2004.

36. For an excellent study of this dynamic, see Lenore Terr, *Too Scared to Cry: Psychic Trauma in Childhood* (New York: Basic Books, 1990). Also see Leonard Shengold, *Soul Murder: The Effects of Childhood Abuse and Deprivation* (New Haven: Yale University Press, 1989).

37. See, e.g., Judith L. Herman, M.D., and Bessel A. van der Kolk, M.D., "Traumatic Antecedents of Borderline Personality Disorder," in Bessel A. van der Kolk, M.D., ed., *Psychological Trauma* (Washington, D.C.: American Psychiatric Press, 1987) pp. 111-26.

38. See Philip A. May, "The Epidemiology of Alcohol Abuse among American Indians: The Mythical and Real Properties," in Duane Champagne, ed., *Contemporary Native American Cultural Issues* (Walnut Creek, CA: Altamira Press, 1999) pp. 227-44; R. Bachman, *Death and Violence on the Reservation* (New York: Auburn House, 1992); David Lester, *Suicide in American Indians* (New York: Nova Science, 2001). Relatedly, see U.S. Dept. of Health and Human Services, Indian Health Service, *A Roundtable Conference on Dysfunctional Behavior and Its Impact on Indian Health* (Albuquerque & Washington, D.C.: Kauffman/Public Health Service, 1991); *Trends in Indian Health* (Washington, D.C.: Public Health Service, 1995).

39. By his own account the personal dimension of this understanding crystallized for Churchill through the psychological suffering and greatly premature death of his wife, Kizhiibaabinesik (Leah Renae Kelly), the daughter of residential school survivors. See his essay, "Kizhiibaabinesik: A Bright Star,

She Burned Too Briefly," which serves as the preface to Leah Renae Kelly, *In My Own Voice: Explorations in the Sociopolitical Context of Art and Cinema* (Winnipeg: Arbiter Ring, 2001). On the transmissibility of psychological trauma from parents to children, see Ann Buchanan, "Intergenerational Child Maltreatment," and Kathleen Olympia Nader, "Violence: Effects of Parents Previous Trauma on Currently Traumatized Children," in Yael Danieli, ed., *International Handbook of Multigenerational Legacies of Trauma* (New York: Plenum Press, 1998) pp. 535-52, 571-83.

40. Viewed in terms of symptomatology, Donnie's behavior conforms quite well with that attributed to "Complex PTSD." The same may be said with regard to every "drunken Indian" I've known. See Judith Herman, M.D., *Trauma and Recovery* (New York: Basic Books, [2nd ed.] 1997) p. 121. For another very useful reading, see M. Seligman, "Depression and Learned Helplessness," in R.J. Friedman and M. M. Katz, eds., *The Psychology of Depression* (New York: Wiley, 1974) pp. 85-113; H. Rosenthal, "The Learned Helplessness Syndrome," *Emotional First Aid*, Vol. 3, No. 2, 1986, pp. 5-8.

41. In Indian Country, this is a very common theme. See J. Westermeyer and E. Peake, "A Ten-Year Follow-Up on Alcoholic Native Americans in Minnesota," *American Journal of Psychiatry*, No. 140, 1983, pp. 189-94; P.A. Kettl and E.O. Bixler, "Alcohol and Suicide in Alaska Natives," *American Indian and Alaska Native Mental Health*, Vol. 5, No. 2, 1993, pp. 34-45; W.H. Sack, M. Beiser, G. Baker-Brown, and R. Redshirt, "Depressive and Suicidal Symptoms in Indian School Children," *American Indian and Alaska Native Mental Health Research*, Monograph No. 4, 1994, pp. 81-96.

42. For background on the St. Francis mission school, see Mary Crow Dog with Richard Erdoes, "Civilize Them with a Stick," in Susan Lobo and Steve Talbot, eds., *Native American Voices: A Reader* (New York: Longman, 1998) pp. 241-8.

43. The scenario is typical. Ample documentation will be found in Assembly of First Nations, *Breaking the Silence: An Interpretive Study of Residential School Impact and Healing as Illustrated by the Stories of First Nations Individuals* (Ottawa: Assembly of First Nations, 1994). Also see Suzanne Fournier and Ernie Crey, *Stolen From Our Embrace: The Abduction of First Nations Children and the Restoration of Aboriginal Communities* (Vancouver, B.C.: Douglas & McIntyre, 1997) pp. 115-42.

44. The "soul rape" metaphor has been used in related contexts, vis-à-vis the residential schooling of aboriginal children in Australia for example. See, e.g., Peter Read, *A Rape of the Soul So Profound: The Return of the Stolen Generations* (St. Leonard's: Allen & Unwin, 1999). For a succinct clinical summary, see Beverly Raphael, Pat Swan, and Nada Martinek, "Intergenerational Aspects of Trauma for Australian Aboriginal People," in Danieli, *Multigenerational Legacies of Trauma*, pp. 327-41.

45. Again, this is standard fare. See C.A. Elliot, "Sexually and Physically Abused Native Youth," in David Lester, ed., *Suicide '92* (Denver: American Association of Suicidology, 1992) pp. 61-2; C. Kaverola, "Sexual Abuse as a Precipitant of Suicide in Native Youth," *AAS Newslink*, Vol. 20, No. 2, 1994, 9-10; N.G. Dinges and D.T. Quang, "Stressful Life Events and Co-occurring Depression, Substance Abuse and Suicidality among American Indian and Alaska Native Adolescents," *Culture, Medicine and Psychiatry*, No. 16, 1992-3, 487-502; N.G. Dinges and D.T. Quang, "Suicide Ideation and Suicide Attempt Among American Indian and Alaska Native Boarding School Adolescents," *American Indian and Alaska Native Mental Health Research*, Monograph No. 4, 1994, pp. 167-88.

46. In effect, Donnie was suffering a variant the "Survivor Syndrome" displayed by former prisoners in concentration camps, combat veterans and others afflicted with acute/complex PTSD. See William G. Niederman, "Clinical Observations on the 'Survivor Syndrome'," *International Journal of Psycho-Analysis*, No. 49, 1968, 313-5; Henry Krystal and William G. Niederman, "Clinical Observations on the Survivor Syndrome," in Henry Krystal, ed., *Massive Psychic Trauma* (New York: International Universities Press, 1968) pp. 327-48.

47. A good discussion of this factor will be found in T.D. O'Nell's "Feeling Worthless," *Culture, Medicine and Psychiatry*, No. 16, 1993.

48. For cogent analysis, see Albert Memmi, *Dominated Man* (Boston: Beacon Press, 1976). Many of Memmi's thematics are developed and refined in Thomas Gladwin with Ahmad Saidin, *Slaves of the White Myth: The Psychology of Neocolonialism* (Atlantic Highlands, NJ: Humanities Press, 1980).

49. Such dynamics are explored against the analogous—albeit, less totalizing—backdrop of East India by Ashis Nandy in his *The Intimate Enemy: Loss and Recovery of Self Under Colonialism* (New York: Oxford University Press, 1983).

50. The sense of this is captured quite well in the concluding chapter of Agnes Grant's superbly titled *No End of Grief: Indian Residential Schools in Canada* (Winnipeg: Pemmican, 1996). For a good case-study, see Marie-Anik Gagné, "The Role of Dependency and Colonialism in Generating Trauma in First Nations Citizens: The James Bay Cree," in Danieli, *Multigenerational Legacies of Trauma*, pp. 355-72.

51. The setting at issue, common to all colonized societies, was most famously depicted by Frantz Fanon in his *The Wretched of the Earth* (New York: Grove Press, 1966).

52. Rennard Strickland, "Indian Law and the Miner's Canary: The Signs of Poison Gas," *Cleveland State Law Review*, No. 39, 1991, pp. 486-9.

53. A good selection of readings in this connection will be found in Stephen Greymorning, ed., *A Will to Survive: Indigenous Essays on the Politics of Culture, Language and Identity* (Boston: McGraw-Hill, 2004).

54. In this connection, see my own *Spirit and Resistance: Political Theology and American Indian Resistance* (Minneapolis: Fortress Press, 2004).

55. See Paul Chaat Smith and Robert Allen Warrior, *Like a Hurricane: The American Indian Movement from Alcatraz to Wounded Knee* (New York: New Press, 1996).

56. See Geoffrey York and Linda Pindera, *People of the Pines: The Warriors and the Legacy of Oka* (Boston: Little, Brown, 1991). On a subsequent, and in some ways similar armed confrontation between native people and state authorities in Canada, see Janice G.A.E. Switlow, *Gustafson Lake: Under Siege* (Peachland, B.C.: TIAC Communications, 1997).

57. For contextualization of this and related initiatives, see Glenn T. Morris, "Vine Deloria, Jr., and the Development of a Decolonizing Critique of Indigenous Peoples and International Relations," in Richard A. Grounds, George E. Tinker, and David E. Wilkins, eds., *Native Voices: American Indian Identity and Resistance* (Lawrence: University Press of Kansas, 2003) pp. 97-154.

58. Although it is badly marred by the political biases of its author, the most comprehensive history of Thomas' ecumenical organizing is James Treat's *Around the Sacred Fire: Native Religious Activism in the Red Power Era: A Narrative Map of the Indian Ecumenical Conference* (New York: Palgrave, 2003). On Thomas himself, see Samuel Stanley, "Staying the Course: Action and Reflection in the Career of Robert K. Thomas," and Tom Holm, "Politics Came First: A Reflection on Robert K. Thomas and Cherokee History," both in Steve Pavlic, ed., *A Good Cherokee, A Good Anthropologist: Papers in Honor of Robert K. Thomas* (Los Angeles: UCLA American Indian Studies Ctr., 1998) pp. 3-8, 41-56,

59. Linda Tuhiwai Smith, *Decolonizing Methodologies: Research and Indigenous Peoples* (London: Zed Books, 1999); Ngugi wa Thiongo, *Decolonizing the Mind: The Politics of Language in African Literature* (London/Nairobi/Portsmouth, NH: James Curry/EAEP/Heinemann, 1986).

60. For more of King's insights, see Harvey Arden, ed., *Noble Red Man: Lakota Wisdomkeeper Mathew King* (Hillsboro, OR: Beyond Words, 1994).

61. See esp. the transcriptions of several of Churchill's public lectures, collected under the title *Speaking Truth in the Teeth of Power* and forthcoming from AK Press.

62. For a particularly useful collection of his essays, see *Acts of Rebellion: The Ward Churchill Reader* (New York: Routledge, 2003). Also see Ward Churchill, *From a Native Son: Selected Essays in Indigenism, 1985-1995* (Cambridge, MA: South End Press, 1996).

63. Churchill has published two major pieces exploring the definitional criteria of genocide. See "Defining the Unthinkable: Towards a Viable Understanding of Genocide," in his *A Little Matter of Genocide*, pp. 339-444; and "Genocide: Toward a Functional Definition," in David O. Friedrichs, *State Crime, Vol. 1: Defining. Delineating and Explaining State Crime* (Aldershot, UL: Ashgate, 1998) pp. 95-118. A version of the latter piece was originally published in *Alternatives*, No. XI, 1986, pp. 403-30.

64. For additional samples of Churchill's rebuttals of those who would deliberately distort the definition of genocide for political reasons, see "It Did Happen Here: Sand Creek, Scholarship and the American Character," in his *Fantasies of the Master Race: Literature, Cinema and the Colonization of American Indians* (San Francisco: City Lights, [2nd ed.] 1998) 19-26; and "Lie for Lie: Linkages Between Holocaust Deniers and Proponents of the 'Uniqueness' of the Jewish Experience in World War II," in his *A Little Matter of Genocide*, pp. 63-80.

65. A partial exception will be found in Roland Chrisjohn and Sherri Young with Michael Mauran, *The Circle Game: Shadows and Substance in the Indian Residential School Experience in Canada*

(Penticton, B.C.: Theytus Books, 1997). Although an excellent study in its own right, *The Circle Game*, as is indicated by its subtitle, does not deal at all with the U.S. system of Indian residential schooling. It therefore lacks the comparative dimension of the present volume.

66. For death rates in the nazi concentration camps, see Michael Burleigh, *Ethics and Extermination: Reflections on the Nazi Genocide* (Cambridge, UK: Cambridge University Press, 1997) p. 211.

67. These commonalities between the residential school experience on the one hand, and the experiences of those interned in concentration camps maintained not only by nazi Germany but a number of other countries (including the U.S.) offers the best—or at least the most obvious—explanation of the striking symptomalogical similarities linking the "Residential School Syndrome" to the "Concentration Camp Syndrome." See, as examples, J. Segal, E.J. Hunter and Z. Segal, "Universal Consequences of Captivity: Stress Reactions Among Divergent Populations of Prisoners of War and Their Families," *International Journal of Social Science*, No. 28, 1976, pp. 593-609; W.W. Eaton, J.J. Sigal, and M. Weinfeld, "Impairment in Holocaust Survivors After 33 Years: Data from an Unbiased Community Sample," *American Journal of Psychiatry*, No. 139, 1982, pp. 773-7; J.D. Kenzie, R.H. Frederickson, R. Ben, et al., "PTSD Among Survivors of Cambodian Concentration Camps," *American Journal of Psychiatry*, No. 141, 1984, pp. 645-50; J.C. Kluznik, N. Speed, C. Van Valkenberg, et al., "Forty Year Follow Up of U.S. Prisoners of War," *American Journal of Psychiatry*, No. 143, 1986, pp. 1443-6; Donna K. Nagata, "Intergenerational Effects of the Japanese American Internment," in Danieli, *Multigenerational Legacies of Trauma*, pp. 119-24.

68. It will no doubt be protested that the comparison is grotesque, since there was no mention at Lake Mohonk of killing any, much less all, American Indians. As historian David Stannard points out, however, the record of the Wannsee Conference, which is "commonly regarded as the 'smoking gun' for those seeking solid evidence for the Nazi plan to kill all the Jews of Europe," is equally sterile. "Never, in this, the key document establishing the plan for a Final Solution, are the outright killing of Jews discussed." The meaning of Wannsee—and Lake Mohonk as well—must be adduced from what ensued. See David E. Stannard, "Uniqueness as Denial: The Politics of Genocide Scholarship," in Alan S. Rosenbaum, ed., *Is the Holocaust Unique? Perspectives on Comparative Genocide* (Boulder, CO: Westview Press, 1996) pp. 186-7.

69. On the SS bureaucrat who managed the logistics system which made the nazi genocide possible, see Hannah Arendt, *Eichmann in Jerusalem: A Report on the Banality of Evil* (New York: Penguin, 1964). Friere, of course, was a liberatory educator. See his *Pedagogy of the Oppressed* (New York: Herder and Herder, 1972).

70. A perfect illustration will be found in the argument advanced by Belgium as part of its diplomatic effort to retain its colony in the Congo during the early 1950s; see Foreign Office of Belgium, *The Sacred Mission of Civilization: To Which Peoples Should the Benefit be Extended?* (New York: Belgian Government Information Center, 1953). This, after a half-century's wholesale perpetration of genocide against the native population; see Adam Hochschild, *King Leopold's Ghost: A Story of Greed, Terror, and Heroism in Colonial Africa* (Boston: Houghton Mifflin, 1998).

71. Russell Means, talk at the University of Denver, Apr. 1995 (tape on file).

72. By the same token, as Jews confronted with the phenomenon of neonazi Holocaust denial will readily attest, the already excruciating effects of trauma are amplified immeasurably when the nature—or even the very fact—of one's victimization publicly is denied; see, e.g., Deborah Lipstadt, *Denying the Holocaust: The Growing Assault on Truth and Memory* (New York: Free Press, 1993).

73. In the book cited in the preceding note, Lipstadt was unsparing in naming those guilty of Holocaust denial, among them David Irving, an ostensibly reputable English historian specializing in the German experience of World War II. Irving promptly sued for libel. To her eternal credit, Lipstadt went to England to face her accuser, made her case at trial, and thoroughly discredited her opponent (among other things, establishing to a judicial certainty that he had systematically distorted—and in some instances fabricated—the data underpinning several books which had been previously accepted by the profession as "benchmark" works). See Richard J. Evans, *Lying About Hitler: History, Holocaust, and the David Irving Trial* (New York: Basic Books, 2001). A better example of "making it stick" would be hard to find.

74. This is most powerful when it emerges in the form of imminent critique. Karl Jaspers, for instance, did a superb job with this in his postwar tract, *The Question of German Guilt* (New York: Fordham University Press, 2002). Members of the North American settler societies would do well to heed his example.

75. See Eric Lister, "Forced Silence: A Neglected Dimension of Trauma," *American Journal of Psychiatry*, No. 139, 1982, pp. 872-6. Consider in this light the implications of the Assembly of First Nations having selected *Breaking the Silence* as the title of its groundbreaking publication on the residential schools. Other groups—Japanese Americans with regard to the World War II internment, for instance— have shown the same pattern; see, e.g., Janice Mirikitani, *Shedding Silence: Poetry and Prose* (Berkeley, CA: Celestial Arts, 1987).

76. See Mike Kaye, "The Role of Truth Commissions in the Search for Justice, Reconciliation and Democratization: The Salvadoran and Honduran Cases," *Journal of Latin American Studies*, No. 29, Oct. 1997, pp. 693-716; Priscilla B. Hayner, "Fifteen Truth Commissions—1974-1994: A Comparative Study," *Human Rights Quarterly*, No. 16, 1994, pp. 597-655.

77. In Canada, the Royal Commission on Aboriginal Peoples, which conducted nationwide series of hearings during the early '90s, was largely designed to serve the purpose at issue (see its official report, published in 5 vols. by Canada Communication Group in 1996 and '97). Since then, there have been an all but endless stream of smaller-scale conferences—most of them government-funded—which have pursued the theme of "healing and reconciliation." What might be described as a "native healing industry"—accompanied by a burgeoning literature on the topic—has also taken hold. See, e.g., Nechi Institute, Four Worlds Development Project, Native Training Institute, and New Direction Training, *Healing Is Possible: A Joint Statement on the Healing of Sexual Abuse in Native Communities* (Edmonton: Nechi Institute, 1988).

78. See Neil J. Kritz, ed., *Transitional Justice: How Emerging Democracies Reckon with Former Regimes*, 3 vols. (Washington, D.C.: U.S. Institute for Peace Press, 1995).

79. This is a point that seems lost on all too many would-be therapists. The convention seems to be to adopt a rhetoric of "postcoloniality"—for context, see note 14—while studiously ignoring the reality that the relations of internal colonial domination remain unchanged. See, as a prime example of this trend, Eduardo F. Duran and Bonnie M. Duran, *Native American Postcolonial Psychology* (Albany: State University of New York Press, 1995). Also see Eduardo F. Duran, *Transforming the Soul Wound: A Theoretical/Clinical Approach to American Indian Psychology* (Berkeley, CA: Folklore Institute, 1990); Bonnie Duran and Eduardo Duran," "Applied Postcolonial Clinical and Research Strategies," in Marie Battiste, ed., *Reclaiming Indigenous Voice and Vision* (Vancouver: UBC Press, 2000) pp. 86-100; Eduardo Duran, Bonnie Duran, Maria Yellow Horse Brave Heart, and Susan Yellow Horse-Davis, "Healing the American Indian Soul Wound," in Danieli, *Multigenerational Legacies of Trauma*, pp. 341-54. Suffice it here to observe that any therapy undertaken on the premise that wounds can be healed without eliminating their source is, at best, accommodationist in the sense described by Thomas Szasz in his *The Therapeutic State: Psychiatry in the Mirror of Current Events* (Buffalo, NY: Prometheus Books, 1984).

80. For those who continue to subscribe to the archaic notion of female subjugation in marriage, of course, the proposition will no doubt seem entirely reasonable. During the mid-19th century, it was considered a legal truism that, insofar as she was "naturally obligated" to provide him with sex on demand, "a husband could not be guilty" of raping his wife; Matthew Hale, *History of the Pleas of the Crown*, 2 vols. (Philadelphia: H.R. Small, 1847) Vol. 1, p. 628. Although such laws have been repealed, their legacy is enduring. Until rather recently, it remained therapeutic orthodoxy that women who found themselves in sexually/physically abusive marriages should be advised to "make the best of it"; see, e.g., J.E. Snell, R.J. Rosenwald, and A. Robey, "The Wife-Beater's Wife," *Archives of General Psychiatry*, No. 11, 1964, pp. 107-12. Hence, it remains all too common to find wives who are routinely raped and/or battered regularly seek to "reconcile" with their abusive spouses. Fortunately, there is now a growing consensus among mental health professionals—not to mention feminists—that such behavior is pathological, *not* evidence of "healing." See Diana E.H. Russell, *Rape in Marriage* (New York: Macmillan, 1982); David Finkelhor and Kirsti Yllo, *License to Rape: Sexual Abuse of Wives* (New York: Holt, Rinehart & Winston, 1985). Also see Lenore Walker, *The Battered Woman* (New York: Harper & Row, 1979).

81. Such construal of consent is analyzed in Susan Brownmiller, *Against Our Will: Men, Women and Rape* (New York: Simon and Schuster, 1975) pp. 384-6.

82. Put most crudely, she was "asking for it," so how's a guy to know? Ibid., p. 312.

83. As in, "If you're going to be raped, you might as well relax and enjoy it." Ibid., p. 313.

84. This, of course, takes us right back to the rape in marriage scenario discussed in note 80.

85. See Royal Commission on Aboriginal Peoples, *Restructuring the Relationship: Report of the Royal Commission on Aboriginal Peoples, Vol. 2* (Ottawa: Canada Communications Group, 1996).

86. A classic example is that of procedure through which the U.S. purportedly admitted and redressed the wrong done to Japanese Americans interned in concentration camps during World War II. Not only did the commission established to "set the record straight" attribute the internment of only the Japanese Americans to "war hysteria" rather than racism—a matter which hardly squares with the far more threatening German American population having been treated with kid gloves—it dodged the substantial economic motives underlying the maneuver. To top off the whole charade, although U.S. officials at the time, from Pres. Roosevelt on down, routinely described the facilities to which the Japanese Americans were being sent as concentration camps, the "truth commission" refused to do so (insisting instead that the camps be referred to as "relocation centers"). See Commission on Wartime Relocation and Internment of Civilians, *Personal Justice Denied: Report of the Commission on Wartime Relocation and Internment of Civilians* (Seattle: University of Washington Press, 1982).

87. While this goes without saying under the conditions prevailing in North America, it is also true more generally. Even in South American countries where a change of regime has occurred, blanket amnesties are the rule. See Geoffrey Robertson, *Crimes Against Humanity: The Struggle for Global Justice* (New York: New Press, 2000) pp. 267-70.

88. It is perhaps instructive in this sense that the most highly-touted of all such entities, the Commission on Truth and Reconciliation established in 1995 under authority of Nelson Mandela's post-apartheid South African government, was conceived and organized by Bishop Desmond Tutu. In principle, it "offered immunity from prosecution only to political criminals prepared to earn it by testifying fully and frankly, and if necessary testifying as prosecution witnesses at subsequent trials. This is not so much an amnesty as a form of plea-bargaining, familiar for centuries in most common law countries; conspirators may turn informers, acknowledge their guilt and earn their pardon by convicting their associates." Tutu, however, has proven less than enthusiastic for actual prosecutions, meanwhile "waxing overlyrically about the virtues of forgiveness" and thereby converting the proceedings into a confessional, pure and simple. While purporting to have adopted this stance for "the greater good," the Bishop seems to have completely lost sight of the principle that "forgiveness is the prerogative of the victims, not of the majority of members of the society in which they happen to live, let alone of any government." Robertson, *Crimes Against Humanity*, pp. 272-3.

89. Tellingly, such testimonies have lately begun to gain popularity as commodities—i.e., collected as books—within certain, possibly sadistic, sectors of the settler population. See, as examples, Fournier and Crey, *Stolen From Our Embrace*; Robert Benson, ed., *Children of the Dragonfly: Native Voices on Child Custody and Education* (Tucson: University of Arizona Press, 2001).

90. Their more draconian "educational" objectives now complete, the North American settler states have placed an increasing emphasis on Macaulay's idea of cultivating a narrow sector of the native population to perform the technical functions necessary for their colonies to be self-administering (see note 2 and accompanying text). Although there are antecedents, the real kick-off of this trend in the U.S. came with passage of the Indian Self-Determination and Educational Assistance Act of 1975 (88 Stat. 2203, codified at 25 U.S.C. 450a and elsewhere at Titles 25, 42 and 50, U.S.C.A.). When all else fails, of course, they still have the usual roster of Great White Experts to fall back on.

91. For explication in a related context, see A.J. Cienfuegos and C. Monelli, "The Testimony of Political Repression as a Therapeutic Instrument," *American Journal of Orthopsychiatry*, No. 53, 1983, pp. 43-51; Inger Agger and Soren B. Jensen, "Testimony as Ritual and Evidence in Psychotherapy for Political Refugees," *Journal of Traumatic Stress*, No. 3, 1990, pp. 115-30.

92. For related analysis, see Evan Stark and Anne Flitcraft, "Personal Power and Institutional Victimization: Treating the Dual Trauma of Woman Battering," in Frank Ochberg, ed., *Post-Traumatic Therapy and Victims of Violence* (New York: Brunner/Mazel, 1988) pp. 115-51.

93. Here, we've doubled back once again, this time to the situation described in note 88. In this instance, however, professions of forgiveness have been cunningly extracted from the victims—or enough of them to create the appearance—by preying upon their psychoemotional vulnerabilities rather than depending upon their hewing to the "principles" of an institutionalized religion that, with regard to the residential schools, has been among the worst offenders.

94. Although there are other vectors of the settler society in which the parenthetical plays out, the presumption seems to center among those fancying themselves to be of the "New Age." Interestingly enough, their collective notion of a "healing therapy" appears hinge upon the "sharing"—read, appropriation—of indigenous spiritual practices. See Wendy Rose, "The Great Pretenders: Further Reflections on Whiteshamanism," in M. Annette Jaimes, ed., *The State of Native America: Genocide, Colonization and Resistance* (Boston: South End Press, 1992) pp. 403-22. Also see Ward Churchill, "Indians 'R' Us: Reflections on the 'Men's Movement,' " in his *From a Native Son*, pp. 367-408.

95. In his *The Colonizer and the Colonized* (Boston: Beacon Press, 1965), the Tunisian anticolonial theorist Albert Memmi provides much incisive analysis of precisely this phenomenon. Also see Memmi, *Dominated Man*; Gladwin with Saidin, *Slaves of the White Myth*; Carnoy, *Education as Cultural Imperialism*.

96. Framed politically, the process is one of "cooptation," wherein the existing structure of power relations is strengthened through implementation of cosmetic adjustments to its operational system. Such "reforms" are specifically designed to preempt systemically marginalized/external opponents, diverting the energy of the opposition itself into a reinforcement or completion of the status quo. Currently, the application of such methods are most commonly veiled in a rhetoric of political "inclusiveness" attended by ostentatious—but altogether vacuous—"celebrations" of "cultural diversity." For useful insights on how cooptive techniques were employed to neutralize the transformative potential inherent to international revolutionary movements during the 1960s and '70s, see George Katsiaficas, *The Imagination of the New Left: A Global Analysis of 1968* (Boston: South End Press, 1987) esp. pp. 156-64, 186-97, 209-11. A more theoretical analysis will be found in Michael Saward, *Co-optive Politics and State Legitimacy* (Hanover, NH: Dartmouth Group, 1991).

97. As the matter has been put elsewhere and relatedly: "One should not speak lightly of 'cultural genocide' as if it were a fanciful invention. The consequence in real life is far too grim... The cultural mode of group extermination is genocide, a crime. Nor should 'cultural genocide' be used in the game: 'Which is more horrible, to kill and torture; or, remove the reason and will to live?' Both are horrible." Robert Davis and Mark Zannis, *The Genocide Machine in Canada: The Pacification of the North* (Montréal: Black Rose Books, 1973) p. 20.

98. See Robert Jay Lifton and Eric Markusen, *The Genocidal Mentality: Nazi Holocaust and Nuclear Threat* (New York: Basic Books, 1988).

99. I mean this in the most literal way. Sartre's observation that "colonization...is necessarily a cultural genocide [which cannot be maintained] without systematically destroying the particular characteristics of native" societies remains as valid today as it was when he wrote it. Any strategy of native accommodation to the internal colonial structure of the North American settler states must therefore be autogenocidal. See Jean-Paul Sartre, "On Genocide," in Ken Coates, Peter Limqueco and Peter Weiss, eds., *Prevent the Crime of Silence: Reports from the Sessions of the International War Crimes Tribunal Founded by Bertrand Russell* (London: Allen Lane/Penguin, 1971) p. 353.

100. See generally, Hussein A. Bulhan, "Revolutionary Psychiatry of Fanon," in Nigel C. Gibson, *Rethinking Fanon: The Continuing Dialogue* (New York: Humanity Books, 1999) pp. 141-75. Also see Bulhan's *Frantz Fanon and the Psychology of Oppression* (New York: Plenum, 1985).

101. The idea congeals in *Wretched of the Earth* at pp. 293-6.

102. That the dynamics producing Wounded Knee and Oka are threatening to rather than reinforcing of the stability of the North American settler states is best reflected, perhaps, in the magnitude of state repression visited upon the participants. See, e.g., Ward Churchill, "The Bloody Wake of Alcatraz: Repression of the American Indian Movement during the 1970s," in his *Acts of Rebellion*, pp. 163-82.

103. The nexus of Fanon's discourse on the therapeutic effect upon the colonized of "equalizing" colonial violence through counterviolence is generally attributed to the first chapter of his *Wretched of the Earth* (the throat-slitting phraseology is at p. 61, and again at p. 297). A better articulation, however, will be found in an earlier essay, "Algeria Unveiled," included in Frantz Fanon, *A Dying Colonialism* (New York: Grove Press, 1965) pp. 35-67. For theoretical contextualization, see Marie Perinbaum, *Holy Violence: The Revolutionary Thought of Frantz Fanon* (Washington, D.C.: Three Continents Press, 1982); Samira Kawash, "Terrorists and Vampires: Fanon's spectral violence of decolonization," in Anthony C. Alessandrini, ed., *Frantz Fanon: Critical Perspectives* (New York: Routledge, 1999) pp. 235-57.

104. This proposition, again, derives from Fanon. For explication, see Lewis R. Gordon, *Fanon and the Crisis of European Man: An Essay on Philosophy and the Human Sciences* (New York: Routledge, 1995).

105. Churchill has elsewhere set forth this argument in greater detail. See his *On the Justice of Roosting Chickens: Reflections on the Consequences of U.S. Imperial Arrogance and Criminality* (Oakland, CA: AK Press, 2003) esp. pp. 5-25, 269-76.

106. See "Notes on Man and Socialism in Cuba," in George Lavan, ed., *Che Guevara Speaks: Selected Writings and Speeches* (New York: Merit, 1967) pp. 121-38, term at 128. Ché's conception of the "new man" was originally and more fully posited in his "El socialismo y el hombre en Cuba," *Marcha*, Mar. 12, 1965. It is worth noting that on the final page of *Wretched of the Earth*, and also at p. 310, Fanon also calls for creation through anticolonial struggle and consequent liberation of a "new man" similar to Guevara's.

107. "At the risk of seeming ridiculous, let me say that the true revolutionary is guided by a great feeling of love. It is impossible to think of a genuine revolutionary lacking this quality... Our vanguard revolutionaries must idealize this love of the people, this most sacred cause, and make it one and indivisible." Guevara, "Notes on Man and Socialism," p. 136.

INTRODUCTION

That Little Matter of Genocide Revisited
Contours of a Hidden Holocaust in Native North America

> Genocide is genocide, no matter what form it takes
> and no matter what you call it.

> —Sharon H. Venne
> residential school survivor
> June 2000

In 1997, I published *A Little Matter of Genocide: Holocaust and Denial in the Americas, 1492 to the Present*, a rather hefty volume devoted to describing, comprehensively and in stark relief, the processes through which the peoples indigenous to the Western Hemisphere have been systematically subjugated, and in many instances eradicated altogether, over the past five centuries.[1] As a corollary, I sought to place the holocaust of American Indians firmly within its proper analytical context — that of genocide scholarship, per se — while stripping bare the methods and motives uniting "mainstream" academic/ political commentators in a common pretense that, however else it might be characterized, the unrelenting and ongoing liquidation of Native American societies cannot be "properly" depicted as embodying "real" genocide. Especially in the latter connection, my approach was and remains unabashedly confrontational, consisting as it does of an insistence upon calling the duplicities of orthodox "interpretation" — and thus its proponents themselves — by their right name(s), with the hope of debunking all they've said and stand for in the process.[2]

For a book of its type, *A Little Matter of Genocide* has been remarkably successful. More striking still, given the harshness of the critique advanced in the book, it has been seriously and often quite favorably received by a broad range of prominent genocide researchers, most notably those situated within the nonexclusivist sectors of Jewish Holocaust scholarship.[3] Among the upshots of this response have been my own inclusion on the advisory board of the Institute on Holocaust and Genocide in Jerusalem, repeated invitations for me to address major convocations of holocaust/genocide scholars,[4] and the incorporation of several of the issues I'd raised into Israel Charny's massive double-volume *Encyclopedia of Genocide*, published in 1999.[5] Hence, to the extent that any single effort might be reasonably expected to accomplish the somewhat overly ambitious objectives I posed for it, *A Little Matter of Genocide* can be seen to have done so.

That said, it must be acknowledged that for all the scope with which I sought to imbue it, *A Little Matter of Genocide* was an incomplete study, sometimes dramatically so. Indeed, in certain respects it replicates errors I critiqued in others, exhibiting too great a concentration upon the raw physicality of killing rather than the more insidious cultural dimensions of the genocide suffered by the peoples indigenous to this hemisphere. As well, I tended to historicize the genocide of Native Americans at the expense of analysis devoted to exploring the perpetuation/evolution of genocidal processes in contemporary settings. True, a substantial chapter was devoted to the impact of U.S. mining and milling of uranium, as well as nuclear weapons production and testing, upon the "national sacrifice peoples" of Native North America during the second half of the twentieth century.[6] Exactly one phrase in the entire 531-page book was devoted to the ongoing scourge of alcohol in American Indian communities, however.[7]

Similar examples abound: a solitary sentence went to noting a federal program that resulted in the involuntary sterilization of about 40 percent of all native women of childbearing age in the United States during the early 1970s;[8] another sentence went to mentioning the "termination" initiatives of the 1950s and 60s through which more than a hundred targeted native peoples were unilaterally dissolved and thereafter declared to be "extinct" by the U.S. government;[9] a single paragraph went to pointing out the official and rather flagrant use of native children for purposes of medical experimentation in the U.S.;[10] no notice at all was given the implications attending assertions of control by both the U.S. and the Canadian governments over Indian identity criteria, a situation positioning either or both to engage in manipulations precipitating the "definitional extermination," either of selected indigenous target groups or, potentially, "their" respective native populations, en toto.[11] An itemization of matters given comparably short shrift could be extended to considerable length.

The present volume is thus in a very real sense compensatory. Taking as its focus the system of residential schooling imposed upon North America's indigenous peoples for more than a century—a topic in which just three sentences were invested in *A Little Matter of Genocide*[12]—it seeks to rectify what was perhaps the most serious of the numerous deficiencies encompassed within my earlier effort. I say this because, of all the malignancies embodied in twentieth-century U.S./Canadian Indian policy, the schools were arguably the worst. The profundity of their destructive effects upon native people, both individually and collectively, not only in the immediacy of their operational existence but in the aftermath as well, was and remains by any reasonable estimation incalculable. Ultimately, neither the nature nor the magnitude of the genocide suffered by Native North Americans can be truly appreciated unless the impact of the residential schools is understood. The essay that follows thus constitutes a component absolutely essential to completion of the record I've set out to build.

At one level, my intention has more than anything else been to reinforce, amplify and extend the assault I commenced even before writing *A Little Matter of Genocide* upon those who seek to mask genocidal realities—especially those, like the residential schools, not marked by direct killing on a mass scale—behind the sophistries of definitional distortion and the semantic veil attending the use of terms like "ethnocide."[13] In pursuit of this objective, I have by design engaged in no new research while assembling my essay. Instead, to underscore the obviousness of what is being obfuscated and denied by "responsible" scholars, I've chosen to rely exclusively on previously published data, most of it long and readily accessible to anyone willing to consider its implications. My main contribution to the literature, I think—aside from offering the first comparative assessment of residential school operations and impacts covering both the U.S. and Canada[14]—is thus to have effected a synthesis of the relevant information, configuring it in a manner facilitating its being scrutinized through the lens of legality.

My approach in this regard is quite straightforward. Beginning with the original explication of its meaning offered by Raphaël Lemkin, the jurist who coined it in 1944,[15] and a quick tracing of its codification in black letter international law—i.e., the second article of the 1948 Convention on Prevention and Punishment of the Crime of Genocide[16]—I (re)establish the *actual* definition of the word "genocide." Since this definition comes equipped with an array of rather specific criteria, it becomes a relatively simple matter to match them up, point by point, to conditions well-documented as having prevailed in the schools. Both the conclusions drawn at the end of the essay and its title—"Genocide by Any Other Name"—follow, directly and unavoidably, from the results of the procedure employed. The truth of Sharon Venne's observation, quoted above as an epigram, is thereby both illuminated and validated in the clearest possible terms.

This, it seems to me, represents a proper antidote to the performance of the all too many analysts who have treated the same phenomena discussed herein, often far more exhaustively than I, while remaining unable to bring themselves[17]—in some cases openly refusing[18]—to employ the "g-word" in characterizing what they'd so thoroughly described.[19] Since, as Venne observes, genocide remains genocide, no matter what you call it, then, by the same token, those who call it by some other name, or who decline to name it at all, must take their place within the sordid ranks of holocaust deniers. No less than when neonazi trash like Arthur Butz or Ernst Zündel claim that the judeocide perpetrated by Hitler's Reich never happened,[20] this is so, when the offender is a respected member of the mainstream North American academic establishment who pretends—seeking all the while to reassure or convince others—that the form and function of the genocide wrought against American Indians was, is, or might have been anything other than it was and is.[21] Just as those whose trade is the deliberate denial of truth must be revealed as the liars they are, so, too, must the "interpretations" of history and the nature of the social order it has produced be rejected on the basis of their sheer and inherent falsity.

In effect, North America's settler society must be forced to confront fullface the actualities attending its creation and maintenance, stripped of the triumphal and altogether loathsome smugness with which the pathology of denial has imbued it. It must, in other words, be compelled to see and recast itself in terms diametrically opposed to those which have heretofore comprised the hideous lethality of its essence. I say this, not out of vindictiveness, nor of a narrow sense of propriety demanding adherence to baseline standards of honesty and accuracy, nor even of the admitted fervency of my desire to see the dignity of truth at last bestowed upon the victims of what my friend David Stannard refers to as "The American Holocaust,"[22] but because, as Leo Kuper, Israel Charny and others have long and rightly insisted—and as I myself emphasized in *A Little Matter of Genocide*—such horrors must be understood in *all* their many facets if ever their repetition is to be prevented.[23] It is in this spirit, and to this end, that *Kill the Indian, Save the Man* has been written.

—Ward Churchill
Boulder, Colorado
February 2004

Notes

1. Ward Churchill, *A Little Matter of Genocide: Holocaust and Denial in the Americas, 1492 to the Present* (San Francisco: City Lights, 1997).

2. See especially the chapters entitled "Lie for Lie: Linkages Between Holocaust Deniers and Proponents of the 'Uniqueness of the Jewish Experience in World War II'" and "Defining the Unthinkable: Towards a Viable Understanding of Genocide," both in ibid., pp. 81-96, 399-444.

3. See, e.g., the review essay by Israel Charny entitled "Is Genocide Curable?" in *Readings*, Vol. 15, No. 1, Mar. 2000.

4. Among these have been talks delivered at the 30th Annual Scholars' Conference on the Holocaust and the Churches conducted at St. Joseph's University in Mar. 2000; the Genocide Studies Program at Yale University in Oct. 2000; the Westchester (NY) Holocaust Commission in Apr. 2001; and the 32nd Annual Scholars' Conference on the Holocaust and the Churches held at Kean University in Mar. 2002.

5. See the entries entitled "Denials of the Holocaust," "Denials of the Genocides of Non-Jewish Peoples in the Holocaust," "Genocide of South American Indians," "Genocide of Indians in the Caribbean, Mexico and Central America," "Genocide of Indians of the United States" and "Genocide of Canadian Indians," all in Israel Charny, ed., *The Encyclopedia of Genocide* (Santa Barbara, CA: ABC-CLIO, 1999).

6. "Cold War Impacts on Native North America: The Political Economy of Radioactive Colonization," in *A Little Matter of Genocide*, pp. 289-362. For preliminary explorations of the same subject matter, see, as examples, see my and Winona LaDuke's "Radioactive Colonization and Native Americans," *Socialist Review*, No. 81, May 1985; "Native America: The Political Economy of Radioactive Colonization," *Journal of Ethnic Studies*, Vol. 13, No. 3, Fall 1985; also my "American Indian Lands: The Native Ethic and Resource Development," *Environment*, Vol. 28, No. 6, July-Aug. 1986. Since *A Little Matter of Genocide* was released, I've further developed certain aspects of the material; see the chapter entitled "A Breach of Trust: The Radioactive Colonization of Native North America," in my *Perversions of Justice: Indigenous Peoples and Angloamerican Law* (San Francisco: City Lights, 2003) pp. 153-200.

7. *A Little Matter of Genocide*, p. 247.

8. Ibid., p. 249.

9. Ibid., p. 248.

10. Ibid., p. 249.

11. This lapse was subsequently addressed in a pair of major essays; see the chapter entitled "The Nullification of Native North America? An Analysis of the 1990 American Indian Arts and Crafts Act," in my *Acts of Rebellion: The Ward Churchill Reader* (New York: Routledge, 2003) pp. 23-42; "The Crucible of American Indian Identity: Native Tradition versus Colonial Imposition in Postconquest North America," in my *Perversions of Justice*, pp. 201-46.

12. *A Little Matter of Genocide*, p. 246.

13. See my "Genocide: Toward a Functional Definition," *Alternatives*, Vol. XI, No. 3, July 1986 (reprinted in David O. Friedrichs, ed., *State Crime, Vol. I: Defining, Delineating and Explaining State Crime* (Aldershot, UK: Ashgate, 1998) pp. 119-46). A more thorough analysis of the duplicity imbedded in attempts to classify certain forms of genocide under seemingly less significant headings like "ethnocide" will be found in *A Little Matter of Genocide*, pp. 414-5.

14. "Canadian Indian school experiences cry out for systematic comparisons with counterparts in the United States"; Michael C. Coleman, *American Indian Children at School, 1850-1930* (Jackson: University of Mississippi Press, 1993) p. 196. Although such observations have accrued with increasing regularity over the past decade or more, I appear to be the first to undertake the task (however partially).

15. Raphaël Lemkin, *Axis Rule in Occupied Europe: Laws of Occupation, Analysis of Government, Proposals for Redress* (Washington, D.C.: Carnegie Endowment for International Peace, 1944) pp. 79-80.

16. 1948 Convention on Prevention and Punishment of the Crime of Genocide (UN GAOR Res. 260A (III) 9 Dec. 1948 (78 U.N.T.S. 277); effective 12 Jan. 1951).

17. A hallmark of nearly every existing study of the residential schools is a distinct evasion of the word "genocide." This is so, even where descriptions of the circumstances involved are so graphic as to virtually compel its usage. Consider, as a prime example, the closing passages of what might be considered

the benchmark examination of the U.S. system of Indian residential schooling: "For tribal elders who had witnessed the catastrophic developments of the nineteenth century—the bloody warfare, the near-extinction of the bison, the scourge of disease and starvation, the shrinking of the tribal landbase, the indignities of reservation life, the invasion of missionaries and white settlers—there seemed no end to the cruelties perpetrated by whites. And, after all this, the schools. After all this, the white man had concluded that the only way to save Indians was to destroy them, that the last great Indian war should be waged against children. They were coming for the children"; David Wallace Adams, *Education for Extinction: American Indians and the Boarding School Experience, 1875-1928* (Lawrence: University Press of Kansas, 1995) pp. 336-7. Suffice it to observe that, despite his explicit depiction of a genocidal context, the word "genocide" appears nowhere in Adams' text. Indeed, he avoids using even so dilute a substitute as "ethnocide." The same principle prevails with regard to what should be considered the two best overall studies of the Canadian system; see J.R. Miller, *Shingwauk's Vision: A History of the Indian Residential Schools* (Toronto: University of Toronto Press, 1996); John S. Milloy, *"A National Crime": The Canadian Government and the Residential School System, 1879 to 1986* (Winnipeg: University of Manitoba Press, 1999).

18. There are, to be sure, exceptions to the more general rule of silence discussed in the preceding note. When the word "genocide" is used at all, however, it is typically for purposes of rejecting its appropriateness and utility in describing the residential school phenomenon. Robert Trennert presents a striking example by lambasting an unnamed "tribal official" who dared to describe what happened in the Phoenix Indian School as "cultural genocide." From there, he goes on to assert—contrary to his own evidence, which depicts the imposition of a "disciplinary" régime so harsh that children were on occasion literally beaten to death—that "there was nothing…evil [or] shameful" about the school; Robert A. Trennert, Jr., *The Phoenix Indian School: Forced Assimilation in Arizona, 1891-1935* (Norman: University of Oklahoma Press, 1988) pp. 206, 207, 212. So far as I know, the only book to date that actually frames Indian residential schools as a genocidal process is *The Circle Game: Shadows and Substance in the Indian Residential School Experience in Canada* (Penticton, B.C.: Theytus Books, 1997), coauthored by Roland Chrisjohn and Sherri Young with Michael Maraun.

19. It should be noted that it is actually illegal in Canada to use the term "genocide" in accordance with the definition articulated in international law. There, pursuant to an April 1998 decision entered by Judge J.T. MacPherson in *Daishowa Inc. v. Friends of the Lubicon* (Ontario Court of Justice (Gen. Div.), File No. 95-CQ-59707) it is a criminal offense to refer to anything other than mass killing as constituting genocide; see my "Forbidding the 'G-Word': Holocaust Denial as Judicial Doctrine in Canada," *Other Voices*, Feb. 2000.

20. Butz is author of *The Hoax of the Twentieth Century: The Case Against the Presumed Extermination of European Jewry* (Torrance, CA: Institute of Historical Review, 1976). Zündel is author of *The Hitler We Love and Why* (Toronto: Samisdat, 1984) and one of North America's major purveyors of material denying the nazi judeocide. For incisive analysis of these and a range of comparable figures, see Deborah Lipstadt, *Denying the Holocaust: The Growing Assault on Truth and Memory* (New York: Free Press, 1993).

21. Consider the following passage, penned by one of Euroamerica's preeminent "ethnohistorians": "The…problem with 'genocide' as a description of, or even analogy to, the post-Columbian loss of Indian life is that the moral onus it tries to place on European colonists, equating them with the Nazi S.S., is largely misdirected and inappropriate… [We] make a hash of our historical judgments because we continue to feel guilty about the real or imagined sins of our fathers and forefathers and people to whom we have no relation whatsoever… Despite the resort to universalizing labels such as 'Imperialism' and 'Colonialism,' most of the battles of the sixteenth and seventeenth centuries are behind us… [We] can stop flogging ourselves with our 'imperialistic' origins and tarring ourselves with the broad brush of 'genocide' "; James Axtell, *Beyond 1492: Encounters in Colonial North America* (New York: Oxford University Press, 1992) pp. 262-3. Such sentiments are truly ubiquitous in "reputable" academic circles.

22. David E. Stannard, *American Holocaust: Columbus and the Conquest of the New World* (New York: Oxford University Press, 1992).

23. Leo Kuper, *The Prevention of Genocide* (New Haven, CT: Yale University Press, 1985); Israel Charny, ed., *Toward the Understanding and Prevention of Genocide: Proceedings of the International Conference on Holocaust and Genocide* (Boulder, CO: Westview Press, 1984); *A Little Matter of Genocide*, pp. 52-3.

I can understand now why there appears to be such a widespread prejudice on the part of the Indians against residential schools. Such memories do not fade out of the human consciousness very rapidly.

—R.A. Hoey
Canadian Indian Department official
June 1942

Genocide by Any Other Name
American Indian Residential Schools in Context

> We must begin with the misrepresentation and transform it into what is true. That is, we must uncover the source of the misrepresentation; otherwise, hearing what is true won't help us. The truth cannot penetrate when something is taking its place.
>
> —Ludwig Wittgenstein

The word "genocide" is among the more profoundly misunderstood in the English language. Most often, the term has been cast as no more than a synonym for mass murder—albeit mass murder of the most extreme sort—and considerable scholarly energy has been expended in debating the scale of killing or proportionality of its impact upon victim groups necessary for one or another slaughter to qualify as "truly" genocidal rather than simply blending into the vast panorama of butchery with which history is replete.[1] More refined—or tedious—lines of analysis have devolved upon such questions as whether certain modes or methods of killing must be present if a given "exterminatory phenomenon" is to be considered "genuinely" genocidal.[2] Still others have delved into the function(s) served by mass murder in what are taken to be genocidal settings[3] and, most ambiguously, the nature of the intentions which must guide perpetrator groups if their actions are to be construed as genocidal.[4]

While it has been argued that such inquiries are undertaken for purposes of making our understanding of genocide more "rigorous,"[5] they have for the most part had a decisively exclusionary effect, establishing definitional/conceptual threshold criteria for what has been in this sense aptly described as the "incomparable crime" so narrow that supposedly reputable researchers were asserting in all apparent seriousness by the mid-1990s that the nazi-perpetrated judeocide of World War II was "phenomenologically unique."[6] In substance, and more clearly put, the conclusion embodied in such contentions is that "real" genocide "has happened [only] once, to the Jews under Nazism."[7] Not even the fate of the Sinti and Romani (Gypsies), simultaneously exterminated by the nazis in a proportion entirely comparable to that of the Jews—and in the same camps, by the same methods and under the same official decrees—is accorded equal footing.[8] Similar absurdities abound.[9]

The motives underlying imposition of such radical constraints upon the meaning of genocide have been anything but pure. On the one hand, as Edward Alexander has approvingly observed, their development has been a key element in a conscious strategy designed to invest the Jewish people with a monopoly on the sort of "high-grade moral capital" attending genocidal victimization, a matter translating into certain of the political advantages enjoyed by the State of Israel.[10] On the other hand, the result is plainly exculpatory, allowing virtually every perpetrator régime or society other than the Germans under Hitler to dodge not only the stigma of their history but other potential consequences of their crime(s).[11] Small wonder, given the utility inherent to a truncating and thus deforming the definition of genocide, that doing so has long since become a practice enthusiastically and all but universally embraced by the world's ruling élites and the "responsible" intellectual establishments they sponsor.[12] Indeed, in many quarters, it amounts to official policy.[13]

That the policy at issue amounts to the "routine denial" of a plethora of genocides—not least in countries such as France and Canada, where comparable denials of the nazi judeocide constitute a statutory offense—should be self-evident.[14] The implications, as Roger Smith, Eric Markusen and Robert Jay Lifton have pointed out in connection with the much-denied 1915-18 Turkish genocide of Armenians, are exceedingly grim.[15]

> Where scholars [and other ostensibly reliable commentators] deny genocide, in the face of decisive evidence that it has occurred, they contribute to a false consciousness that can have the most dire reverberations. Their message is: [genocide] requires no confrontation, no reflection, but should be ignored, glossed over. In this way, scholars lend their considerable authority to the acceptance of this ultimate human crime. More than that, they encourage—indeed invite—a repetition of the crime from virtually any source in the immediate or distant future. By closing their minds to the truth, that is, scholars contribute to the deadly psychohistorical dynamic in which unopposed genocide begets new genocides.[16]

Clearly, such denial is diametrically opposed to the openness described as essential by Leo Kuper, Israel Charny and others who have devoted themselves to the task of conceiving ways and means of preventing the recurrence of "the human cancer."[17] Because, as Irving Louis Horowitz has noted, "genocide is always and everywhere an essentially political decision," and since, to quote Huey P. Newton, politics itself must be seen as an "ability to define a phenomenon and cause it to act in a desired manner," the need to approach eradication of genocide from the vantage point of definitional viability—thence precision—is undeniably of cardinal importance.[18] Hence, we would do well to review the actual meaning of the term as it was set forth by Raphaël Lemkin, the man who coined it in 1944.[19] From there, it will be possible to apply Lemkin's concept in analyzing a process falling well beyond the parameters of what has become the norm of genocide scholarship, thereby restoring to his formulation something of its original efficacy and promise.

Form and Scope of the Crime

The first and most striking of aspect of Lemkin's explanation of the neologism he created by combining "the ancient Greek word *genos* (race, tribe) and the Latin *cide* (killing)" was the care he took to distinguish it from being strictly associated with descriptors of literal murder (irrespective of the scale on which the murder was committed).[20] Rather, he was at pains to emphasize that he was addressing virtually *any* policy undertaken with the intention of bringing about the dissolution and ultimate disappearance of a targeted human group, *as such*.

> Generally speaking, genocide does not necessarily mean the immediate destruction of a nation, *except* when accomplished by mass killing. . . It is intended rather to signify a coordinated plan of different actions aiming at the destruction of the essential foundations of the life of national groups, with the aim of annihilating the groups themselves. The objectives of such a plan would be disintegration of the political and social institutions, of culture, language, national feelings, religion, and the economic existence of national groups, and the destruction of personal security, liberty, health, dignity, and even the lives of the individuals belonging to such groups. Genocide is directed against the national group as an entity, and the actions involved are directed against individuals, not in their individual capacity, but as members of the national group [emphasis added].[21]

Thus, while Lemkin acknowledged that outright physical extermination was one means by which genocide might be perpetrated, he was quite unequivocal in his insistence that it was not a necessary ingredient of the crime, far less that it was the "essential" feature. What was essential in Lemkin's conception was that extinguishing the existence of a target group be undertaken as a matter of policy. Insofar as any such policy was in evidence, it fell within the rubric of genocide, "even though the individual members survived" the process of group liquidation.[22] There is in fact every indication that Lemkin saw the physical survival of all or most members of groups subjected to genocide as being normative, their physical extermination exceptional. Consider what may be taken as the very core of his definition.

> Genocide has two phases: one, destruction of the national pattern of the oppressed group; the other, the imposition of the national pattern of the oppressor. This imposition, in turn, may be made on the oppressed population which is allowed to remain, or upon the territory alone, after the removal of the population and colonization of the area by the oppressor's own nationals.[23]

Thus, as Zygmunt Bauman has noted, Lemkin was primarily concerned with depicting the essential ingredients of what might be termed "ordinary genocide," a process which is "rarely, if at all, aimed at the total annihilation of the group" in physical terms.[24]

> The purpose of violence (if the violence is purposeful and planned) is to destroy the marked category (a nation, a tribe, a religious sect) as a viable community capable of self-perpetuation and defense of its own identity. If this is the case, the objective of the genocide is met once (1) the volume of violence has been large enough to undermine the will and resilience of the sufferers, and to terrorize them into surrender to the superior power and into acceptance of the order it imposed; and (2) the marked group has been deprived of the resources necessary for the continuation of the struggle. With these two conditions fulfilled, the victims are at the mercy of their tormentors. They may be forced into protracted slavery, or offered a place in the new order on terms set by the victors—but which sequel is chosen depends solely on the conquerors' whim. Whichever option is selected, the perpetrators of genocide benefit. They extend and consolidate their power, and eradicate the roots of their opposition.[25]

So decisive was the nonlethal dimension of ordinary genocide in Lemkin's estimation that he observed how the term "denationalization" might have sufficed to encompass what he meant were it not for the fact that "in connoting the destruction of one national pattern, it does not connote the imposition of the national pattern of the oppressor."[26] Similarly, he observed that "denationalization," sometimes taken to connote a mere deprivation of citizenship, failed to encompass the fact that genocide, in some instances at least, involved "destruction of the biological structure" of the target group.[27] It is important to note that much more than killing is at issue in this last connection. Involuntary sterilization and other measures designed to prevent births among the target group falls within the scope of "biological genocide."[28] Not all of these all of these are even physical in any literal sense. Lemkin held the nazi refusal to permit marriage between Poles to be genocidal, for example.[29]

> In the occupied countries of "people of non-related blood," a policy of depopulation is pursued. Foremost among the methods employed for this purpose is the adoption of measures calculated to decrease the birthrate of the national groups of non-related blood, while steps are taken to encourage the birthrate of [ethnic Germans] living in these countries . . . Different methods are adopted to [this] end. Special subsidies are provided in Poland for German families having at least three minor children. Because the Dutch and Norwegians are considered to be of related blood, the bearing, by Dutch and Norwegian women, of illegitimate children begotten by German military men is encouraged by subsidy . . . The special care for legitimation of children in Luxemburg, as revealed in the order concerning changes in family law of March 22, 1941, is dictated by the desire to encourage extramarital procreation with Germans.[30]

Such understandings have from the outset informed the international legal discourse on genocide. In 1947, the Secretary General of the newly formed United Nations, pursuant to Economic and Security Council (ECOSOC) Resolution 47(IV), retained Lemkin to head up a committee of experts charged with drafting a law to define, prevent and punish the crime of genocide (this was the so-called Secretariat's Draft of the present Genocide Convention).[31] Here, Lemkin offered substantial clarification of what is entailed, elaborating the nature of the protected classes involved—which he'd earlier referred to simply as "national" or "oppressed" groups—by listing "racial, national, linguistic, religious [and] political groups" as falling under the law's rubric (by implication, economic aggregates were included as well). Genocide itself is defined in a two-fold way, encompassing all policies intended to precipitate "1) the destruction of [such] a group" and "2) preventing its preservation and development."[32] The modes through which such policy objectives might be attained are then delineated in tripartite fashion and in considerable detail.

1. *Physical Genocide* includes both direct/immediate extermination (à la Auschwitz and the nazis' *einstatzgruppen* operations in the USSR) and what are referred to as "slow death measures": i.e., "subjection to conditions of life which, owing to lack of proper housing, clothing, food, hygiene and medical care or excessive work or physical exertion are likely to result in the debilitation [and] death of indi-

5

viduals; mutilations and biological experiments imposed for other than curative purposes; deprivation of [the] means of livelihood by confiscation, looting, curtailment of work, and the denial of housing and of supplies otherwise available to the other inhabitants of the territory concerned."[33]

2. *Biological Genocide* includes involuntary "sterilization, compulsory abortion, segregation of the sexes and obstacles to marriage," as well as any other policies intended to prevent births within a target group."[34]

3. *Cultural Genocide*—which encompasses the schema of denationalization/imposition of alien national pattern Lemkin had described as being the central feature of the crime in 1944—includes all policies aimed at destroying the specific characteristics by which a target group is defined, or defines itself, thereby forcing them to become something else. Among the acts specified are the "forced transfer of children . . . forced and systematic exile of individuals representing the culture of the group . . . prohibition of the use of the national language . . . systematic destruction of books printed in the national language, or religious works, or the prohibition of new publications . . . systematic destruction of national or religious monuments, or their diversion to alien uses [and] destruction or dispersion of objects of historical, artistic, or religious value and of objects used in religious worship."[35]

Significantly, no hierarchy is attached to these classifications. The perpetration of cultural genocide is presented as an offense every bit as serious—and subject to exactly the same penalties—as perpetration of physical or biological genocide. This was so in part because Lemkin was of the view that the crux of what others would later call "the genocidal mentality" resides squarely within the cultural domain,[36] and because he understood that there is ultimately no way of segregating the effects of cultural genocide from its physical and biological counterparts.

> A culture's destruction is not a trifling matter. A healthy culture is all-encompassing of human lives, even to the point of determining time and space orientation. If a people suddenly lose their "prime symbol," the basis of culture, their lives lose meaning. They

become disoriented, with no hope. As social disorganization often follows such loss, they are often unable to ensure their own survival . . . The loss and human suffering for those whose culture has been healthy and is suddenly attacked and disintegrated are incalculable.[37]

In other words, the deliberate destruction of cultures kills individuals just as surely as do guns and poison gas, especially when combined with imposition of the sorts of slow death measures which all but invariably attend such undertakings.[38] There is thus no way in which cultural genocide may be reasonably set apart from physical and biological genocide as a "lesser" sort of crime. Nor is there a basis for the now fashionable practice of declaring it to be "ethnocide," an as yet uncodified category of offense which is supposedly different from genocide, per se.[39] In this regard, it should be noted that Lemkin coined the term "ethnocide" on the very same page as that on which he offered up the word "genocide" itself, *not* to describe some other process, but as a *synonym*.[40] In view of the centrality of the cultural mode of genocide to Lemkin's conception of the crime as a whole, analysts such as Yehuda Bauer have also argued that certain approaches to physical genocide should be segregated from Lemkin's existing triad and bestowed with a separate—and elevated—classification called "Holocaust."[41]

In any event, Lemkin's draft was submitted to ECOSOC in November 1947, and, in turn, the Council subjected it to review by a seven-member ad hoc committee chaired by the U.S. representative.[42] During this process, the Soviet Union delegate managed to have political groups removed from the list of protected classes, while the delegate of the United States gutted the entire category concerning cultural genocide.[43] Lemkin had also included an article specifying that charges of genocide would be referred to an international tribunal maintained for this and related purposes (i.e., adjudicating cases involving crimes against humanity).[44] This idea was scuttled in favor of the courts of each signatory country, although provision was made for genocide to be considered an extraditable offense, and for "appropriate intervention" by "competent organs of the United Nations"—e.g., the Security Council—in cases where compliance was refused.[45]

The revised draft convention, which was unanimously adopted by the U.N. General Assembly on December 9, 1948, nonetheless retained just enough of Lemkin's thinking to be (barely) workable. Even in the dilute form in which it was adopted, the second article of the 1948 Convention on Prevention and Punishment of the Crime of Genocide defines the crime as being "any of the following acts committed with intent to destroy, in whole or in part, a national, ethnical, racial or religious group, as such."[46]

(a) Killing members of the group;
(b) Causing serious bodily or mental harm to members of the group;
(c) Deliberately inflicting on the group conditions of life calculated to bring about its physical destruction in whole or in part;
(d) Imposing measures intended to prevent births within the group;
(e) Forcibly transferring children of the group to another group.

It is worth remarking the obvious at this juncture: killing is only one of five criteria, or twenty percent of the total. The other four—80 percent of the entire definition of genocide posited in international law—although (b) and (c) overlap with Lemkin's "slow death measures," consist of or devolve upon explicitly nonlethal lines of action. It is also worth noting that not only perpetration of any of these acts, but attempting to commit them, conspiring to do so, incitement of them,[47] or any other sort of complicity in their commission are all advanced as criminal offenses under the convention's third article. Under Article IV, it is specified that "persons committing genocide or any of the other acts enumerated in Article III shall be punished, whether they are constitutionally responsible rulers, public officials or private individuals."

Genocide in North America

Both the United States and Canada have dodged implementation of the genocide convention from the outset, albeit in somewhat different ways. In Canada, the strategy was to foster an illusion of acceptance—Parliament voted to ratify the convention on May 21, 1952—while quietly redefining the crime in the country's domestic enforcement statute so as to omit any mention of policies and actions in which Canada was and is engaged. Thus, the convention's prohibitions of policies causing serious bodily or mental harm to members of a target group and/or effecting the forcible transfer of their children were from the first moment expunged from Canada's "legal understanding."[48] In 1985, the Canadian statute was further "revised" so as to delete measures intended to prevent births within a target group from the list of proscribed policies/activities. In its present form, Canadian law admits only items (a) and (c) among the criteria posited under the convention's sec-

8

ond article as being constitutive of the crime of genocide.[49] At least one Canadian court, moreover, has recently entered a decree making it a criminal offense for anyone to employ the term in any other way.[50]

The sheer disingenuousness imbedded in this definitional distortion is abundantly reflected in the parliamentary debates leading up to the 1952 "ratification." Although the official position was that only those provisions of the genocide convention "intended to cover certain historical incidents in Europe that have little essential relevance in Canada" were being excised,[51] it was clearly noted that then-current "proposals to impose integrated education upon [American] Indian children, for example, might fall within [the Convention's] prohibition" against forced transfer of children.[52] Since the government had in fact been doing far more than entertaining proposals in this regard for the better part of a century at that point—and would continue to do so for another thirty years—its claim that "mass transfers of children to another group are unknown . . . in Canada" can only be seen as a bold-faced lie.[53] In effect, the Canadian statute was knowingly crafted not as an instrument of prevention or punishment, but rather as a mask for the fact that Canada was consciously committing genocide—as the crime was enunciated in black letter international law—and had every intention of *continuing* to do so.

As for the U.S., having led the way in watering down the convention during the U.N. revision process,[54] it refused even to pretend to accept the resulting instrument for forty years. And, when the Senate did finally vote for ratification on February 19, 1986—the ratifying instrument was not deposited with the United Nations Secretariat until November 1988—it did so on the basis of an attached reservation, referred to as the "Sovereignty Package," which purported to set the U.S. constitution at a level above that of international law and to render the country self-exempting from compliance.[55] This stunning regurgitation of the nazi theory of legality[56] prompted strenuous complaints by numerous prior signatories. As of December 1989, Denmark, Finland, Ireland, Italy, the Netherlands, Norway, Spain, Sweden and the United Kingdom had all entered formal objections with the Secretariat challenging the validity of the U.S. ratification.[57] Several countries also noted that the genocide convention holds the force of customary law and is therefore binding upon the U.S., whether or not its government eventually proves willing to effect a valid ratification (the same rule pertains to Canada, the circumscribed definition contained in its domestic statute notwithstanding).[58]

The record of preratification debates conducted by U.S. senators from 1950 onward is even more illuminating than is that of their counterparts in the Canadian parliament. A major sticking point for two successive generations was whether the convention's stipulation that killing members of a target group solely on the basis of their group membership is a genocidal act irrespective of the numbers involved meant that the thousands of lynchings of African Americans carried out by the Ku Klux Klan added up to genocide and would thus require the U.S. to declare the Klan a criminal organization in the same sense the nazi SS had been declared such at Nuremberg.[59] Another was whether, given the precedent set at Nuremberg in the Streicher case, the convention's prohibition on incitement of genocide would require the government to prosecute purveyors of white racist literature for crimes against humanity.[60] Still another, in view of the country's posture of Jim Crow segregation/discrimination, and the serious physical/psychological harm this was well-documented as inflicting on racial minorities, was whether the entire corpus of U.S. race law and policy might not be construed as genocidal.[61]

Less discussed, but as much or more to the point, was the relationship of the U.S. to American Indians. Here, the country was in violation of every one of the criteria posited in the convention's second article. While direct killing of the sort evidenced in scalp bounties and military extermination campaigns had mostly ended by the early twentieth century,[62] the U.S. imposition of slow death measures upon Native North Americans was quite clear-cut in 1950, and to a considerable extent remains so today. The policy basis for this situation rests in the unilateral extension of federal "trust authority" over what remained of Indians' lands and other assets pursuant to a Supreme Court opinion rendered in the 1903 *Lone Wolf v. Hitchcock* case,[63] a maneuver through which the government empowered itself to license the exploitation of indigenous resources by preferred corporations at a small fraction — usually no more than 10 percent — of the royalty rates prevailing on the open market.[64] Even this pittance did not go to the Indians themselves, but was placed instead in "trust accounts" administered "in behalf of" their native owners by the U.S. Interior Department's Bureau of Indian Affairs (BIA). From there, some 90 percent of it — nearly $140 *billion*, by current estimates — has been "lost" (that is, expended for purposes other than the wellbeing of the Indians whose money it was/is).[65]

The upshot of this has been that as the U.S. economy bloated itself on the wealth of native people, the people themselves have been driven into the depths of a destitution resembling that prevailing in the Third World.[66] As but one example, it was recently estimated that nearly 90 percent of the dwellings on the Pine Ridge Reservation in South Dakota, location of Shannon County, the poorest in the country for more than fifty years, were effectively uninhabitable. Basic sanitation and water purification facilities were all but nonexistent, as was anything resembling adequate nutrition or medical care.[67] Such conditions are by no means atypical of reservation settings throughout the U.S., and the impacts upon the health and longevity of native people have been predictably severe.

> The Indian health level is the lowest and disease rates the highest of all major population groups in the United States. The incidence of tuberculosis is 400 percent higher than the national average. Similar statistics show that the incidence of strep infections is 1,000 percent, meningitis is 2,000 percent higher and dysentery is 10,000 percent higher. Death rates are shocking when Indian and non-Indian populations are compared. Influenza and pneumonia are 300 percent greater killers among Indians. Diseases such as hepatitis are in epidemic proportions, with an 800 percent higher chance of death. Diabetes is almost a plague.[68]

Overall, according to official census data, reservation-based American Indians experience an average lifespan one-third shorter than the general U.S. population, with a marginally better ratio prevailing in Canada.[69] Clearer examples of the "deliberate infliction of conditions of life calculated to bring about [a target group's partial] physical destruction" and the imposition of policies "causing serious bodily and mental harm" to the rest are difficult to imagine. Under such conditions, population outflow from the reservations—or reserves, as they are called in Canada—has become increasingly pronounced over the past half-century, partly as the result of government relocation programs designed to accelerate the trend.[70] The result has been that more than half of all the people indigenous to North America have by now been dispersed into the "Indian ghettoes" found in. cities across the country, most of them coerced into a permanent separation from their own communities and traditions, their children therefore raised with little or no direct experience of their cultures.[71]

The rate of "outmarriage" has increased apace, with all the consequences this entails for a target group which has been formally defined in racial—i.e., biological—terms by its oppressor.[72] Meanwhile, it has been well documented that the U.S. conducted a program during the early-to-mid-1970s in which upwards of 40 percent of all native women of childbearing age were involuntarily—and in many cases unwittingly—sterilized (the emphasis seems to have been on those with a high "quantum" of native "blood"; the likelihood that Canada has resorted to the same practice is evident in its above-mentioned 1985 revision of its genocide statute).[73] In sum, all the earmarks of what Lemkin described as "a coordinated plan of different actions aimed at destroying the essential foundations of [existence] of national groups, with the aim of [eliminating] the groups themselves," remain ongoing realities in both the settler states asserting contemporary hegemony over the North American continent.[74]

"To Kill the Indian. . ."

Since the end of the "Indian Wars" in 1890, by which point the indigenous population of North America had been reduced to 5 percent or less of its preinvasion total,[75] the weight of policy in the U.S. and Canada alike has been placed on "assimilating"—"digesting" might be a better word—the residue of survivors.[76] Described in 1910 by one of its chief practitioners, U.S. Indian Commissioner Francis Leupp, as "a mighty pulverizing engine for breaking up [the last vestiges of] the tribal mass,"[77] the objective of assimilation policy was from the outset to eliminate all American Indians culturally recognizable as such by some point in the mid-twentieth century.[78] That its proponents failed to completely achieve this goal is due to a number of mediating factors, not least the depth and degree of resistance mounted by the victims themselves, but never for lack of a sustained and often concerted effort to accomplish it.

Beginning with the unilateral extension of U.S. jurisdiction over Indian Country in 1885[79]—actually, the process commenced much earlier in Canada[80]—several components have featured prominently in giving assimilation policy its shape and substance. These include a comprehensive program to abolish the traditional indigenous practice of holding land in common, imposing in its stead an Anglicized system of individual property titles which undermined the cohesiveness of native societies, laid the groundwork for expropriation of more than two-thirds of the territory remaining in Indian hands at the turn of the century, and spawned an intractable "heirship problem" precluding effective use by the nominal owners of what little remained.[81] Concomitantly, programs were adopted to supplant the traditional mode of defining group members by genealogy (kinship) with the above-mentioned "blood quantum" (racial) criteria,[82] to prohibit traditional spiritual practices and virtually compel the adoption of Christianity,[83] to reshape traditional modes of governance along the lines of corporate boards,[84] to disperse the native population as widely as possible,[85] and, mostly during the 1950s, to "terminate" the existence of more than a hundred distinct "bands" and "tribes" (i.e., they were simply declared "extinct").[86] All of this was undertaken on the basis of a self-ordained "plenary"—that is to say, "unlimited and absolute"—power of federal authorities over American Indian lands and lives.[87]

So, too, was the program that served as the linchpin of assimilationist aspirations. This was an initiative begun both north and south of the border during the 1870s, and lasting over a century, in which it was ideally intended that every single aboriginal child would be removed from his/her home, family, community and culture at the earliest possible age and held for years in state-sponsored "educational" facilities, systematically deculturated, and simultaneously indoctrinated to see her/his own heritage—and him/herself as well—in terms deemed appropriate by a society that despised both to the point of seeking as a matter of policy their utter eradication.[88] That some native children escaped such processing had far less to do with the ambitions of those administering the system than with the fact that the U.S./Canadian settler states ultimately proved unwilling to allot sufficient resources to the task.[89] Still, at its peak, the complex of Indian residential schools—"boarding schools," as they were called in the U.S.—was large enough to accommodate about half of all Native North American children at any given moment, and something on the order of eighty percent of several succeeding generations of native youngsters underwent some portion of their schooling therein.[90]

The nature of the "national crime" bound up in this coldly calculated "education for extinction" was put quite bluntly by Captain Richard Henry Pratt, the army officer selected by the U.S. to create and supervise its system in 1879.[91] The objective, Pratt publicly declaimed in 1895,

Architect of the U.S. system, Captain Richard Henry Pratt, once warden of the Fort Marion military prison, later appointed superintendent of the prototype Indian Industrial School at Carlisle, Pennsylvania. (Cumberland County Historical Society)

13

was to "kill the Indian, save the man" in every pupil.[92] Or, to rephrase, as U.S. Indian Commissioner William A. Jones did in 1903, the goal was to "exterminate the Indian but develop a man."[93] The core thinking of those running the system could not have been framed more clearly: to be discernibly Indian was to be other than human; to be human, one could not be discernibly Indian. The formulation, and the mentality it reflects, is identical at base to that displayed in General Phil Sheridan's earlier and much-celebrated observation that "the only good Indian is a dead one,"[94] an enunciation but a bare step removed in sensibility from Colonel John Chivington's infamous order, issued just prior to the Sand Creek Massacre of 1864, that his troops should slaughter Indian babies right along with their parents and other adults because, after all, "nits make lice."[95]

Pratt's selection as the founding head of the U.S. effort to "educate" native children is instructive in other ways as well, given that his major qualification for the job could only have been that he'd previously served as warden of the army prison at Fort Marion, Florida, to which those viewed as the most "recalcitrant" figures among what was left of Native North America's military resistance were often sent to be "broken."[96] In this capacity, he'd demonstrated considerable success, pioneering techniques for compelling "ideological conversion"—or, in the alternative, reducing prisoners to a permanent state of "psychological incompetence"—that are employed in certain of the harsher U.S. penal institutions to this day.[97] Another still popular innovation of the Pratt régime at Fort Marion was establishment of "prison industries" in which the veritable slave labor of inmates was/is utilized both to offset the cost of running such facilities and in some cases turn them into profit-making ventures.[98] That this was the man federal authorities deemed "most fit" to oversee the handling of tykes as young as five years of age speaks volumes as to what was officially intended.

While Commissioner Jones' Canadian counterpart, Duncan Campbell Scott, did not select a military man *cum* penal expert to implement his policies, Canada in most other respects modeled its system on that of the U.S.[99] Proceeding first under the mantle of the 1857 Act to Encourage the Gradual Civilization of the Indian Tribes in the Province,[100] and then under the 1884 Indian Advancement Act,[101] the Indian Department took as its goal "tribal dissolution, to be pursued mainly through the corridors of residential schools."[102] Pratt's notion of killing Indians to save men was frequently voiced within the circles of those charged with "educating" Indians,[103] while

Cheyenne Dog Soldiers upon arrival at Fort Marion, Florida, in 1875. (Beinecke Rare Book and Manuscript Library, Yale University)

Several of the same Dog Soldiers after undergoing Pratt's regimen at Fort Marion for less than a year. (U.S. National Park Service, Castillo de San Marcos national Monument, St. Augustine, Florida)

Scott himself announced that the goal was "to be rid of the Indian question. That is [the] whole point Our objective is to continue until there is not a single Indian in Canada that has not been absorbed into the body politic, and there *is* no Indian problem [emphasis added]."[104] Such endeavors, he explained at another point, were quite consistent with the fact that "progress"—i.e., consolidation of the Canadian state—would be unnecessarily difficult "so long as the Indians remain a distinct people and live as separate communities."[105]

Given the overtly genocidal character of such pronouncements, and the absolute centrality of the residential school system to Indian policy implementation in both the U.S. and Canada for a sustained period, it is important to delve more deeply into the details of the system's functioning in order to appreciate the extent to which rhetoric and reality coincided in the schools themselves. In this way, and *only* in this way, can their implications be properly understood.[106] And only in such understanding can there be hope that certain of the residential schools' lingering effects may be in some way redressed,[107] a consciousness inculcated within the public mind that may in the end afford a prophylactic of first resort against the in many ways still "unthinkable" horrors of genocidal continuation or recurrence.[108] Be that as it may, a straightforward exposition of the facts seems the most appropriate response to the ubiquitous posture of misrepresentation and denial which has for so long been adopted with regard to what was actually done in the schools.[109]

Forcing the Transfer of Children

There can be no question whether the transfer of children upon which the residential school system depended was coercive, that it was resisted by indigenous parents and other adults—and often, to the extent they were able, by the youngsters themselves—or that physical force was used to overcome that resistance. Beginning in 1891, the U.S. Commissioner of Indian Affairs was authorized by Congress to "make and enforce . . . such rules and regulations as will ensure the attendance of Indian children of suitable age and health at schools established and maintained for their benefit."[110] Legislators followed up in 1893 by putting teeth into their earlier decree, authorizing the BIA to "withhold rations, clothing and other annuities from Indian parents or guardians who refuse or neglect to send and keep their children of proper school age in school."[111] Canada followed suit with an amendment to its Indian Act in 1894 that authorized the cabinet to "make regulations, which shall have the force of law, for the commitment by justices or Indian agents of children of Indian blood under age of sixteen years to [an] industrial school or boarding school, there to be kept . . . for a period not extending beyond the time at which such children shall reach the age of eighteen years."[112]

In some cases, the basic elements of coercion built into such legislation were sufficient to produce compliance. Where resistance was concerted—or threatened to be—however, direct applications of force were not infrequent. One of the more flagrant examples is that of the Hopis, a group of whom spent years in the military prison on Alcatraz Island for the "offense" of refusing to surrender their children.[113] At the Fort Peck Reservation, the local Indian agent "sent the police to round up the children, denied rations to the parents, and then, to drive the point home, locked several of the more intractable fathers in the agency guardhouse."[114] A typical scene was recorded by the agent of the Mescalero Apache Reservation in 1886.

> Everything in the way of persuasion and argument having failed, it became necessary to visit the [Indians'] camps with a detachment of police, and seize such children as were proper, and take them away to school, willing or unwilling. Some hurried their children off to the mountains or hid them away in camp, and the police had to chase and capture them like so many wild rabbits. This proceeding created quite an outcry. The men were sullen and muttering, the women loud in their lamentations, and the children almost out of their wits with fright.[115]

At Fort Hall Reservation in 1892, Agent S.J. Fisher proudly reported that he'd "taken quite a number of school children by force," even going so far as to "choke a so-called chief into subjection" before carrying away the man's youngsters.[116] Such tactics was met with "open rebellion" by resident Shoshones and Bannocks and a refusal by most of the reservation's Indian police force to participate in further "recruitment" of students. "Order" was finally restored only in September 1897, when a troop of soldiers from the 4th Cavalry Regiment was dispatched to the reservation, promising publicly to "kill and scalp" anyone who dared oppose them. At that point, "some 40 students were collected in a single day," a total of 207 within the next few weeks.[117] The situation at Fort Hall differed in degree, not in kind, from that prevailing on every reservation in the U.S. The official records are replete with illustrations drawn from all corners of the country, and virtually every memoir produced by a former boarding school student contains a section recounting the official use of force to compel enrollment.[118]

Although the military was not used to impound native children in Canada, the history there is otherwise quite similar. In 1893, for example, the Cree leader Star Blanket was deposed from his position as chief of his band and informed by the Indian Department that he would be reinstated only if he helped secure students for the residential schools.[119] Officials routinely "withheld food rations from parents who resisted the removal of their children," and there are numerous accounts of the Royal Canadian Mounted Police (RCMP) "herd[ing] children onto . . . trains like cattle" in the process of transporting them to institutions that "none of [them] wanted to go to . . . any more than [they] wanted to go to hell or a concentration camp."[120] Overall, "compulsion . . . has generally been the way that both government and churches [have] reacted to Indians' refusal to respond" favorably to demands for their children.[121] So pervasive was the use of force and coercion that in 1908 the recruitment methods employed by the Red Deer Industrial School in Alberta, which consisted of "coaxing and persuading instead of bribery and kidnapping," were officially highlighted as a marked exception to the rule.[122]

Aside from the emotional trauma afflicting any family or community whose children are being "stolen from [their] embrace,"[123] the resistance mounted by Native North Americans to the removal of their children for "education" in residential facilities was usually based in a firm understanding that the process was consciously genocidal. Analyst John Milloy has observed that "reaction to [residential schooling] from First Nations governments across the southern part of [Canada] was resolutely negative. They recognized immediately its implications for continued tribal existence."[124] As a now anonymous native leader put it as early as 1858, the purpose of the whole procedure was self-evidently to "break [indigenous societies] to pieces."[125] David Wallace Adams has reached the same conclusion regarding the U.S.: "a major motivation for resistance [was] that a significant body of tribal opinion saw white education for what it was: an invitation to cultural suicide."[126]

That the native assessment was entirely accurate is borne out in the earlier-quoted statements of purpose offered by officials like Richard Henry Pratt, William Jones and Duncan Campbell Scott. Reinforcement and amplification of their views by lesser figures abounds, as when in 1945 a little-known "Indian affairs specialist" named Allan Harper, writing of Canada,

18

noted that "the extinction of the Indians *as Indians* [emphasis original]" remained "the ultimate end," not only of residential schooling, but of the country's Indian policy as a whole.[127] The same, of course, applied in equal measure to the U.S. Further questions as to whether the forced transfer of children at issue should rightly be considered genocidal are addressed by both the longterm and daily operational realities of the schools themselves.

Destroying the National Pattern of the Oppressed Group

In psychological terms, the regimen was deliberately and relentlessly brutal. From the moment the terrified and bewildered youngsters arrived at the schools, designed as they were to function as "total institutions,"[128] a comprehensive and carefully-calibrated assault on their cultural identity would commence. For boys and girls alike, this began with a thorough scrubbing and "disinfection"—alcohol and kerosene were among the astringents used for the latter purpose[129]—often accompanied by staff commentary about "dirty Indians."[130] For boys, the next step was to undergo the humiliating experience of having their heads shorn, military-style.[131] Although the shearing was/is usually passed off as more "hygiene," it was not typically done to girls except as punishment,[132] and must therefore be considered to have served a different purpose: "At the heart of the policy was the belief that the [boys'] long hair was symbolic of savagism; removing it was central" to destroying their sense of themselves as Indians.[133]

The same was true of their clothing and other personal items, all of which were taken from them. In exchange, they were issued uniforms expressly intended to separate them from the "excessive individualism" of their own traditions by reducing them "to sameness, to regularity, to order."[134] Then came their names. Those with "savage" or "unpronounceable" identifiers like Chesegesbega or Sitahpetale, which included the great majority of new arrivals, quickly found themselves saddled with Anglicized replacements like "Smith" and "Miller" (renaming the children after U.S. presidents and literary or historical figures like Henry Ward Beecher or Julius Caesar also seems to have been a source of amusement for many school staffers).[135] A consistent theme running through autobiographical material written by former students is how this procedure in particular engendered an abiding sense that they'd "lost" themselves and were thus "stranger[s,] with no possibilities" for the future.[136]

19

A young Cree named Thomas Moore as he appeared upon his arrival in 1910 at the Regina Indian Industrial School, Saskatchewan, and three years later. Such "before and after" photo sequences, supposedly providing graphic evidence of the "progress" made by children committed to residential institutions, were produced in the hundreds by school administrators both north and south of the U.S./Canadian border. (Provincial Archives of Alberta, Oblates Collection)

Such despair, in that it rendered the already malleable children still more so, was perfectly in keeping with the desires of those in charge. The schools operated under the mandate of effecting a "complete change" in their charges,[137] a matter described in Canada—under the premise that "true civilization must be based on moral law, which Christian religion alone can give"[138]—as the "building and developing character on the foundation of Christian morality, making Christian faith and love the wellspring and motive of conduct."[139] In the U.S., more secular objectives were additionally set forth.

> It is of prime importance that a fervent patriotism be awakened in [the children's] minds. . . They should be taught to look upon America as their home and the United States government as their friend and benefactor. They should be made familiar with the lives of great and good men and women in American history, and be taught to feel pride in all their great achievements. They should hear little or nothing of the "wrongs [done] the Indians," and of the injustice of the white race. If their unhappy history is alluded to it should be to contrast it with the better future that is within their grasp.[140]

All of this was calculated to take considerable time, even under optimal conditions. Hence, from the outset, it was standard practice that the students be kept in the schools year-round and for as long as a decade, without neither visits to their homes nor visits from their families where possible—even letters were sometimes withheld[141]—because of the "deleterious influences" such interactions might exert.[142] As early as 1863, U.S. Indian Commissioner William P. Dole complained that any other course led to repeated "infection" of the youngsters with "the filthy habits and loose morals of their parents."[143] By 1888, the message was being framed even more bluntly: "Children leaving even the best of training schools for their homes [are] like swine return[ing] to their wallowing filth, and barbarism."[144] The stated goal was to place the students "under the entire control of their teachers," thereby preventing "backsliding" or "retrogression" at any point in the process of their being "raised and educated [to think] like white children."[145]

With the youngsters thus isolated, and otherwise stripped of the most immediate links to their cultural identity, a deeper and more comprehensive demolition was undertaken. This devolved upon absolute prohibitions on the speaking of indigenous languages and the knowledge/practice of native spirituality. Although instruction was already delivered exclusively in that language,[146] the BIA promulgated a regulation in 1890 requiring that "pupils be compelled to converse with each other in English, and should be properly rebuked or punished for persistent violation of this rule."[147] Canada, which followed suit in 1896, was even more explicit, positing not only the inculcation of English and/or French but destruction of students' ability to speak their own languages as goals.[148] Almost universally, "school staff in addition to their other responsibilities were assigned the duty of preventing pupils from 'using their own languages'," even in private conversations (or prayer).[149] Doing so, of course, meant that the children had to be placed under virtually continuous surveillance,[150] while other measures were still more draconian.

> By far the most common experience was that boarding-school students were sternly forbidden to speak their language. They were usually punished, sometimes severely, if they broke the rule. School records and student recollections agree that vigorous disciplinary action was taken to discourage the use of Aboriginal languages. . . It is also clear that the attack on Native languages was part of a broader assault on Aboriginal identity and the individual Native person's sense of worth as an Indian or Inuit.[151]

The resulting stew of fear, loneliness and obliterated self-esteem, sustained for most students over periods of years, was, as is evident in survivor testimonies collected by Canada's Assembly of First Nations, the Royal Commission on Aboriginal Peoples and other such entities over the past decade,[152] quite literally devastating to all who underwent it.

> A man who had attended Chooutla [Carcross] school [in the Yukon] recalled with a mixture of pain and bewilderment how the older students took the novices aside and explained to them that they could escape . . . punishment by learning to speak English quickly. Still more unsettling were the recollections of a female Saulteaux who attended the Oblates' St. Philip's School [Ontario]. This woman recalled that she'd been raised to respect her elders, her own people, and other peoples' ways of doing things. Her first experience at school was to have her braided hair cut short and coal oil poured over her head, and given a bath and provided new clothes. Another female student warned her, "You've got to try and learn how to talk English because you're going to be punished if you talk your own language." She "didn't even know what 'yes' and 'no' meant. I was so scared I wouldn't talk" [for a considerable period]. When she forgot and was caught talking Saulteaux, she would be punished . . . strapped, or made to kneel in a corner for half an hour.[153]

What was worst for this woman was that her "family's entire way of life was denigrated."[154]

> At home she'd been taught to believe in a single Creator, and enjoined to respect the white people's way of worshipping because it was merely another form of giving reverence to the same deity. But at [school] she was told that "our language belonged to

The separation of children from their parents entailed far more than physical distance, a matter dramatically illustrated by this photo of a Cree man named Quewich during a visit with his offspring at the Qu'Appelle Indian School in Saskatchewan, *circa* 1910. (Saskatchewan Archives Board)

the devil," as did all the Saulteaux religious observances. "They told us that our parents, our grandparents, all our people, they were chanting to the devil". . . At school she was taught that all the things she'd learned at home were "ugly" and "meant for the devil," with the result that she "became ashamed of being Indian."[155]

Long before she'd completed her schooling, "she learned to hate, not simply the people who oppressed her, but herself and her race as well."[156] Alienated in the extreme, overflowing with inchoate rage and self-loathing, she soon began a prolonged bout with alcoholism, experienced correspondingly severe problems in her personal/family life, and very nearly consummated her aimless drift towards a final self-nullification on several occasions.[157] Her story, irrespective of its unique twists and turns, is to all intents and purposes endlessly repeated in the narratives offered by other former residential school students. In that sense at least, it can be considered normative (meaning, among other things, that it is by no means the worst the record has to offer).

Imposing the Nation Pattern of the Oppressor

The resemblance of residential schools to military facilities extended far beyond haircuts and uniforms. Captain Pratt's prototypical Carlisle Indian Industrial School, which opened its doors in November 1879 and in many respects served as the template for what followed, was actually established in an unused army barracks in Pennsylvania.[158] So, too, were a number of others, such as those at Fort Shaw, Montana, and Fort Lewis, Colorado. Even those, like the Chilocco Indian Agricultural School (Newkirk, Oklahoma) and the Phoenix Indian Industrial School (Arizona), constructed specifically for the purpose to which they were put, were visibly patterned after military compounds.[159] Although less conspicuous there, the situation in Canada—insofar as "dormitories" were typically built along the lines of barracks bays, if nothing else[160]—was similar. The layouts of most "campuses," geometrically precise and incorporating such features as parade grounds , were thus unabashedly designed to convey a sense closer to regimentation than to mere "orderliness."[161]

More to the point, perhaps, was the fact that the children actually *were* regimented in military fashion. Almost without exception, photos of the youngsters attending Carlisle during Pratt's tenure show them assembled in ranks, awaiting inspection or instructions, or marching in lockstep from one point to the next.[162] Moreover, as every newcomer quickly discovered, "nearly every aspect of his [or her] daily existence—eating, sleeping, working, learning, praying—would be rigidly scheduled, the hours of the day intermittently punctuated by a seemingly endless number of bugles and bells demanding this or that response."[163]

Morning drill at the Sherman Institute, Riverside, California, *circa* 1910. (Courtesy of Harvey Oster)

The children were awakened between five and six in the morning and went to bed between eight and nine at night. In between there was little time for recreation. The daily routine was very much like a military school. "You are drilled to the dining room for breakfast . . . and then you are drilled to the school yard," a Santa Clara woman recalled of the Santa Fe Indian School. During the Sunday dress parade at the Albuquerque Indian School, each student carried a "dummy rifle" and was "dressed up like a regular army." At Haskell Institute the military organization was even more rigorous. Every student at this school was in a regular army outfit, and in 1922 eighty of the older students were in a special machine-gun company, which had undergone two weeks training with the Kansas State Militia the previous summer.[164]

" 'It was a military school,' wrote Helen Sekaquaptewa of the Phoenix Indian School, which she began to attend in 1915. 'We marched to the dining room three times a day to band music. We rose to a bell and had a given time for making our beds, cleaning our rooms, and being ready for breakfast. Everything was done on schedule, and there was no time for idleness.' Boys *and* girls lined up in uniform each Sunday morning. The boys saluted and the girls held out their hands to be checked; the 'officers' noted every flaw in appearance [emphasis original]."[165] "We dressed, we ate, we drilled, we studied and recited our lessons with a precision that left not one minute without its duties," recounted another former student.[166] "Pupils needed a pass to leave the campus, and were expected to salute teachers, officers, and fellow students 'with proper respect.' "[167] Others have written bitterly about the "cold and bullying staff, more like army superiors than mentors."[168]

Pratt and his superiors sought to justify their imposition of a "Prussian" régime with glowing descriptions of the "health benefits, ability to concentrate, and self-confidence" supposedly imparted thereby,[169] while more candid—or honest—observers extolled the "virtues" of "patriotism" and

Captain Pratt's charges at drill. Youngsters at the Carlisle Indian School are put through their morning paces on a specially designated parade ground, backdropped by a 10' student-built fence. The main campus is in the far background. (Cumberland County Historical Society, Pennsylvania)

"obedience" being systematically hammered into previously "wild" young-sters.[170] As students at the Sherman Institute (Riverside, California) were informed in 1910:

> Obedience is the foundation of the great law of life. It is the common fundamental law of all organization, in nature, in military, naval, commercial, political, and domestic circles. Obedience is the great essential to securing the purpose of life. Disobedience means disaster. The first disastrous act of disobedience brought ruin upon humanity and that is still going on. "The first duty of a soldier is obedience" is a truth forced upon all soldiers the moment they enter military life. The same applies to school life. The moment a student is instructed to do a certain thing, no matter how small or how great, immediate action on his part is a duty and should be a pleasure . . . What your teachers tell you to do you should do without question. Obedience means marching right on whether you feel like it or not.[171]

A free-hand drawing class, 1900. This was a typical classroom situation for male and female students, who were expected to acquire some of society's refinements as well as learn to read and write. (U.S. National Archives)

Echoes of Commissioner Thomas Morton's earlier demand that the residential schools take all possible steps to infuse native children with a "fervent" U.S. patriotism are unmistakable. As might be expected, these reverberations spilled over into the roughly two hours per day which in most schools were devoted to "academic" instruction. Here, first emphasis was on the "Three Rs"—reading, 'riting and 'rithmetic—with the goal of bringing all students up to the rudimentary levels of proficiency necessary to allow them to meet the needs of potential employers in the "real world."[172] As the children progressed, increasing weight was placed on what were called the "lessons of citizenship" or "civilization," using texts like Horace E. Scudder's *A History of the United States of America* for the purpose.[173] There, the youngsters learned that the country was "peopled by men and women who crossed the seas in faith [and that] its foundations [were] laid deep in a divine order." The "nation has been entrusted with liberty," and that "carries with it grave duties: the enlargement of liberty and justice is the victory of the people over the forces of evil."[174]

What indigenous students were to make of the fact that their own people—and thus they themselves—had not "crossed the sea" to get to America, and whether it meant that they weren't *really* "people," but rather formed the "forces of evil" that had to be overcome, were questions none too subtly answered by Scudder's depiction of the "Indian race": "While the tribes differed from one another, all the Indians were in some points alike. They were brave, but they were treacherous. They could bear hunger and torture in silence, but they were cruel in their treatment of captives . . . [they were] ignorant barbarians . . . like wild animals [who perpetrated gratuitous] massacres," and so on.[175] Small wonder that the children came to identify far more with the mythic legions of noble white men populating their textbooks and classroom lectures than they did with the grotesquely distorted caricatures of their own ancestors and traditions presented therein.[176]

The incantation of "faith" and "divine order" as cornerstones in the "proper" understanding of history and civics dovetailed perfectly with the lessons delivered during the second half of the typical instructional day—again, about two hours—which was explicitly devoted to the proselytizing of Christianity.[177] This, in

A classroom scene at the Hay River Indian School, Northwest Territories, *circa* 1900. (Anglican Church of Canada, General Synod Archives)

turn, conformed not only to the fact that implanting the "true faith" was integral to the overseers' mandate to "impose the national pattern" they represented,[178] but with the fact that the churches had established Indian residential schools as part of their missionary programs long before governments of either the U.S. or Canada had set out to do so.[179] In both countries—partly

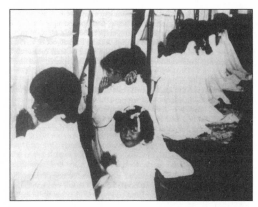

to acquire the benefit of their experience, partly as a cost-constraining expedient—these preexisting institutions and their staffs/faculties were simply incorporated, usually on a contract basis, into the official system with the result that the churches were in this sense made responsible for the fulfillment of official policy.[180] Conversely, church representatives were positioned to exert decisive influence in the formation of educational policy as it pertained to Indians.[181]

Prayers before bedtime at the Phoenix Indian School, Arizona, 1900. Roughly half of the "academic" instruction given students in residential institutions consisted of indoctrination in Christianity, always at the expense of their own spiritual traditions. (U.S. National Archives, Bureau of Indian Affairs Collection)

In Canada, "the residential school system was a creature of the federal government even though the children in the schools were, in most cases, in the care of the churches,"[182] while, in the U.S., the reverse may ultimately have been the case. "Even as the government edged the mission societies to the margin" in the U.S., however, "its teachers also sought to imbue pupils with some form of Christianity. For most secular as well as missionary educators, 'civilization' was inconceivable unless grounded in Christian . . . values."[183] Consequently, and regardless of whether church or state was ascendant in operating the schools at any given moment or location, the result was the same. Even as they underwent a harsh and thoroughgoing process of deculturation (or "denationalization") the children were systematically "reenculturated" to function in psychointellectual terms as "little white people."[184] Given the virulently racialist constructions of role and place by which the U.S. and Canadian settler societies were/are defined, of course, "white" was/is something an American Indian child could *never* become.[185] Thus, the youngsters, both individually and collectively, were forced into the impossible position of "fitting in" to neither their own society nor its ostensible replacement.[186]

The "Slow Death Measure" of Starvation

In the boarding schools, "hunger was a continual and symptomatic problem."[187] By this, it is not meant that the children were denied treats, snacks and such indulgences. A 1944 report submitted to Canada's Department of Indian Affairs by Dr. A.B. Simes, medical superintendent of the Qu'Appelle Indian Hospital, concluded that "28% of the girls and 69% of the boys [were] underweight" in the nearby Elkhorn School (Manitoba).[188] The same or worse was true of virtually every Indian residential facility in the country, and the reason is not hard to find: having forced thousands of native youngsters into the schools, the government was willing to spend almost nothing to feed them: the department's per capita allocation for Indian residential school support—*all* support, that is, not just food—at the time of Simes' report was forty-nine cents per day (and in many schools, only a fraction of that meager sum was actually being spent on students).[189]

Things had never been better. Before 1910, per capita rates in Canada were assigned by the Indian Department in an ad hoc fashion, adding up to as little as $60 annually.[190] In 1911, a more uniform contract system was adopted, fixing Ontario rates at $80-100 per year (depending on school location), "western" rates at $100-125, and "northern" rates at $125, with the great majority receiving a flat $100 per student/year.[191] In 1917, an across-the-board increase of $10 was applied, and another in 1919. Others followed in 1921, 1924, 1926 and 1931, raising the annual tally per student to $172, and then $180 in 1938 (this was the rate prevailing when Simes' report was submitted).[192] Inflation, of course, had the effect of holding the buying power of the monies allotted at a more or less constant level (it may in fact have declined somewhat).[193]

It has since been argued that, given its overall economic situation during most of the period in question, this was "the best Canada could do."[194] At the time, however, even Indian Department officials acknowledged that the rates applied to supporting native residential students was "exceptionally low."[195] The truth of this admission is revealed in a comparison of annual allocations made to sustain white children in residential facilities in 1938, the year the all-time high rate of $180 was applied to Indians: a per-capita rate of $550 was allotted to the Manitoba School for Boys, to name one example, while the provincial School for the Deaf received a governmental subsidy of $642 per student (about *three and a half times* the rate paid to support a native child). Church-sponsored facilities serving white children also did far better than those to which Indian youngsters were consigned: St. Norbert's Orphanage in Winnipeg received $294 per student; St. Joseph's, $320.[196]

In the U.S., things were even worse. Although the Child Welfare League of America reported that the average expenditure per white child in a residential institution ranged from $313 to $541 annually,[197] the 1928 Meriam Report concluded that as little as nine cents per day ($32.85 per year) was being expended on the feeding of a native child in a government boarding school.[198] Even assuming that triple this amount was involved by the time a child's clothing, medical care and the like were added in—a wildly optimistic expectation, under the circumstances—the annual per capita expenditure on a native youngster was still less than $100, or about one-quarter the amount expended on the average white child in a residential facility.[199] In 1929, moreover, Representative Louis C. Cramton, chair of the House Subcommittee on Appropriations for the Department of Interior, argued vociferously—and unopposed by Indian Commissioner Charles Burke—that even this meager sum was "extravagant."[200] Plainly, it is not without reason that the indigenous children herded into U.S. boarding schools have been referred to as "Uncle Sam's Stepchildren."[201]

The results of such governmental "frugality" were as grim as they were predictable. As Dr. Simes discovered at the Elkhorn School, "there was not enough milk, no potatoes or other vegetables on stock, and . . . the children never received eggs."[202] If anything, Simes' findings understated the case: at the Regina Industrial School (Saskatchewan), a "regulation school meal" in 1904 consisted, according to the principal (a "Rev. Mr. Sinclair"), of "bread and drippings or boiled beef and potatoes."[203] At the Round Lake School (Saskatchewan), "breakfast" consisted in 1929 of three tablespoons of "porridge, bread, lard and tea—nothing else."[204] At Christmas time, 1923, a little boy lodged in the Onion Lake Residential School (Saskatchewan) wrote a plaintive letter to his father:

> I am always hungry. We only get two slices of bread and one plate of porridge. Seven children run away because there [sic] hungry. . . We are treated like pigs, some of the boys eat cats and [raw] wheat. . . Some of the boys cried because they are hungry. Once I cry to [sic] because I was very hungry.[205]

This letter, along with many others, ended up in the hands of Indian Affairs Director Duncan Campbell Scott. The director, although he certainly knew better, dismissed them as "exaggerations," even "libels," claiming in the face of all evidence that "ninety-nine percent of the Indian children at these schools are too fat."[206] Hence, no departmental action was taken. Year after year, school by school, the situation remained the same. This was only partly due to the fact that the "reality of the economics of the schools did not change between 1915 and 1938."[207] The children were not receiving even such food as was allotted by Scott's bureaucrats in Ottawa. The ninety children lodged in the Regina School were allocated 21,580 pounds of beef in 1904, for example, but were served only 13,866; they were allotted 515 pounds of cheese, but were served 73; of 1,236 pounds of beans, they were served 700; of 1,236 pounds of rice, they were served 730.[208]

The reason for this otherwise inexplicable situation is clear. The staff, already provisioned far more generously than the children—a staff member was allotted 540 pounds of flour for the year, for instance, as compared to a teenage student's 360 pounds—were spending the monies budgeted to feed students on luxury items for themselves. The school's invoices for the year included substantial expenditures on "marmalade, sardines, lemons, oranges, shelled walnuts, icing sugar, lunch tongue, canned salmon, toilet cream, bananas, Frye's chocolate, olives, candies, tobacco, jelly powder, canned peas . . . oysters and grapes . . . syrup, strawberries, raspberries, blueberries, peaches, plums, red cherries, pears, pineapples, apricots, raisins, figs, tomatoes, corn, macaroni, kippered herrings, dates, honey and toothpicks," *none* of which was shared with the youngsters subsisting on meals of "bread and drippings."[209] Since the Indian Department's accountants were undoubtedly aware of what was going on—it was legally required that detailed summaries of expenditures be submitted to Ottawa at the end of each fiscal year—and no corrective action was taken, it can only be concluded that such practices, if not actively encouraged by Scott and his underlings, were at least tacitly endorsed.[210]

Variations on the theme are endless, not only in Canada but also in the U.S., where "standard dinner fare [was] bread baked at the school and a stew or meat gravy [and although] many board schools . . . operated dairies, students often drank coffee rather than fresh milk."[211] A May 1925 survey revealed that of the ninety children enrolled in the Flandreau Indian School (South Dakota), for example, "80-odd," most of them from utterly destitute Lakota communities where malnutrition was notoriously endemic, ended up weighing *"less* than when they entered in September [1924; emphasis added]."[212] School officials, meanwhile, had ordered that its dairy products be converted into butter, consumed by staff and sold in a nearby town populated by whites, but unavailable to students.[213] Much the same conditions prevailed at Haskell and many other BIA-run schools.[214]

At the United Church Brandon School (Manitoba) "whole milk was fed to the school's cattle herd and the remainder separated, with the skim milk going to the children and the cream made into butter for the staff dinner table. 'Beef dripping is our substitute for butter for the pupils,' noted [the principal] at Brandon. Lard was another common butter replacement on [the children's] tables at many of the schools."[215] Nor were such things relegated to the "bad old days" before World War II, as is representatively attested by the recollection of a woman who attended the Catholics' Shubenacadie School (Nova Scotia) during the early 1960s: before breakfast, the girls assigned kitchen duty "separated milk—Nuns and Priests got the cream."[216] In 1966, there were reports that "90% of the children" at the Mohawk Academy (Brantford, Ontario) suffered "dietary deficiency" so severe that many of them had been reduced to

A typical prison-style dining hall, this one at the Qu'Appelle Industrial School, Saskatchewan. (Western Canada Pictorial Index)

"eating from the swill barrel, picking out soggy bits of food that was [sic] intended for the pigs."[217]

The quality of such food as the children received was also a serious issue. Accounts of bug-ridden and spoiled foodstuffs abound, as when most of the students at Shubenacadie became violently ill after being served liver so tainted that it had taken on a greenish cast.[218] At the Kamloops Industrial School (British Columbia), when a girl found a "big worm, like a big grub [in her] yellow porridge" one morning, she was instructed by the staff member on hand, a Sister Caroline, to "eat it anyway [and] be thankful" (another student, professing hunger, did in fact eat the vermin).[219] Inability of the children to stomach such fare sometimes generated dire consequences. A young girl at Shubenacadie who, "unable to swallow some soggy bread," vomited in her plate, found her face pushed into the mess by a nun supervising the dining room and was forced to eat what she'd regurgitated.[220] Nor was this the only report of such methods being used to prevent "food wastage."

A Sister of Charity at the Shubenacadie school ordered a boy who had accidentally spilled the salt from the shaker while seasoning his porridge to eat the ruined food. He declined, she struck him, and told him to eat it. When he downed a spoonful and then vomited into his bowl, the sister hit him in the head and said, "I told you to eat it!" A second attempt produced the same result. On his third try, the student fainted. The sister then "picked him up by the scruff of the neck and threw him out to the centre isle" of the dining hall.[221]

The number of American Indian children who actually died of starvation during their time in the residential schools is unknown. Probably, from that cause alone, not many. The "link between poor diets and poor health" was well known to officials in both the U.S. and Canada from a point long before either had imposed its residential education system upon native children, however.[222] The implications tend to speak for themselves, not only in view of the staggering disease-driven mortality rates within the schools discussed in the next section, but also with respect to the sharply reduced life expectancy afflicting survivors from start to finish. It is also worth noting that the effects of chronic malnutrition would unquestionably have been far worse had the children in most schools not devised ways of supplementing their diets by foraging and/or "stealing" from institutional larders.[223]

It should also be noted that in many cases the children's families and communities tried to help, sometimes successfully, as when local native men near the Moose Factory School (Québec) took it upon themselves to provide water fowl, fish and game during the 1930s.[224] More often, however, such efforts were rebuffed; when native deacon John Martin attempted to organize a similar provisioning for the Chooutla School and the Anglican Church refused to authorize his endeavor, for example.[225] More striking still was the message sent by Indian Affairs Minister Ellen Fairclough in 1959, informing the Catholic Oblate that the principal of its Fort George School (Québec) had "broken the law" by feeding his students moose meat delivered by native hunters.[226] Far better, apparently, that the memory of the schools for all concerned be nothing so much as that of "ragged, ill-kempt and sickly looking" little waifs "who cried in vain for food."[227]

"Indirect Killing" by Disease

Since at least as early as 1763, when Lord Jeffrey Amherst ordered smallpox-infected blankets distributed to the Ottawas as a means of "extirpat[ing] this execrable race," the spread of disease has been a conscious part of the Euroamerican/Eurocanadian approach to facilitate the "vanishing" of Native North America.[228] Probably not the first, and certainly not the last time epidemics were deliberately unleashed, Amherst's gambit serves simply as an especially crystalline example of a larger whole. Although there are other instances in which contaminated items are known to have been intentionally introduced among healthy people—at Fort Clark in 1836, for example, in northern California a couple of decades later, and in British Columbia a few decades later still—they are difficult to pin down.[229] Most often, the methods employed were less direct, as when the U.S. Army interned the entire Navajo population at the Bosque Redondo for four years (1864-68) under conditions that left half their number dead of malnutrition, exposure and, most of all, disease.[230] All things considered, the residential schools must take their unfortunate place in this latter queue.

Mortality rates in the schools were, from the beginning, appalling. While comprehensive data for the U.S. is sketchy—partly because of a policy of sending terminally ill children home to die, their deaths thus lumped in with reservation statistics rather than the institutions'[231]—no less an authority than Duncan Campbell Scott observed that, in Canada, "fifty percent of the children who passed through these schools did not live to benefit from the education they received therein."[232] To place this startling proportion in proper perspective, it should be borne in mind that the death rate at the infamous nazi concentration camp at Dachau was 36 percent, mostly from disease. At Buchenwald, another notorious example, the rate was nineteen percent. At Mauthausen, described by historian Michael Burleigh as exhibiting "the harshest regime of all the concentration camps," the death rate was 58 percent (again, mostly from malnutrition and attendant disease).[233]

What *is* known of the U.S. experience suggests that conditions and outcomes there were, at best, only marginally better than those pertaining under Scott's régime in the north. During the first part-year of its operation, for instance, six of Pratt's original 136 students at Carlisle died on campus, another fifteen were sent home to die, and "in the winter of 1880 the situation worsened."[234] Of 73 Shoshone and Arapaho children from the Wind

River Reservation who were sent to Carlisle, the Genoa Indian Industrial School (Nebraska) and the Santee Indian Boarding School (Nebraska) between 1881 and 1894 "only twenty-six survived the experience."[235] "Haskell, Carlisle, Chemewa [Salem, Oregon], and other Indian schools maintained cemeteries to bury the many students who succumbed to sickness and disease. . . Between 1885 and 1913, one hundred Indian students were buried in the Haskell cemetery alone."[236] The roll of the dead is heartwrenching.

> The youngest students buried in the cemetery were six and seven years of age. Lem Cage, a Pawnee, was six years old when he died at the Haskell school in 1887. Nettie Pequah, a Kickapoo girl, died in 1895 at seven years of age. Mary Pahmahine, of the Potawatomi [people], was also seven when she died in 1900. Ada Mohajah was nine years old when her sister May passed away at Haskell in 1887 at the age of seven. Six years later, in 1893, Ada also died and was buried next to her sister. The Cheyenne children Susie and Ollie Walker both died at Haskell in 1886 and are buried together. Susie was eight when she died, and her brother, born in 1875, was eleven.[237]

The vast majority of fatalities among youngsters in the schools were caused by the rampant spread of contagious diseases, primarily tuberculosis (although influenza had its moments as a major killer, and smallpox made an occasional appearance).[238] At the Crow Creek School (South Dakota), for instance, it was reported in 1897 that nearly all the children there "seem[ed] to be tainted with scrofula and consumption."[239] Overall, a 1908 study undertaken by the Smithsonian Institution concluded that by that year only one in every five students was likely to be "entirely free" of tubercular symptoms.[240] An official study conducted in 1912 both confirmed the Smithsonian's findings and added that thirty percent of all boarding school students had contracted trachoma, a nonlethal but extremely ugly eye disease that unless properly treated leads to blindness; in 37 schools, the rate was over

A typical class in the Sarcee Indian School, Alberta, 1912. The two boys with bandages are suffering active tuberculosis sores. (Anglican Church of Canada, General Synod Archives)

50 percent; in all thirty of the schools located in Oklahoma, it had climbed to just under 70 percent.[241]

Beginning in 1882, when the tuberculosis bacillus was first conclusively identified, a medical consensus rapidly formed holding that among the best defenses against the disease were "strict hygiene, a nutritious diet . . . and well-ventilated living quarters."[242] Conditions in U.S. boarding schools, where "the diet of the children [sometimes] consisted of bread, black coffee and syrup for breakfast; bread and boiled potatoes for dinner; more bread and boiled potatoes for supper," and which were consistently "overcrowded by almost 40 percent," went in exactly the opposite direction, a circumstance greatly compounded by a gross underfunding of medical services.[243] So blatant was the cause/effect relationship involved that, by 1899, even a BIA inspector, William McConnell, was openly denouncing the whole residential education system as embodying a policy of deliberate slaughter.

> The word "murder" is a terrible word, but we are little less than murderers if we follow the course we are now following after the attention of those in charge has been called to its fatal results. Hundreds of boys and girls are sent home to die so that a sickly sentiment may be patronized and that institutions where brass bands, foot and base ball are the principle advertisements may be maintained.[244]

"Those in charge," repeatedly—although seldom so bluntly—informed of the silent holocaust occurring as a result of their methods and priorities, not only ignored it but, whenever possible, actively suppressed the information (as when, after requesting the American Red Cross to conduct a comprehensive Indian health survey submitted in 1924, Commissioner Charles Burke "buried" its inconvenient findings[245]). More damning still is the pattern of promotion prevailing in the BIA throughout the entire system, a process which saw some of the most egregious offenders elevated to higher and broader realms of responsibility. Haskell Superintendent Hervey B. Peairs, to name but one example, was appointed director of education for the entire Indian Bureau in 1925, despite—or because of—his glaring record of "endanger[ing] the lives of healthy and sick pupils by ignoring the presence of tuberculosis among [them, and having] repeatedly ignored the advice of the school doctor who recommended the quarantine of students obviously suffering the disease."[246]

In 1929, Peairs stood, along with Commissioner Burke and Representative Cramton, at the forefront of those defending the boarding school system, claiming that any appreciable change in conditions therein would be an "unnecessary extravagance."[247] On balance, then, there can be no reasonable dispute of the fact that responsible U.S. officials knew *exactly* what they were doing when, during the half-century lasting from 1880-1930, they continued to feed other people's children like fodder into the maw of their residential facilities as fast or faster than beds were vacated by dead or dying young-sters.[248] Nor, did the vaunted reforms marking America's "New Deal" of the 1930s mean an abandonment of the system. In 1941, 49 schools were still operating, some 14,000 native youngsters were still consigned to them, and conditions, although noticeably improved, still produced rates of death by dis-ease markedly higher than the norm.[249] And so it would remain, to one extent or another, until 1990, when the Phoenix Indian School finally closed its doors.[250]

In Canada, where things have been rather better documented—albeit far from adequately—the full horror of what was happening both there and in the U.S. comes into clearer focus. This is in substantial part due to a study of fifteen residential schools undertaken in 1907 by Dr. P.H. Bryce, chief medical officer of the Indian Department. The *Bryce Report*, as it's usually called, revealed that of the 1,537 children who had attended the sample group of facilities since they'd opened—a period of ten years, on average—42 percent had died of "consumption or tuberculosis," either at the schools or shortly after being discharged.[251] Extrapolating, Bryce's data indicated that of the 3,755 native children then under the "care" of Canada's residential schools, 1,614 could be expected to have died a miserable death by the end of 1910.[252]

In a follow-up survey conducted in 1909, Bryce collected additional information, all of it corroborating what he'd initially reported. At Old Sun's School and an Anglican facility on the Piegan Reserve, both in Alberta, 64 and 65 students respectively had died of tuberculosis by 1909, giving each a mortality rate of 47 percent.[253] Of 264 children who had attended the Kuper Island Industrial School (British Columbia), 107 were dead of the same cause.[254] At the Crowfoot Indian Boarding School (Alberta), eight of 52 stu-dents were already dead and 22 others had been diagnosed with tuberculo-sis.[255] At the Qu'Appelle School, the principal, a Father Hugonard, announced that his facility's record was "something to be proud of" since "only" 153 of the 795 youngsters who'd attended it between 1884 and 1905 had died in school or within two years of leaving it.[256] And so it went.

The reasons were neither hard to find, nor constrained to glaring dietary deficiencies. In 1908, a departmental accountant, E.F. Paget was assigned to conduct a survey of the system's "physical plant" in western Canada. Having examined 21 facilities in Alberta and Saskatchewan, he reported that most were in "deplorable" condition. Built with "an eye to economy," they were in the main "quite unfit for the purpose [they were] being used for."[257]

> At File Hills, the dormitories were too small, Cowesses needed brick cladding, Crowfoot was too small and badly ventilated, Sarcee could not be heated, was unfit to be used as a school and could not be modernized. . . Red Deer was "not modern in any respect." Regina was a sorrowful school: "Driving up it looked more like a deserted place than a Government Institution". . . Old Sun's Boarding School was "found to be all that had been said of it by others in regard to being unsanitary and in every way unsuitable for such an institution". . . Finally, the report indicated what was by 1908 a commonplace, the connection between the condition of the schools and the ill-health of children, particularly through tubercular infection.[258]

This, indeed, was by no means the first time Indian Department officials had been informed of the situation. As early as 1890, a school inspector had reported severe "ventilation problems" at the Kamloops Industrial School (Elkhorn was constructed on the same design);[259] 1893 and 1894 reports on Crowstand Boarding School identified drainage and water systems that were threatening students' health;[260] in 1897, an internal assessment conducted by departmental bureaucrat Martin Benson concluded that as a rule the schools had been "hurriedly constructed of poor materials, badly laid out without provision for lighting, heating or ventilation";[261] in 1903, the newly-arrived principal of the Red Deer School reported that the "sanitary conditions of the buildings are exceedingly bad."[262] An 1895 report submitted by a Dr. M. Seymore on the Qu'Appelle Industrial School in 1895 is indicative of the more general conclusion drawn: that "the schools themselves were expeditors" of tuberculosis, a plague already afflicting and killing native people at more than eight times the rate evident among Eurocanadians.[263]

> [Seymore] calculated that the boys dorm was four times too small for the number of children assigned to it. Out of necessity, "the beds are packed in as closely as they can be and the ceiling only about eight feet [high], and from the deficient ventilation the boys have consequently to breathe and rebreathe the same air during the night." Before morning, the air would be "simply awful." Overcrowding and the breathing of "vitiated air" constituted the main factors that facilitated the spread of tuberculosis. There would be little hope of "lessening the present very high death rate from this disease" until the children were "provided with such room as will allow them to be in a healthy atmosphere both day and night."[264]

Even the press drew the appropriate conclusions from all this when the *Bryce Report* was published in 1907, reporting that "Indian boys and girls [were] dying like flies" because of an "absolute inattention to the bare necessities of [their] health" in "schools that aid [the] white plague," and noting how "even war seldom shows as large a percentage of fatalities as does the education system imposed on our Indian wards."[265] Echoing William

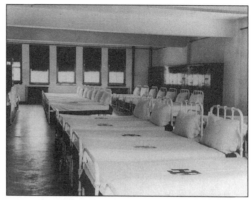

Boys' dormitory at the Kamloops Indian School, British Columbia, *circa* 1940. Such living conditions, all but guaranteed to facilitate epidemics, were standard in both Canada and the U.S. (Kamloops Museum and Archives)

McConnell's charge against the BIA a few years earlier, a Toronto attorney named Samuel H. Blake joined in, publicly asserting that "in doing nothing to obviate the preventable causes of . . . the appalling number of deaths among young children," the Indian Department had brought itself within "unpleasant nearness to the charge of manslaughter,"[266] while the *Ottawa Citizen* added that the "situation [was] disgraceful to the country."[267]

The response of "those in charge," once the flurry of public attention had passed, was to do nothing.[268] Or, more accurately, they did nothing constructive. As in the U.S., they *did* continue to facilitate a steady *increase* in the number of native children lodged in the schools.[269] Beyond that, their main effort appears to have been aimed at discrediting Bryce as a "medical faddist" who had brought the system into "undeserved disrepute," and with painting a patently false portrait of conditions prevailing in residential facilities.[270] One ranking bureaucrat actually went on record describing the "jolly, healthy children fairly bubbling over with vitality" supposedly inhabiting Manitoba's boarding schools.[271] By 1914, the author of the *Bryce Report* had been pushed out of the Indian Service altogether, forced to watch from the sidelines in mounting rage and frustration as the business of "educating" Indians went on as usual.[272]

By 1922, Bryce had had enough, publishing a searing tract entitled *The Story of a National Crime* in which the mechanics of death in the schools was laid bare and responsibility placed squarely on Duncan Campbell Scott's conscious and undeviating blend of "thrift" with ever greater numbers of com-

The cemetery at the Lac La Ronge Indian School, Saskatchewan, *circa* 1920. The youngest child buried there was six years old. (Anglican Church of Canada, General Synod Archives)

pulsory enrollments.[273] Among other things revealed was that in several of the schools upon which Bryce had reported in 1907, conditions had grown demonstrably worse over the intervening decade-and-a-half. At Old Sun's School, to take a representative example, F.C. Corbett, an Indian Department contract physician, had reported in 1920 that 70 percent of the students were infected with tuberculosis, suffering "enlarged lymphatic glands, many with scrofulous sores requiring prompt medical attention" which they were not receiving.[274] Such conditions "seemed to shock even the doctor himself . . . but it was the discovery that 60 percent of the children had 'scabies or itch . . . in an aggravated form' that most upset Corbett, for this was . . . a sign of gross neglect."[275]

> This skin infection, caused by the itch mite and usually found among children living in overcrowded and unhygienic conditions, had "been neglected or unrecognized and had plainly gone on for months." Corbett noted: "The hands and arms, and in fact the whole bodies of many of the children [were] covered with crusts and sores from this disgusting disease. Two of the girls [had] sores on the back of their heads fully three inches across and heaped up with crusts nearly a half inch deep". . . The remedy was simple cleanliness.[276]

The Sarcee Boarding School, near Calgary, was worse still, with 33 of 57 students "much below even a passable standard of health. . . All but four [were] infected with tuberculosis, [in] a condition bad in the extreme [and] fighting a losing battle with the disease."[277] Sixteen of those diagnosed with TB were still forced to attend classes despite being obviously afflicted with "suppurating glands or open sores" and had to sit "at their desks with unsightly bandages around their necks to cover up their large swellings and foul sores."[278] Only those no longer able to stand were "retired" to the school infirmary, there, shortly, to die. Corbett sometimes sketched haunting portraits of the dying youngsters.

> The condition of one little girl [eight years old] found in the infirmary is pitiable indeed. She lies curled up in a bed that is filthy, in a room that is . . . dirty and dilapidated, in the northwest corner of the building with no provision of . . . sunshine or fresh air. Both sides of her neck and chest are swollen and five foul ulcers are discovered when we lift the bandages. This gives her pain, and the tears from her fear of being touched intensifies the picture of her misery.[279]

Overall, "apparently robust children weakened shortly after admission" to most residential schools and "eventually became so sick" they had to be confined to sick bays where "the dead, the dying, the sick and convalescent,

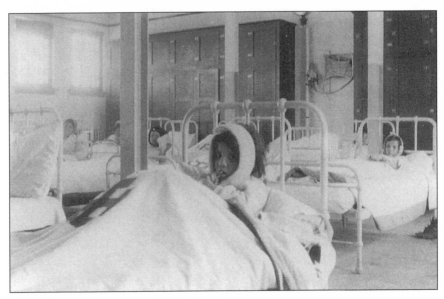

The infirmary at Old Sun's School in Alberta where so many children died. This photo was taken during an epidemic of the mumps in the mid-1930s. (Anglican Church of Canada, General Synod Archives)

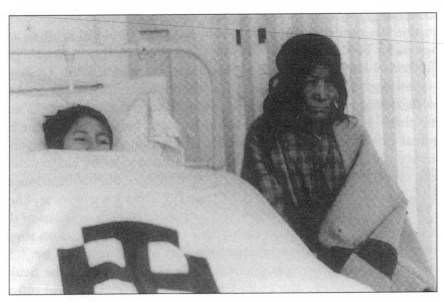

Death watch: A tubercular child and his grandmother, Sarcee Indian School, Alberta, 1913. (Anglican Church of Canada, General Synod Archives)

were all [lumped] together in the same room" in order to hold down the cost of their "care."[280] Sometimes they were then "buried two [or more] in a grave" to reduce the expense entailed in disposing of their corpses.[281] Topping things off, Scott had ordered that departmental medical services be *cut back* in 1918—the position of medical inspector was eliminated altogether—"for reasons of economy."[282] Indeed, while the number of students rose steadily during the years of World War I (1914-18), expenditures on residential facilities *declined* by about one-third.[283] Truly, the "scandalous procession of Indian children to school and on to the cemetery" remarked in the press upon publication of the *Bryce Report* in 1907 was continuing unabated when Bryce released *The Story of a National Crime* fifteen years later.[284]

While in 1922, just as it had in 1907, the Indian Department mounted a vituperative defense of its policies and practices for public consumption, it is worth noting that Scott himself had in the meantime privately conceded the substance of Bryce's charges. Writing behind a shroud of presumed confidentiality in a 1918 report to Superintendent General Arthur Meighan, he readily admitted that the buildings to which his minions were sending more and more native children were already seriously overcrowded and otherwise "inadequate," and that the resultant "unsanitary [conditions therein] were undoubtedly chargeable with a very high death rate among pupils."[285] Thus informed, Meighan took no more corrective action than had his predecessors. Indeed, it would be another sixteen years before monies were set aside to establish the first tuberculosis sanatorium for the ravaged youngsters, and even then no special funds were designated to improve conditions in the schools themselves.[286] That would have to wait until "comprehensive reforms" were finally undertaken in 1957.[287] Still, as late as 1969, reports on a number of schools revealed conditions were not especially different from those recorded by Bryce, Paget and others at the beginning of the century.[288] So it would remain until the last of Canada's Indian residential facilities was closed in 1984.[289]

Viewed in the whole, and especially in light of Scott's sharing of critical information with Arthur Meighan and other such highly placed officials, there can be no real question of the onus of blame resting upon the Indian Department alone. If it was not literally a policy consensus in Canada that residential schooling should be used as a handy medium through which to physically liquidate an appreciable segment of the country's aboriginal population, then their mass death was undeniably treated as an "acceptable" byproduct of the government's broader drive to culturally annihilate them. To refocus analyst John Milloy's apt assessment of the priorities displayed by the principal of Old Sun's School in 1922, Canadian officials as a group were plainly "determined that, with slates and chalk in hand, the children would die on the road to civilization."[290]

As to Canada's "general public," leaving aside the transient and largely pro forma expressions of outraged "concern" attending release first of the *Bryce Report*, and later *The Story of a National Crime*—manifestations which in themselves prove that average settlers knew, or had reason to know, what was being done "in their name"—"the deaths, and the condition of the schools pricked no collective conscience, wrought no revolution," nor even sustained pressure for a reformulation of policy.[291] As in the U.S., the fate of native people, children included, was simply not discussed within the polite circles of Good Canadians. Instead, such issues, like those contemporaneously pertaining to Jews and other "undesirables" in Germany, were swept, quietly and conveniently, "into the darker reaches of the national consciousness."[292] A better illustration of "the genocidal mentality" at work is difficult to imagine.[293] By the same token, the fact that Indian residential schools served as instrumentalities of genocide in both Canada and the U.S. stands muster under all but the narrowest definitions of the term.

The "Slow Death Measure" of Forced Labor

Amplifying the debilitating effects of continuous anxiety and stress, malnutrition and the near-total absence of basic sanitation in the fostering of rampant disease among residential school students was the substantial work regimen imposed in most such institutions. A number of facilities were from the outset explicitly designated as "industrial schools"—Pratt's prototype at Carlisle is a classic example; there were 25 such entities in the U.S. and 22 in Canada by 1907[294]—but those not endowed with that telltale descriptor ultimately functioned in much the same way.[295] Overall, the situation in the U.S. was such that in 1935 BIA employee Oliver LaFarge went on record describing the board school system as being composed of "penal institutions—where little children [are] sentenced to hard labor for a term of years for the crime of being born of their mothers."[296] In Canada, residential school survivors have also not infrequently compared their experience to imprisonment—in 1991, the Musqeam leader Wendy Grant-John referred to them as "internment camps for children"[297]—although as those who had actually been incarcerated in both types of facility usually observed, "the food was better in prison."[298]

Whether or not they were formally designated as purveyors of "industrial training," virtually all residential facilities were, by design, "frankly supported in part by the labor of their students," who, by the time they reached fifth grade, "work[ed] for half a day and [went] to school for half a day."[299] In other words, having completed their four hours of basic academics and Christian indoctrination, and fed their lunch of bread and boiled potatoes, boys as young as ten in the industrial institutions were promptly dispatched to spend another four hours manufacturing commercial wares in metal, wood or leather shops, while the girls went to garment shops, kitchen work or laundries.[300] In nonindustrial boarding schools, agricultural work usually replaced the shops for boys, while the girls' tasks remained more or less the same.[301] In both types of facility, providing domestic services to the staff, and maintenance of campus buildings were typically viewed as student responsibilities.[302]

The shop facilities at Carlisle where male students as young as nine were assigned to daily labor. (Cumberland County Historical Society, Pennsylvania)

> Students not only labored in the laundries, dairies and gardens of the schools, they also built and repaired many of their campus buildings. During 1910, in what appears to be an average work year, the Haskell boys constructed a two-story building addition . . . They also remodeled the boys' dormitory, laid new floors in its halls and in some rooms, repainted all the employees' quarters, fixed roofs, remodeled a shed, built a new hay barn and guard house, manufactured seventy-five sets of animal harnesses, made new furniture such as tables, chairs, desks, cupboards, and bookcases, and laid six hundred square feet of cement sidewalk.[303]

As a U.S. investigating commission found in 1928, "much of the work of Indian children in boarding schools would . . . be prohibited in most states under child labor laws."[304] The official justification in the U.S. and Canada alike for exempting native children from such protections was that, in the course of their "employment," they were being prepared for future self-suffi-

ciency by "learning a trade."[305] The trades taught, however—children made and repaired harnesses at Flandreau until 1936, for example, long after the internal combustion engine had displaced the horse on both road and farm[306]—often bore no relationship to the prospect of future employment. An obvious question also arises concerning the repetitive nature of the tasks assigned: "How many pillowcases did a girl have to make to become proficient at making pillowcases? How

Piecework production is performed in the sewing room at the Shugenacadie Indian School, Nova Scotia, *circa* 1930. At most schools, female students were assigned to undertake "instruction in the domestic arts," day after day, for years on end. (National Archives of Canada)

many shirts to become expert at shirtmaking?"[307] Plainly, production rather than "education," "vocational" or otherwise, was at issue. As one analyst has put it, "The student worked for the school rather than the school for the student."[308]

The sheer scale of output is in some ways indicative of what was going

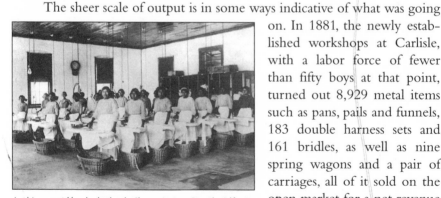

on. In 1881, the newly established workshops at Carlisle, with a labor force of fewer than fifty boys at that point, turned out 8,929 metal items such as pans, pails and funnels, 183 double harness sets and 161 bridles, as well as nine spring wagons and a pair of carriages, all of it sold on the open market for a net revenue of $6,333.46.[309] In 1890, the

A girls' commercial laundry detail at the Sherman Institute, Riverside, California, *circa* 1910. (U.S. National Archives, Bureau of Indian Arffairs Collection)

sixteen girls working in the Albuquerque Indian School's garment shop produced 170 dresses, 93 chemises, 107 hickory shirts, 67 boy's waists, 261 pairs of drawers, 194 pillow cases, 224 sheets, 238 aprons, 33 sheets and 38 towels.[310] At the Genoa Indian School, where agricultural rather than industrial work prevailed, 300 acres were under cultivation by 1890, producing corn, oats, wheat, potatoes and sorghum, virtually all of it sold at market.[311] At Haskell, where nearly 600 acres were under cultivation, revenues from the sale of hay, wheat, oats, corn and potatoes reached $14,000 in 1925.[312] At Chilocco, where even more land was under cultivation and there was a better growing environment, sales of farm products alone had risen to an amazing $48,467 a year earlier.[313] Nor was this by any means the end of it.

> The amount of material produced by student labor [at Chilocco] was astonishing: twelve boys in the bakery each week produced 2,000 loaves, 2,000 buns, 900 cinnamon rolls, 220 pies, 900 cookies, 900 slices of gingerbread and cake, and 1,800 pieces of cornbread. The laundry annually processed 475,000 towels; 98,000 sheets; 35,000 shirts and tens of thousands of nightgowns, pillowcases, bloomers and long underwear.[314]

As was mentioned earlier, almost none of this was dedicated to improving student nutrition. Even at the Sherman Institute, reputedly providing the best diet of any Indian residential facility on the continent in 1928, the vast bulk of the produce and dairy items generated through student labor were sold for a profit while the children themselves remained demonstrably malnourished.[315] No better case can be made for the disposition of revenues accruing from sales. At Chilocco, for instance, the BIA "adjusted" its own funding of the school each year in direct proportion to the amount gleaned from agricultural and industrial enterprises the year before.[316] Hence, rather than working to feed themselves, or to acquire such "luxuries" as adequate clothing,[317] the children were collectively harnessed to the task of paying staff salaries and otherwise underwriting their own confinement by providing a low-cost diversity of foodstuffs and other commodities enhancing to the quality of life enjoyed by surrounding white communities. As was candidly admitted by Canadian Indian Service official W.H. Graham in 1930, residential schools often functioned as "workhouses" in which children were reduced to the status of "slaves."[318]

The goal, openly and repeatedly stated on both sides of the border, was to make each school "financially self-sufficient," or even profit-making.[319] Toward this end, where students were paid for their labor at all—some administrators apparently believed token "wages" might provide incentive to

Harvest time at the Brocket Indian School in Alberta, *circa* 1920. Girls as young as eight were assigned to field labor. Such practices were standard. (Provincial Archives of Alberta, Oblate Collection)

greater productivity—the compensation was abysmally low. According to 1897 BIA guidelines, students new to a job should never be paid, but might receive 1¢ per hour thereafter. Children with two years experience might receive a "raise" to 1.5¢ per hour. That was the suggested limit for student "farm-hands"—other than at harvest time, when they might receive 25¢ per 10-hour workday—while those assigned to "skilled" positions in the industrial shops might receive 3¢ per hour after three years.[320] Even these tiny sums did not go to the youngsters who earned them, however. Rather, they were deposited in no-interest "savings accounts" (mis)managed by school administrators.[321]

The same applied to the "outing" program, originally devised by Pratt as means of retaining children in the system year-round while augmenting their total immersion in Euroamerican social and cultural mores.[322] While the program did in fact accomplish these objectives to one or another extent, it ultimately served more as a "pernicious form of involuntary servitude . . .

Boys on work detail at the Alert Bay Indian School, British Columbia, *circa* 1925. (Anglican Church of Canada, General Synod Archives)

that prevailed in many schools from the 1880s until the 1940s. Making male students available during the summer to work on farms owned by non-Natives, or putting a young woman out at service with a family in town, [was] a method of furnishing cheap, semi-skilled labour" to whites.[323] By 1900, schools like Genoa, Chilocco and Albuquerque were—in a manner entirely similar to the notorious "convict leasing" system then functioning in more than thirty U.S. states—"farming out" work gangs of up to 100 boys each to Colorado and Nebraska beet growers at harvest time, "there to labor monotonously in the hot sun from daybreak to sunset, sleeping in barns or tent camps at night," at wages so low they became a matter of concern to regional union organizers.[324] The girls, meanwhile, were placed as servants in middle-class homes to perform fulltime domestic drudge work for as little as $4 per month.[325]

Whether during the school year or during summer "outings," the labor demanded of children in residential institutions was not only dreary and demeaning, but often gut-bustingly difficult. In a single year, the 38 "working age" boys at the Fort Stevenson Indian Boarding School (North Dakota), to offer just one illustration among many, "in addition to cutting and hauling 300 posts, fencing in twenty acres of pasture, cutting over 200 cords of wood, and

The sheer quantity of labor demanded of students could be staggering. Consider this trove of timber harvested by barely two dozen boys at the Chooutala Indian School in the Yukon during the fall semester of 1934. (Archives of the Yukon, Anglican Diocese Records)

storing away 150 tons of ice . . . mined 150 tons of lignite coal. Proud of this accomplishment, the superintendent boasted that 'a vast amount of hard labor' was required to extract the coal, partly because 'about 9 feet of earth had to be removed before the vein was reached.' "[326] The debilitating effect of such rigors upon youngsters subsisting on fewer than 1,500 calories per day goes without saying.[327] Even when sheer brute labor was not involved, the survivor record is replete with accounts of being sickened by working conditions—spending hours each day in the steam of industrialized laundry rooms, for example, or spending endless hours standing at ironing boards—and of being too fatigued to do anything but nod off to sleep at the end of every "school day."[328]

It is impossible to calculate with precision the extent to which the conditions of forced labor imposed upon residential school students, rather than the malnutrition and other adverse conditions to which they were all but universally subjected, proved decisive in lowering their resistance to the diseases that at times claimed half their number.[329] Probably the best approach is, as historian David E. Stannard recommends, to treat the combination of factors as a inseparably interactive whole.[330] Be that as it may, any notion that the schools' work régime was intended in some sense to be genuinely "educational" for the children burdened with it is disabused both by the weight of associated facts and by numerous statements on the part of the "those in charge" themselves. "By the turn of the century, the balance between academics and [labor] was clearly shifting toward the latter," with the result that BIA educational superintendent Warren Hailman explicitly instructed his subordinates to "downplay literary advancement" among residential school students.[331] Hailman's Canadian counterpart, Hayter Reed, put it somewhat more delicately, but meant the same thing, when he observed in 1891 that "instruction in industries is of much more value to the ordinary Indian than in literary subjects."[332]

Compounding the situation was the fact, quite predictable under the circumstances, that many students were literally too exhausted by the end of each day's work to even try and study.[333] As such patterns solidified, some schools — Qu'Appelle, for instance, where in 1916 students attended a half-day's worth of classes only nine times during a 42-day period[334]—simply abandoned all pretense of being anything other than "workhouses." Unsurprisingly, all things considered, standardized test results revealed in the mid-1930s that many native students in the U.S. who had been in residential facilities long enough to have reached tenth grade had yet to acquire fundamental arithmetical or reading proficiencies.[335] In Canada, things were as bad or worse. A 1945 Indian Department survey concluded that of 9,149 students then in the residential schools, *none* demonstrated the equivalent of grade ten proficiencies, and barely a hundred had reached grade nine.[336]

> Research conducted in the 1980s by [Jean] Barman, [Yves] Hébert and D. McCaskill has added much greater definition to this Departmental sketch. They estimate that in the period between 1890 and 1950 at least 60 percent, and in some decades over 80 percent, of the children in federal [Indian] schools . . . failed to advance past grade three [even though many were teenagers]. They acquired no more than "basic literacy."[337]

Such outcomes were, of course, in many respects entirely consistent with a broader "philosophy" embraced by "educators" on both sides of the border that, in "civilizing" native children, utmost care should be taken not to "educate [them] above the possibilities of their station."[338] In general, this meant that the goal was for those who survived the ordeal of their processing to have gained *only* such rudimentary knowledge/skills as were necessary for them, indoctrinated as they were to view their lot as being both right and inevitable, to make their way in later years as "contributing citizens" on an extremely "limited family income."[339] More specifically, as was stated in the Flandreau's *Student Handbook* for 1938-39, girls were being deliberately drilled from an early age for lives spent "as cooks, waitresses, and maids."[340] As for boys, it was openly anticipated that upon leaving school they would take their "natural place" in the always necessary pool of permanently marginalized, expendable and, most of all, *lowly paid* menial laborers performing the kinds of industrial/agricultural tasks that "no self-respecting white man" might reasonably be expected to undertake.[341]

The tombstone of Joseph Rousseau, a 16-year-old Chippewa boy who died of unknown causes at the Haskell Indian School, Kansas, in 1902. One in two children entering such facilities shared his fate. (Brenda J. Childs)

Torture

To be sure, native children were not merely the passive victims of all that was being done to them. Virtually without exception, survivor narratives include accounts of subversion, both individual and collective, most commonly involving such activities as "stealing" and/or foraging food, possessing other "contraband," persistence in the speaking of native languages and running away. In many — perhaps most — residential schools, such activities were so common and sustained as to comprise outright "cultures of resistance."[342] And in most instances, the official response was to intensify the already harsh disciplinary regimen by which institutional life was defined, resorting to "corrective measures" exceeding any reasonable limit or proportion. Many of the methods routinely employed not only went beyond the usual standards of "cruel and unusual punishment" prohibited under Angloamerican law for application to convicted felons in penal facilities,[343] but violated the prohibitions against torture found in international legal custom and convention.[344]

Although in the U.S. an 1898 BIA handbook formally forbade institutional staff from "resort[ing] to abusive language, ridicule, corporal punishment, or any other cruel or degrading measures,"[345] such lofty-sounding prose was nullified by a series of "exceptions" promulgated several years earlier. Under the 1890 guidelines, the schools were licensed to inflict corporal punishment, literal imprisonment in a "guardhouse," and other such penalties on students believed "guilty of persistently using profane or obscene language; lewd conduct; stubborn insubordination; lying; fighting; wanton destruction of property; theft, or similar misbehavior."[346] "In other words," observes analyst David Wallace Adams, "just about everything" the children did was subject to discretionary interpretation/punishment by their overseers.[347] The utterly predictable results were condoned at the Bureau's highest levels.[348]

> One Hopi woman who attended boarding school after the turn of the century recalls, "Corporal punishment was given as a matter of course; whipping with a harness strap was administered in an upstairs room . . . One [staff member] held the [student] while another administered the strap." One Navajo woman would never forget the punishment she and some other girls received for leaving the school to pick apples in a nearby canyon. That evening the matron lined the girls up in the dormitory. "She told us to pull our blankets down and lie on our stomachs. She had a wide strap in her hand. She began whipping us one by one [as] we screamed in agony." A former student at Fort Sill, Oklahoma, recalls: "Generally, the officers in charge of the companies gave the whippings. They used either a board or a belt."[349]

The severity of such beatings, sometimes undertaken with fists, rubber hoses and even baseball bats,[350] is more emblematically witnessed by the case of a 13-year-old boy who in 1912 was "held, handcuffed, and almost beaten into 'insensibility' with a strap. The result was that 'the boy collapsed, lay on the floor almost helpless, and . . . after sixteen days, twenty-six cruel scars remained on his body, and eleven upon his right arm.'"[351] In 1914, "at the Walker River Agency School in Nevada, the superintendent, unable to determine which one of ten girls had stolen a can of baking powder, decided to punish the entire group. 'The superintendent ordered these girls, who were between thirteen and eighteen years of age, stripped of clothing to the waist, and each was flogged on the naked body with a buggy whip.'"[352] Such brutality, found by congressionally commissioned investigators to be endemic in 1928,[353] was hardly the end of it. There are many accounts of children as young as eight being shackled to posts, "having a ball and chain tied to their ankle," and other such things.[354]

Richard Kissiti, Apache, at age 4 the youngest "student" at
Carlisle in 1895. (Cumberland County Historical Society)

Although placing students in a school "jail" or "guardhouse" was officially discouraged in the late 1890s, this . . . remained a standard form of punishment [well into the 1930s]. Actually, school officials employed a variety of techniques to keep students in line. . . One woman who attended a boarding school in Oklahoma recalls that students who spoke Kiowa were made to brush their teeth with harsh lye soap. "The kids would end up with the whole inside of their mouth raw." At Albuquerque, the punishment for speaking Indian was [a stint on] bread and water.[355]

Although in 1929 Indian Commissioner Burke made an ostentatious display of renewing the 1898 ban on the worst of such practices,[356] his successor, Charles J. Rhodes, effectively gutted the constraints a year later.[357] As had been the case with the 1898 constraints, Burke's 1929 ban was for the most part ignored anyway (almost invariably without discernible consequences to offenders),[358] and, irrespective of periodic official pronouncements to the contrary, "harsh measures of discipline remained in use" at facilities like the Phoenix and St. Francis (South Dakota) Indian schools into the mid-1980s.[359] And, as always, things were no better in Canada, especially during the tenure of Duncan Campbell Scott as Indian Service director.

> Discipline, regimentation, and punishment in the service of cultural change was the context of the children's lives. It was pervasive in the system and, to some observers, poisonous. G. Barry, the District Inspector for Schools in British Columbia, described the situation at Ahousaht School, "where every member of the staff carried a strap" and where "children [had] never learned to work without punishment." Another critic who saw the same negative implications in this tyranny of routinization, charged that at Mt. Elgin [Ontario], "their whole day in and day out is planned for them."; the children learned "to work under direction which doesn't require, and indeed discourages, any individual acting or thinking on their part. Punishment goes to those who don't keep in line." To keep the children in line, the staff could deprive them of food, or strap them, or confine them [or all three].[360]

The record brims with accounts such as those at the Williams Lake Industrial School (British Columbia) of youngsters regularly "locked in . . . 'cold and dark' room[s], fed bread and water and beaten 'with a strap' . . . [or] saddle whip . . . sometime [sic] on the face," with their "clothes taken off and beat[en]," and so on.[361] A nurse inspecting the Crowfoot School in 1921 discovered, when entering the dining room, " 'four boys chained and chained to the benches.' [She] later returned to the dining room to examine one of the girls reportedly badly marked by a strap. Several marks were found on her lower right limb. Five girls were in chains."[362] At the Kamloops School, adolescent girls were regularly punished for such severe infractions as chewing gum by having their pants taken down in front of the entire student body and then being publicly strapped.[363] At the Shubenacadie School, one huge nun, Mary Leonard (or "Wikew," the "ogre," to her terrified charges) was notorious for "frequently lash[ing] out at students' heads and bodies with her large fists [for offenses like skipping rope], and was prone to us[ing] racially insulting language towards anyone who displeased her."[364] Indeed, according to Canon S. Gould, president of the Canadian Missionary Society in 1920, beatings were the norm, "more or less, in every boarding school in the country."[365]

Mention has already been made of the special torment, such as being forced to eat their own vomit, visited upon children who "spoiled" or "wasted" their sometimes already-rotten food.[366] Speaking their own language also warranted especially vicious treatment, as with a youngster at the Spanish Indian Boys School (near the town of Espanola, Ontario)who in 1924 was first undressed by the Christian Brothers running the facility as a "charity," then "whipp[ed] naked until he became unconscious."[367] Among the worst examples is that of the Alberni Indian Residential School (British Columbia) where, during the 1920s, children caught "talking Indian" suffered the hideous ordeal of having sewing needles pushed through their tongues.[368] At other facilities, scalding seems to have been the preferred method of punishing repeat offenders.[369]

Those who physically resisted such abuse, usually but not always adolescent males,[370] typically came in for still harsher treatment. One young man at the McKay School (Manitoba), who in 1924 fought back against a strapping after he was accused of "slacking" at work—actually, his hands had become too blistered to hold the pitchfork he was assigned to use—ended up bruised "black from his neck to his buttocks."[371] Another boy, upon being cracked across the skull with a cane by a staff thug named Skinner at the Red Deer School, seized the cane and hit his assailant back; shortly thereafter, the youngster was beaten so badly that he was required to undergo cranial surgery.[372] Such atrocities were regularly reported to Scott, but, other than the release of a vacuous 1921 assertion that abuse would not be condoned,[373] no particular action was ever taken.[374] Thus, the torture continued on a system-wide basis, decade after decade, until the very end.

During the late 1960s, for example, a staff member at the Oblates' St. Philip's Residential School (Saskatchewan) regularly burned "recalcitrant" children with his cigarette lighter, and developed a specialized punishment

The youngest child in this group — portrait-center rear, in the checkered shirt — had just turned five when this photo was taken. (Kansas State Historical Society)

"Young men" consigned to St. Paul's Indian School on the Blood Reserve, Alberta, *circa* 1935. (Anglican Church of Canada, General Synod Archive)

called "whipping with five belts" in which a cluster of narrow straps resembling the infamous cat-o-nine-tails—but embellished with metal studs—was used to induce a "proper" degree of submissiveness in the unruly; "It was not at all uncommon for this punishment to leave scabs that stuck to clothing and left scars."[375] Another method of "bringing unduly stubborn youngsters to their senses" during the same period was to place them in restraints and then apply electrical shocks.[376] Those "guilty" of bedwetting—a sure sign of terror or other sorts of deep emotional distress—were punished by "having their faces rubbed in human excrement" and/or being forced to parade around with their wet sheets draped over their heads.[377] And, of course, the "regular" sorts of beatings went on unabated.

By far the most common form of resistance manifested by the children to the overall set of conditions imposed upon them in the schools was to try and escape. Such efforts began almost the moment the first facility opened its doors,[378] and did not cease until the last one was closed. Once again, the literature overflows with confirming data, much of it centering on the extraordinary lengths to which authorities went in seeking to curb the practice.[379] Usually, these went to tracking down, returning, and then making "deterrent examples" of runaways. In 1907, for instance, it was documented that the principal of the Crowstand School "retrieved" boys who'd fled by tying "ropes around their arms and [making] them run behind [his] buggy from their houses to the school."[380] At Old Sun's School in 1919, the common practice was to chain returned students to their beds and beat them with a horse quirt until their backs were bleeding.[381] At the McKay School in 1924, Indian Service official W.H. Graham reported that a boy who'd fled, "almost naked and barefoot," after being "whaled black and blue" over a petty infraction—one of the trackers who caught him compared his condition to that of an "abused dog"—had received even worse treatment upon his return, and that such practices were standard in western Canadian residential facilities.[382]

A representative 1953 report noted that two boys "caught trying to run away" were beaten savagely by the principal of the Birtle School, leaving them with "marks all over [their] bodies, front genitals, etcetera."[383] During the 1960s, the boys' supervisor of the Duck Lake School (Saskatchewan) specialized in forcing recovered runaways to kneel, then "kicking the boys as they knelt in penance before him."[384] At least as late as 1968, there were still numerous accounts such as that of a 12-year-old girl being "punched in the face," then beaten with a strap on the bare back for fleeing the St. Philip's School.[385] And so, school by school, unremittingly, it went.

Another tactic regularly used—especially in the dead of winter—to instill a fear of the consequences of running away in the children was simply to abandon them to their all but inevitable fates. An early illustration is that of 9-year-old Charlie Hines, who fled the school at Norway House (Manitoba) after being "thrashed within an inch of his life," ending up so badly frozen he lost his toes.[386] Worse came in February 1902, when an 8-year-old named Duncan Sticks fled the Williams Lake School and froze to death almost within sight of his home. School officials had neither notified the youngster's family that he was missing nor, to all appearances, made any real effort to look for him themselves.[387]

> Nearly four decades later, on New Years Day, 1937, at the Lejac School [British Columbia], four boys—Allen Willie, Andrew Paul, Maurice Justin, and Johnny Michael—ran away and were found frozen to death on a lake within half a mile of their village. When Harry Paul saw his son on the ice, the boy was wearing summer clothes, "no hat and one rubber missing and his foot was bare." Another found his boy "lying face down with his coat under him . . . He was the only one with a cap on. He had his running shoes on with no rubbers." The boys—"only little tots" was how Police Constable Jennings described them—had [been desperate enough to] set out for home in thirty-below weather.[388]

At about the same time, a youngster who'd run from the Round Lake School (Saskatchewan) in 25-degree below zero weather and became lost in a blizzard was found when a search was initiated *four days later*.[389] In 1941, three boys who'd run from St. Anne's School (Ontario) simply vanished, never to be seen again (it is theorized that they drowned, their bodies then washing into Hudson's Bay).[390] In 1947, three boys running from the Kamloops School were killed by a train.[391] In 1959, two sisters drowned while trying to escape the Kuper Island School, and a 13-year-old named Joseph Commanda was struck by a train and killed while attempting the same feat at the Mohawk Academy.[392] Although his death was hardly the last of this sort—two boys died of exposure in November 1970 while trying to escape the Kenora Roman Catholic School (Ontario), to cite just one more example[393]—the 1966 case of 12-year old Charlie Wenjack is probably the best known of all such stories.

> He left Cecelia Jeffrey Residence School [Ontario] bound for his home community, Ogoki Post on the Martin Falls Reserve and "collapsed and died of hunger" beside the

railroad tracks he thought would take him home. When found, "he was lying on his back . . . [wearing only] his thin cotton clothing . . . obviously soaked." He had no identification; he was carrying nothing but "a little glass jar with a screw top. Inside, a half dozen wooden matches." From where he lay, "he had half of Ontario to cross" . . . The [Indian] Department shipped his body home accompanied by his little sisters who had also been students [at Cecelia Jeffrey].[394]

Although the record in the U.S. is far from being as well documented as that in Canada, available evidence suggests that a similar pattern was present. Carlisle reported 45 runaways in 1901, for instance, Chilocco a staggering 111 boys and 18 girls—well over 10 percent of the entire student population—having fled in 1927.[395] And, to be sure, there was a steady stream of fatalities.

In 1891, three Kiowa boys ran away from the boarding school at Anadarko [Oklahoma], presumably in response to harsh punishments handed out by one of the teachers. The runaways' destination was a Kiowa camp some thirty miles from the school. Before reaching the camp, however, a severe blizzard struck and all three boys were later found frozen to death. A similar fate awaited Pius Little Bear, age twelve, who in the dead of winter ran away from the school at Cheyenne River [South Dakota] in 1903 . . . "He died of cold and exhaustion before being found."[396]

During the winter of 1908, the superintendent at the Wittenberg Indian Boarding School (Wisconsin) reported "two Menominee children [having] recently . . . perished with the cold" during an escape attempt,[397] and, a few years earlier, four boys who'd fled the boarding school at Grand Junction (Colorado) disappeared into the fastness of the Rocky Mountains with a mysterious permanence which rivaled that of their three Canadian counterparts in 1941.[398] As in Canada, the flood of runaways from U.S. residential facilities not only continued but *grew* in the face of such grim illustrations of the potential consequences, leading some former students and at least one contemporary analyst to suggest that "at certain times of year attempting to flee school could amount to near- or actual suicide" in a very conscious sense.[399] Whether or not such assessments are correct—and it seems likely that they are to one extent or another—there can be no question but that native residential school children opted all too frequently to embrace this ultimate refusal of the conditions imposed upon them.

In this connection, the record is sufficient to proved only occasional glimpses of what was happening. The first documented suicide at the Phoenix Indian School was that of a Pima boy in 1894, for instance; although school officials professed to have had "no idea what was bothering him," contemporaneous accounts strongly suggest that ending the burden of "severe discipline and punishment" was likely his motive.[400] At the Williams Lake School in 1920, "in the aftermath of severe beatings" nine youngsters attempted mass suicide, one of them successfully, by eating water hemlock.[401] In 1930, another pair of children at Williams Lake used the same means to end their lives.[402] As late as June 1981, "five or six little girls between the ages of 8 and 10 . . . tied socks and towels together and tried to hang themselves" at the Muscowequan Residential School (Saskatchewan), following by only a few months the successful effort of a 15-year-old to do so at the same facility.[403]

While "cause of death" bookkeeping on both sides of the border was ultimately far too shoddy—or deliberately misleading—to allow anything resembling a comprehensive and accurate appraisal of suicide rates in the schools, even such fragmentary evidence as is available plainly belies apologistic screeds like Robert Havighurst's convenient—and therefore influential—1971 study claiming that "virtually no suicides occurred . . . in boarding schools" during the first ninety years of their operation.[404] There is, after all, a considerable distinction to be drawn between the number of suicides attempted on the one hand and the number of attempts recorded on the other, especially in a context where "those in charge" at all levels preferred that things appear to be other than they actually were.[405] Even without hard data on the number of child suicides claimed by the residential schools, the ghastly toll taken by the systematic torture practiced in those institutions for more than a century is quite clear.

Predation

It has been argued that the rampant sadism marking staff behavior in the residential schools from start to finish derived, not from any conscious intent on the part of responsible officials, but "inadvertently," as a byproduct of the same complex of budgetary constraints and other factors that led to endemic student malnutrition, overwork and lack of medical care.[406] There is a certain superficial truth to this. Offering bottom dollar for jobs often situated in "remote" and "backward" locations is a sure recipe for attracting the dregs of any "mainstream" (white) labor pool—i.e., the misfits, incompetents and sociopaths deemed unfit to work in other settings—and it was *always* implicit that the threshold criteria for employment in the schools was that those hired be white.[407] It is thus less than startling to find that, as one survivor of the facility at Alberni recently recalled, most male staffers were "men kicked out of the RCMP or retired from the armed forces. Their jobs had to be the bottom of the work force barrel at the time."[408]

The notion that such outcomes can be somehow separated from official intent breaks down upon being subjected to even minimal scrutiny, however. Both budget allocations and hiring preferences are obviously matters of policy. So, too, then, are the results ensuing from them, especially when the policies at issue are sustained over a long period and, as has already been demonstrated to have been the case with respect to the residential schools, in full view of the consequences.[409] Mere budget considerations, moreover, cannot account for the fact that, as has also been mentioned, although the details of specific atrocities were frequently reported to BIA or Indian Department headquarters, often with the recommendation that the perpetrators should be removed from their positions, no such corrective actions were ever forthcoming.[410] To the contrary, it was the relative handful of "teachers or staff members who sympathized with the children [who] were quietly transferred" or simply fired.[411]

Duncan Campbell Scott's removal of P.H. Bryce from the Indian Service provides an excellent example, already discussed. So, too, does that of Elsie Schmidt, a staff member fired in 1930 after protesting what turned out to be 99 separate instances of severe physical abuse over a five-year period at the Phoenix Indian School. Not only was Schmidt pushed out of the system, although many of her allegations were subsequently confirmed by congressional investigators, but, as was the case with Bryce, officials mounted a concerted effort to discredit her—albeit, she was branded a "Bolshevik" rather than a "medical faddist"—rendering her effectively unemployable in the private sector as well.[412] Those who'd perpetrated the pattern of crimes against children at the Phoenix school were allowed to retain their jobs, while superintendent John B. Brown, the man most directly responsible for what went on in the institution, and guilty of purging the only employee "troublesome" enough to complain about it, was also left in his position until he retired on full pension.[413]

Much the same pertained to those outside the Indian Service who sought to shed light on what was happening in the schools, whether north or south of the border. Bryce, given the official defamation he suffered as the result of publishing *The Story of a National Crime*, again serves as a perfect example. The same can be said of John Collier, W. Carson Ryan and other reformers—all of them labeled "liars," "radicals" and the like by Indian Commissioner Burke and other officials—who published similarly scathing critiques of BIA educational policy/practice in the U.S. a decade later.[414] Thirty years later still, the situation remained unchanged. In 1965, an all but identical assault was mounted by the Canadian officials against journalist Ian Adams—tarring him with the brush of "sensationalism" and "leftism"—for publishing an entirely accurate exposé of the conditions in Cecelia Jeffrey and other Kenora-area residential schools that would underpin the awful case of Charlie Wenjack a year after.[415]

Not to put too fine an edge on it, but to defend a policy is to defend what happens under its mantle; to actively excuse—much less shield and reward—the perpetrators of crimes is to embrace the crimes themselves; to make crimes possible is to be complicit in the very act(s) of their commission. Viewed from this perspective, which, after all, has since Nuremberg constituted a cornerstone element of international legal principle,[416] and which has seen considerable replication in North American statutory codes through laws like the U.S. Racketeer Influenced and Corrupt Organizations Act (RICO),[417] "those in charge" of the BIA and Canada's Department of Indian Affairs could not have entered a clearer statement of their intent to kill, torture and otherwise grossly abuse generations of indigenous children if they'd written it out in so many words. The latter deed is in fact—as many a nazi discovered to his dismay during the postwar trials—*never* really necessary to prove intent.[418] In this sense, if no other, the old adage about actions speaking louder than words holds true.

The implications extend far beyond the sorts of endlessly sadistic horror already discussed. Throughout the entire period in which the residential schools were operating, in virtually every facility, and, perhaps most unspeakably, even as the children were mercilessly flogged for the slightest deviation from the supposed virtues of "strict chastity" and other such aspects of "Christian morality," they were routinely subjected to the attentions of sexual predators among the staff members, quite prominently including priests, nuns and protestant clergy. So ubiquitous was the situation that in 1995 Douglas Hogarth, a Supreme Court judge for British Columbia, went on record describing his country's residential school system as having been "nothing but a form of institutionalized pedophilia" and "sexual terrorism."[419] Although they've adamantly denied it,[420] "those in charge," both of the churches and of the Indian Service, knew about and defended *this* as well.

Early indication that this was so will be found in a 1912 report concerning the Kuper Island School, where two young girls had been "polluted" by a male staff member, but information about the pregnancies and who caused them "kept from the public . . . in the interest of the Depart-

"A studied bleakness." The residential school at Norway House, Manitoba, 1927. (National Archives of Canada)

ment education system."[421] In 1914, a report that a farm instructor at the Presbyterian Crowstand School had engaged in sexual intercourse with at least two young women was similarly hushed up.[422] Even earlier, "a homosexual who worked as a recruiter for the . . . Oblates St Joseph School at High River, Alberta . . . was detected in the sexual exploitation of schoolboys."[423] Sexual "improprieties" were also reported at the Birtle School during the 1890s, and at still another Presbyterian school, this one in northwestern Ontario, it was reported that the principle had molested several female students in 1910.[424] In numerous cases, when sexual predation in a given school was discovered or suspected by native communities whose children were lodged there, the predator was simply moved to another institution and, at least in some instances, promoted.[425]

Similar reports continued to accrue right on into the 1950s, as with a male supervisor at the Shingwauk School who "was in the habit of sitting little boys on his lap and moving them around until he became sexually aroused,"[426] and a female staff member at the Anglicans' Moose Factory Indian Residential School (Ontario) who "would take showers with the younger Cree boys, ordering them to scrub her breasts and pubic area while she moaned."[427]

> A 1991 report by the Cariboo Tribal Council on the results of its interviews with former students at the Oblates' St. Joseph's [Mission] residential school in Williams Lake produced shocking figures. . . In answer to an interviewer's question to a group of 187 people . . . whether they had suffered sexual abuse as children [at the school], 89 answered in the affirmative, 38 in the negative, and 60 refused to answer. Depending

on how the non-respondents are allocated between the "yes" and "no" categories, these data represent a reporting rate of from 48 to 70 percent . . . The chief investigators of a less scientific study of abuse at the Roman Catholic Kuper Island School in British Columbia found that more than half the [seventy] people interviewed had horrendous stories . . . Mel H. Buffalo, an advisor to the Samson [Cree] band in Hobbema, Alberta, reported that "every Indian person I've spoken to who attended these schools has a story of mental, physical or sexual abuse to relate."[428]

Finally, in 1993, three years after investigators for the Ministry of National Health and Welfare had also turned up—and publicly commented upon—evidence that "100% of the children at some schools were sexually abused" between 1950 and 1980,[429] the Indian Service, which had by then been merged into what is called the Department of Indian Affairs and Northern Development (DIAND), turned over the first 35 of its files on suspected molestation cases for further action by the RCMP.[430] Meanwhile, conclusive proof was piling up in court, beginning in 1989, when Oblate priest Harold McIntee pled guilty to allegations that he'd molested more than a score of boys as young as five during his years at the St. Joseph's Mission School.[431] In 1991, an Oblate brother, Glen Doughty, who'd also worked at St. Joseph's, did the same,[432] and, a year later, Hubert O'Connor, a priest who'd been principal of the school before being promoted to serve as the Bishop of St. George, went on trial for raping and otherwise molesting several female students (a mistrial was declared in 1992, but O'Connor was retried and convicted in 1994).[433]

In 1995, "Catholic official Jerzy Maczynski [was] sentenced to sixteen years in jail on twenty-eight counts of sexual abuse at the Lower Post Indian Residential School [British Columbia]," while Arthur Henry Plint, a career supervisor at the Alberni School, entered a guilty plea to having committed serial sexual offenses against the children under his "care" from the moment he was hired until his retirement twenty years later.[434] His case is emblematic of the rest.

> Plint, then seventy-seven, cursed his accusers as he walked into court under the glare of television lights, hitting out with a cane in a final act of contempt and violence. Inside, he pled guilty to sixteen counts of indecent assault of aboriginal boys aged six to thirteen, between 1948 and 1968. Three of the boys were forcibly sodomized, others forced to perform oral sex . . . often daily, for months and years.[435]

As one official had already acknowledged, "only the tip of the iceberg" appeared to have been revealed by such cases.[436] Under these circumstances, Canada's Aboriginal Rights Coalition requested in 1992 that the Indian

Department initiate an official and comprehensive investigation of the extent to which sexual predation had prevailed in the schools.[437] In December of that year, Duncan Campbell Scott's heir, Tom Siddon, continued his predecessor's tradition of hiding the truth by declaring that he did not "believe a public inquiry [was] the best approach" to resolving the issue.[438] Although "by 1992, most of the churches had apologized"—the Presbyterians held out until late 1994—Siddon also made it clear that the Indian Service had no intention of following suit:"There would be no ministerial apology, no apology on behalf of Canadians, and no plans for [providing] compensation" to the victims.[439] The most the department was willing to offer was a carefully worded expression of "regret" that bad things had happened in the schools through no fault of its own.[440]

In substance, while grudgingly conceding that certain crimes "may" have been committed in residential school settings, DIAND insisted that each should be treated as an individual "aberration" rather than as a facet of a systemic condition, much less that the purpose of the system itself had in any way been criminal. Thus, the department would "not without specific cause initiate an investigation of all former residence employees,"[441] or consider the idea that compensation needed to be made collectively, as in a "class action" situation, to the communities targeted for elimination through the forced transfer/destruction of their children. Instead, it was insisted that each individual to receive compensation of any sort should have to go into open court and demonstrate the precise nature of the damage they'd suffered.[442]

With that deterrent procedure in place—two of the first group of former students attempting to establish damages found the experience so humiliating that they shortly committed suicide[443]—the department set about its time-honored strategy of limiting public awareness of the issue's dimensions. Without abandoning its rhetoric concerning the "need" for each allegation to be proven in court, DIAND "negotiators" set out to buy off as many former students as possible among those willing to incur the risks of coming forward, thereby preventing their cases from entering the public record and "unduly" tarnishing the department's image (collaterally, of course, one or more sexual predators was protected from prosecution every time this happened).[444]

> In Saskatchewan, [for example,] the federal government began quietly to pay, without any formal acknowledgement of responsibility, out of court settlements to fifty former students of the government-run residential school on the Gordon reserve north of

Regina. Although the size of the settlements is confidential [as are the details of why they were paid], they are reported to range from $75,000 to $150,000 per person . . . The secretive nature of the pay-out—in the absence of an apology—has angered aboriginal leaders. Blaine Favel, chief of the Federation of Saskatchewan Indians in 1996, renewed a demand for a national inquiry . . . "Indian Affairs is sweeping the issue under the table," said Favel.[445]

Chief Favel was by no means the only indigenous leader infuriated by this blend of official stonewalling and duplicity. Hence, the Assembly of First Nations launched an investigation of its own, publishing its findings in 1994.[446] A number of individual researchers, both native and non-, also took up the issue.[447] Concurrently, and perhaps most impactfully, the Royal Commission on Aboriginal Peoples appointed by Prime Minister Brian Mulroney in response to a protracted 1990 confrontation between armed Mohawks and federal forces at the village of Oka, outside Montréal, did the same.[448] Endowed with far more resources and official prestige than the native assembly, the Royal Commission amassed a much broader data base, and, in its November 1996 report, openly challenged DIAND's position by recommending that the department be instructed to conduct still "further inquiry and investigation into the profound cruelty inflicted on Aboriginal people by [the department's own] residential school policies."[449]

> Our research and hearings indicate that a full investigation into Canada's residential school system, in the form of a public inquiry . . . is necessary to bring to light and begin to heal the grievous harms suffered by countless Aboriginal children, families, and communities as a result of the residential school system. The inquiry should conduct public hearings across the country, with sufficient funding to enable those affected to testify. The inquiry should be empowered to commission research and analysis to assist in gaining an understanding of the nature and effects of residential school policies. It should be authorized to recommend whatever remedial action it believes necessary for governments and churches to ameliorate the conditions created by the residential school experience. Where appropriate, such remedies should include apologies from those responsible, compensation on a collective basis to enable Aboriginal communities to design and administer programs that assist the healing process and rebuild community life, and funding for the treatment of affected people and their families.[450]

Under the pressure attending such exposure, DIAND, now headed by Jane Stewart, abandoned its hard line in favor of a "kinder, gentler" approach to containment. Having asked for a year in which to formulate its response, Stewart in early 1998 produced a document entitled *Gathering Strength*.[451] Therein, without once using the word "compensation," she laid out an "action plan" wherein the department would underwrite a "process of renewal" in which native people could set about "healing" from the "tragedy"—never the *policy*—of what was done to them in the schools, eventually "reconciling" with the very government and churches that had done it.[452] So transparent was this ploy—placing as it did the burden of "adjustment" squarely on the victims while taking the victimizers ever so neatly off the hook (both individually and as a society)—that some analysts immediately compared it to the repressive strategies described by Andrew Polsky in *The Therapeutic State*.[453] Nonetheless, the only official initiative resulting from the report of the Royal Commission has been the endowment of $350 million on what is called the "Aboriginal Healing Foundation," mandated to establish psychological counseling programs for former students and their families.[454]

One can readily imagine world reaction if, in the aftermath of World War II, Germany, without ever really admitting what it had done, had offered a carefully monitored program of adjustive therapy for survivors as the sole "remedy" to what they'd suffered in the camps. All the more so if the Germans, as a concomitant of such "beneficence," had entitled themselves to retain all they'd gained from their victims—land, resources, even personal property—as a result of establishing and maintaining the camp system for years on end.[455] That the perpetrators do no favor to their victims by "helping" them "adapt," "accept" and thereby *legitimate* their loss under such circumstances is surely self-evident.[456] Far from redressing the crimes at issue, such an approach embodies a logical/practical consummation of them, enlisting the victims themselves as often unwitting collaborators in the affixing of an unredeemed and illusory seal of propriety upon the ill-gained power and prosperity enjoyed by their victimizers.[457]

While Canada thus continues to hoist itself on the petard of its own performance, it should be noted that the situation is even more putrid in the United States. There, the wall of silence behind which much of what happened to the north was all too conveniently hidden prior to 1990 remains as much in place as ever.[458] Even amidst a burgeoning scandal concerning endemic sexual predations of priests and others operating in mainstream settings over the past thirty years, and of systematic cover-ups and protection of offenders, most prominently by the Catholic Church, there has been no exploration *at all* of the probability that such abuse of native children was likely as pervasive in U.S. residential schools as in Canada's.[459] To the contrary, such efforts as have been made to "explain" the much better documented—and in that sense unavoidable—phenomena as forced labor and physical torture have been primarily of the sort designed to neutralize rather than elaborate the implications.[460]

Worlds of Pain

It is true that in both Canada and the United States the imposition of residential schooling upon indigenous children ended some twenty years ago. It is *not* true, however, as DIAND's Tom Siddon was already claiming by 1991, that the effects are now "in the past."[461] To the contrary, the ravages of a virulent cluster of psychological dysfunctions that has come to be known in Canada as "Residential School Syndrome" (RSS)—there is no corresponding term in the United States, although the symptomotologies involved are just as clearly present there—not only remains undiminished but may in some respects have intensified during the decades since the last survivors were released from the facilities in which the initial damage was done.[462] Given the proportion of the native population caught up in the residential school system during last two generations of its operation, and the fact that the syndrome is demonstrably transmissible to children and others closely associated with/dependent upon survivors,[463] the magnitude of its ongoing impact upon Native North America is easily discernible.[464]

In its most common manifestations, RSS includes acutely conflicted self-concept and lowered self-esteem, emotional numbing (often described as "inability to trust or form lasting bonds"), somatic disorder, chronic depression and anxiety (often phobic), insomnia and nightmares, dissociation, paranoia, sexual dysfunction, heightened irritability/tendency to fly into rages, strong tendencies towards alcoholism/drug addiction, and suicidality.[465] Here, it is important to emphasize that while the syndrome has been treated as if were something unprecedented and unique by most Canadian researchers—i.e., as a "clinical" phenomenon requiring extensive study before it can be either defined or effectively addressed—such posturing adds up more than anything to a subterfuge designed to divert attention from the fact that there is nothing at all "new" or especially different about RSS.[466]

Rather, it has a number of obvious and well-researched corollaries, including the entirely comparable sets of symptoms afflicting victims of rape, torture, hostage-taking, domestic violence and child abuse, all of which are clearly germane to the experience of residential school survivors.[467] Strong

Culture shock. Ziewie, a 15-year-old Lakota girl, shortly after being delivered to Captain Pratt in 1878. (Hampton University Archives)

similarities also exist between the behaviors exhibited among those suffering RSS and the Post-Traumatic Stress Disorder (PTSD) often associated with soldiers who've undergone heavy combat.[468] Perhaps most significantly, the symptomotologies of RSS are virtually interchangeable with those attending the so-called Concentration Camp Syndrome (CCS) manifested on a collective basis by survivors of both the nazi facilities and their counterparts in the Soviet Union and elsewhere.[469] The motive of officials and "responsible" researchers alike in insisting that the Residential School Syndrome be treated as though it were something new and distinct can thus be viewed as little more than a desire to dodge the implication that if RSS and CCS share a common symptomatology, they would all but inevitably share certain commonalities in causative conditions as well.

An equal or greater unwillingness to engage in symptomatic comparison prevails with regard to the observable similarities between RSS and the effects induced by yet another group of "total institutions," these being the "supermax" prison facilities that have recently proliferated in the United States.[470] On this topic, the hush is palpable since the symptomatological catalogue has been accompanied by clear evidence of an official intent to produce *precisely* the results observed. As noted penal psychologist Richard Korn explained the purpose of such "control units" in 1987:

> [The object is] to reduce prisoners to a state of submission essential for their ideological conversion. That failing, the next step is to reduce them to state of psychological incompetence sufficient to neutralize them as efficient, self-directing antagonists. That failing, the only alternative is to destroy them, preferably by making them desperate enough to destroy themselves.[471]

As was mentioned earlier, a more accurate formulation of the goals embodied in the rhetoric of Richard Henry Pratt and Duncan Campbell Scott, as well as the methods both men used in pursuing them, would be hard to find. One readily observable result of the residential schools, all but unremarked in discussions of RSS, is the existence of an entire strata of native people in both Canada and the United States who were, in what might be seen as a permanent variation of the so-called Stockholm Syndrome with which hostages are sometimes temporarily afflicted, "ideologically converted" by their experience.[472] For the most part deeply Christianized, often just as deeply rejecting of their own peoples/traditions, and primally conditioned to identify their interests as coinciding with those of their oppressors, they have over the past fifty years been increasingly employed by the settler status quo—governmental, corporate and academic—as a sort of "broker class," willing to extend an appearance of "native endorsement" to even the most objectively anti-Indian initiatives.[473] In exchange for their utility in perpetually subverting themselves/their peoples, the "brokers" typically receive incidental monetary compensation and appointments to "prestigious"—but invariably powerless—positions as Indian "leaders." The process steadily deepens their estrangement from native communities—wherein they are usually branded "sell-outs"—and furthers the process of sociopolitical fragmentation within the communities themselves.[474]

A much larger group, with which the first is significantly overlapped, consists of people among whom the "neutralizing" symptomatologies of RSS predominate, either intermittently or continuously. Deculturated to the point of being unable to participate fully in their own societies (at least in their own minds), and congenitally barred by the race codes upon which North America's settler societies continue to function from fitting into them either, such people are trapped in a perpetual limbo of conflicted identity, personal unfulfillment and despair.[475] Seeking some sense of "normalcy" in marriage and the forming of families, they typically discover that a combination of the psychoemotional damage they've suffered in the schools, their all but total lack of experience in actual familial settings, and often their inability to secure the steady work necessary to providing for their dependants, generates catastrophic results.[476] As a rule, they end up visiting upon their offspring some variation of the misery they themselves suffered as youngsters.[477] Aware of this, but incapable of altering the destructive dynamics at play, most compound the problem by seeking the oblivion—or self-nullification—offered by alcohol and/or other substances. Ultimately—or alternatively—they seek the final "closure" of suicide at a rate more than five times the national average.[478]

For the children of residential school survivors, childhood is often an experience worse than it was for one or both their parents. Their suffering/witnessing of traumatic abuse begins much earlier—often at birth—and tends to be sustained longer and in a more intensive fashion. For the residential school children, those tormenting them were at least the aliens who had displaced their parents; for the children of survivors, it is all too frequently their parents themselves.[479] The record of the residential schools is filled to overflowing with poignant accounts of little boys and girls who cried themselves to sleep each night in loneliness for the warmth and affection of the homes from which they'd been torn;[480] the children of survivors

Darlington, a 12-year-old Cheyenne, captured in a
"Napoleonic" pose at Carlisle, *circa* 1895. (Cumberland
County Historical Society)

are home, and must shed their tears in desperate hunger for something they've never known. Children in the schools escaped in droves, almost always trying to return to the places from whence they'd come; when the children of survivors run, as they often do, it is only "away." Increasingly, as native communities throughout North America continue to crumble under the weight of both the residential school legacy and such related factors as disempowerment and dispossession, there is nowhere for them to run *to* other than the pitiless streets of Winnipeg, Denver and Chicago.[481]

It has been reasonably estimated that one in every two adult American Indians suffered acute alcoholism during the twentieth century. In some locales, the Grassy Narrows Reserve (Ontario), for example, as well as Alkali Lake (British Columbia), Norway House (Manitoba) and Cross Lake (Manitoba), the tally was at times 100 percent.[482] Much verbiage—and untold research dollars—have been expended in trying not-so-subtly to affix blame to the victims themselves, a process of seeking/asserting "proof" that native people are "genetically predisposed to alcoholism" or that "there is something in traditional cultures" that obtains the same result.[483] No study has as yet attempted to correlate such obvious facts as that while half of all native people have lately become alcoholics, an equal proportion were also processed through residential schools. In the same vein, although they share neither genetic nor cultural characteristics with Native North Americans, other peoples subjected to longterm colonization on the English model—the Irish, for instance—have been notoriously beset by comparable rates of alcoholism, "schizophrenia" and other such RSS-like maladies.[484]

Pretending that a "genetic link to alcoholism" might cause the self-obliterating rather than social nature of American Indian drinking patterns does nothing, moreover, to explain why an ever-increasing number of native children have taken to inhaling the fumes of gasoline, solvents and other such substances in a deliberate attempt to *permanently* eradicate their consciousness.[485] By the early 1990s, this included seven in every ten indigenous youngsters in northern Manitoba, and, by the end of the decade, *all* the children between nine and twelve years of age in several villages in Labrador (where, instructively, virtually every adult was both a residential school survivor *and* an acute alcoholic).[486] To cap off this dismal picture, it must be noted that the efforts of Native North American children to negate themselves is not always so figurative; the suicide rates among indigenous adolescents in both Canada and the U.S. run at about six-to-ten times the national averages, with suicide

Marching to class at the Blood Anglican School, Alberta, 1916. Even where uniforms were not required — or possible — such regimentation of student life was always evident. (United Church of Canada Archives)

"clusters" among native teenagers sometimes pushing the rate upwards of 100 times that of their counterparts in the settler population.[487]

Probably the best characterization of RSS, encompassing as well the symptomotologies defining CCS and other closely related syndromes already mentioned, is that advanced by Harvard psychiatry professor Judith Herman in her conception of "Complex PTSD."[488] Unlike the "normal" variety of the disorder, which typically results from a single traumatic incident or sometimes, as with many combat veterans, several such incidents grouped closely together in time, complex PTSD arises as the result of a protracted series of such experiences, often accruing from multiple sources. Its effects are thus far more severe than the normal varieties of post-traumatic stress, typically manifesting themselves in such intractable forms as borderline and/or multiple personality disorders.[489] When the trauma begins at an early age, the process of cognitive integration is usually distorted and, at least in many cases,[490] observable alterations in brain structure result.[491] Although a variety of longterm therapeutic approaches offer the prospect of compensating for certain aspects of the damage — it is important to note in this connection that what is at issue are psychoemotional *wounds*, not "illnesses"[492] — none are known to "heal" it.[493]

The major defect in Herman's theory in terms of its ability to describe the actuality of RSS is her affixing of the word "post" as a qualifier to the kind of traumatic stress, no matter how complex, suffered by those she describes. This, despite closure of the residential schools themselves, is something very different from the reality faced by Native North Americans, for whom the sources of associated trauma remain as present as ever. Much has been made, for example, of the exacerbation of symptoms among those suffering CCS when they are exposed to neonazi propaganda wherein it is denied that the Holocaust happened.[494] Imagine the effects upon survivors, their children and the groups of which they are part, if, rather than being confined to the ravings of a much-reviled lunatic fringe, such denial, officially ordained as "truth," were asserted as a socially-normative viewpoint. Imagine in the alternative that, although it was conceded that "something like" the nazi genocide had indeed occurred, it was merely an "understandable mistake," carried out with "the best of intentions for all concerned," including the victims (who, ingrates that they are, habitually "exaggerate" its negative effects).[495] Absurd as such scenarios may sound, this is exactly how the genocide of American Indians is treated by virtually all sectors of the U.S./Canadian settler society.

The nature and magnitude of the ongoing traumatic impact of this seamless wall of perpetrator/beneficiary denial upon the continent's native people, both individually and collectively, may be left to simply speak for itself in many respects. There is still more to it, however. That the "shame" attending the irrational but pervasive social stigma assigned to rape and incest victims greatly compounds/amplifies the original trauma is a matter much remarked by feminist psychologists and others.[496] Imagine the effects if, rather than merely stigmatizing them, society as a whole elected to deal with the uncomfortable fact of their existence by subjecting such victims, not just individually but as a "class," to a continuous and all-encompassing process of denigration and ridicule in which even the most flagrant of their abusers was invited to participate, openly and with obvious glee.

That native people are routinely subjected to precisely this sort of humiliation is apparent at every turn: the evidence will be found among the hundreds of sports teams that have "adopted Indian mascots" and/or anointed themselves with names like the "Chiefs," the "Redskins" and the "Braves";[497] it will be found again among the hundreds of North American place names now bearing the word "squaw," and the cavalier manner in which settlers of all social stations apply the same unspeakably derogatory term to any and all American Indian females;[498] again, it will be found among the thousands of cinematic releases — worst of all the "comedies" — rerun endlessly on television, by which the settler society portrays native people for its own amusement;[499] and still again, it emerges from the eternal procession of brand names — Jeep "Cherokees," "Winnebago" recreational vehicles, "Big Chief" writing tablets, "Red Man" chewing tobacco, and on, and on — through which the dominating society converts indigenous dignity itself into a marketable commodity.[500] Suffice it to observe that no other group in either the U.S. or Canada is degraded in anything remotely resembling this comprehensive a manner.

Suppose now that "average" rape and incest victims—or concentration camp survivors, for that matter—even as they were relentlessly pilloried from all sides, found that both official policy and social consensus held that those who had raped, brutalized and otherwise horribly abused them were *as a result* entitled to "own" whatever property they themselves had previously possessed, and that they—unless, of course, they could somehow "suck it up," "get over it," and go to work for those who had maimed, defiled and dispossessed them[501]—were correspondingly relegated to living out their lives in utter destitution. Would it be at all reasonable to expect that the circumstances just described might tend to accentuate the complex of trauma-induced symptomatologies already besetting victims of incest, rape and nazi-style social engineering? It works no differently for those devastated by RSS, other than that where the effects of such factors on each of the other victim groups are for the most part hypothetical, for those traumatized by what was done to them and/or their parents in the residential schools, such things comprise the concrete matrix of day-to-day existence.

Putting Shape to the Future

Native North Americans are by no means the only people who have been subjected to residential schooling, or something similar, by their colonizers. Certainly, the "station" policy maintained by Australia with regard to the aboriginal populace of that subcontinent during the bulk of the twentieth century bears a more than passing resemblance,[502] as do the results embodied in the Aboriginies' "lost generations."[503] Although residential facilities were not usually employed, the system of compulsory schooling imposed by Britain upon the Irish from the early nineteenth century onward entailed "pedagogical" objectives identical to those pertaining to American Indians: destruction of linguistic and spiritual traditions, undermining of familial/social structures, and so on.[504] The same goals hallmark the modes of schooling more selectively forced by the British upon their colonial subjects in India and West Africa.[505] Occasionally, as with the British "Home Child" program, some of the worst aspects of what was done to American Indian and Australian aboriginal young people have also been visited upon unwanted or "surplus" white youngsters.

> British ["overseas territories" like] Canada, Australia, Rhodesia, New Zealand, and South Africa . . . participated in a white child slavery operation with England for well

over a century, Canada's complicity ending officially in 1924 and unofficially in 1948. . . English orphans or children seized from their [impoverished] parents by "benevolent" organizations were shipped to Canada (at a cost of $2.00 each for the Canadian government) and assigned as farm labourers, domestics, or whatever to the Canadian public at large. The children were, among other outrages, exploited as labourers, occasionally bought and sold [among] the farms upon which they resided, often denied an education, and more than frequently abused (sexually, physically, and emotionally) by their owners . . . The American government had a similar program, scooping up their own inner city children as well as buying some of the English "overflow."[506]

While the fate of the Home Children was an exceptionally ugly manifestation of the vicious class structure by which the "English-speaking world" has organized itself internally, such phenomena have plainly been the rule in colonial settings. Indeed, it has been observed that something akin to the residential school system is *inherent* to any successful order of colonialism.[507] As Sartre noted in his preface to Frantz Fanon's monumental anticolonialist tract, *The Wretched of the Earth* and elsewhere, colonization can only be accomplished by a violent subjugation "internalized as Terror by the colonized."[508]

Colonial violence does not only aim to keep the enslaved people at a respectful distance, it also seeks to dehumanize them. No effort will be spared to liquidate their traditions, substitute our language for theirs, destroy their culture without [admitting them to] ours; they will be rendered stupid by exploitation. Malnourished and sick, if they continue to resist, fear will finish the job: the [natives] have guns pointed at them; along come civilians who settle [upon their] land and force them with the riding crop to farm it for them. If they resist, the soldiers [or police] will shoot and they are dead men; if they give in, they degrade themselves and they are no longer human beings; shame and fear fissure their character and shatter their personality. The business is carried out briskly by experts: "psychological services" are by no means a new invention. Neither is brainwashing.[509]

Eventually, if the colonizers' system functions as intended, the colonized "do not even need to be exterminated any more. No, the most urgent thing . . . is to humiliate them, to wipe out the pride in their hearts, to reduce them to the level of animals. The body will be allowed to live on but the spirit will be destroyed. Tame, train, punish: those are the words that obsess the colonizer."[510] In effect, aside from the "perpetual massacre" through which it is of necessity sustained, colonialism "is by its very nature a [process] of cultural genocide. Colonization cannot take place without systematically liquidating all the [autochthonous] characteristics of the native society."[511] It follows that, for Sartre, colonialism, as such, *equaled* genocide. It may be added, moreover, that there is nothing in his formulation, unlike those advanced from virtually every other quarter during the second half of the twentieth century,[512] which is in the least inconsistent with Raphaël Lemkin's original conception of the crime.

Although Sartre's percipience has been treated as "controversial," especially among self-described "genocide scholars," it seems reasonable to postulate that only those in a state of denial — that is to say, those wedded in one way or ten to an unadmitted but nonetheless potent package of personal privileges they perceive as accruing to them through the continuation of colonial dominance by their own group — might be expected to profess surprise, confusion or the "need for qualification" of the proposition that an inherently genocidal system must produce inherently genocidal results.[513] Worst of all are those who, having looked their own society's genocidal comportment in the eye, harness their intellects to proclaiming it something else.[514] In them, the genocidal mentality, and thus the perpetual recurrence of genocide, may be witnessed at its most distillate.

> When scholars deny genocide, in the face of decisive evidence that it has occurred, they contribute to a false consciousness that [has] the most dire reverberations. Their message is [that genocide] requires no confrontation, no reflection, but should be ignored, glossed over. In this way, scholars lend their considerable authority to the acceptance of this ultimate human crime. More than that, they encourage — indeed invite — a repetition of that crime from virtually any source in the immediate or distant future. By [masking] the truth, that is, scholars contribute to the deadly psychohistorical dynamic in which unopposed genocide begets new genocides.[515]

For those not of this ilk, there can be neither compromise nor equivocation. Given that residential schooling and its corollaries have all along served as a linchpin in the consolidation of colonial order, and that colonialism in itself amounts to genocide, there can be no hedging as to whether either the schools or their aftereffects were/are "really" genocidal. They were, and blatantly so. The "something taking the place of this truth" remarked by Wittgenstein in the epigram to this essay is thereby revealed as the aggregate of "interpretations" holding that the Indian residential school systems maintained by the U.S. and Canada were *anything but* instruments of genocide.[516] The first task, then, is to "uncover the source of the misrepresentation" and "transform it into what is true." Genocide, always and everywhere, must be called by its right name. So, too, must those who would camouflage or deny it be called by theirs. Such insights must be voiced, not "to power"—"those in charge" have always known, and never cared—but in its teeth, so that "truth can penetrate" the minds of *people*.[517]

Having thus "defined the phenomenon" at hand in a fashion common to both Wittgenstein and Huey Newton, the question becomes how it might be caused "to act in the desired manner" (that is, to cease and disappear).[518] The answer, of course, resides in the "source" of both the phenomenon and its misrepresentation. Insofar as the genocide embodied in residential schooling arises as an integral aspect of colonialism, then colonialism must be seen as constituting that source. It follows that the antidote will be found, exclusively so, in a thoroughgoing process of *de*colonization.[519] To be consciously antigenocidal, one must be actively anti-imperialist, and vice versa. To be in any way an apologist for colonialism is to be an active proponent of genocide.[520] In this, given the dynamics of power at play, there are—indeed can be—no bystanders. "If you're not part of the solution," as Eldridge Cleaver once so aptly put it, "you *are* part of the problem."[521]

Rephrased in affirmative terms, decolonization in the context of Native North America means simply the assertion and realization by American Indians of the right to self-determination repeatedly confirmed in international law as being vested in *all* peoples, "by virtue of [which], they freely determine their political status and freely pursue their economic, social and cultural development."[522] More concretely, this means the extension of unfettered indigenous jurisdiction over the full extent of the territories explicitly reserved by native peoples for their own use and occupancy in their treaties with the U.S. and Canada, as well as such territories as were expropriated from them through fraudulent or coerced treaties. Within these reconstituted homelands—an aggregate totaling perhaps half the continent[523]—it follows that indigenous nations, *not* North America's settler state governments, will exercise complete control over everything from natural resource disposition, to their form(s) of government, to the criteria of citizenship.[524] There can be none of the current U.S. subterfuge of pretending that native people are already self-determining,[525] or that they are entitled to exercise only a kind of "internal self-determination" previously unknown to legal discourse.[526]

Restitution in terms of property and jurisdiction are by no means the only elements involved in the decolonization of Native North America. The colonization itself occurred in flagrant violation of international law, not least through the systematic breach of some 400 ratified treaties in the U.S. and scores more in Canada,[527] and has been maintained since 1945 in circumvention of provisions in the United Nations Charter making colonialism itself illegal.[528] To this must be added the implications of sustained and multifaceted violations of the Genocide Convention and numerous other conventions, covenants and declarations by both North American settler states.[529] Under international tort law, offending entities incur a liability with regard to each such breach of legality requiring that, to the extent possible, they repair all damages done as a result of their transgressions.[530] In cases where reparation is not possible—as examples, where land has been rendered uninhabitable by mining and/or contamination, or where the destruction of population is involved—they are obliged to make adequate compensation to the victims/survivors.[531] Under no circumstances is an offending entity entitled to define adequacy of restitution, reparation or compensation; the is the prerogative/responsibility of a neutral third party such as the International Court of Justice ("World Court").[532]

Finally, there is the matter of criminal culpability. Those who formulated and presided over, as well as those who carried out criminal policies are subject to prosecution for their actions. Where domestic tribunals fail to mete out justice in such matters—as those of the United States and Canada invariably have—the authority of the newly constituted International Criminal Court may be invoked (despite an ongoing refusal on the part of the United States in particular to accept its jurisdiction).[533] As to the matter of the culpability lodged in the broader settler populations that have for so long proven themselves accepting of what was/is being done to American Indians, and who have gladly queued up to avail themselves of material benefits plainly accruing at the expense of native people—a posture adding up to complicity, if nothing else—a more metaphysical resolution presents itself. In general, this would assume the form of penance explored quite eloquently by Karl Jaspers in his *The Question of German Guilt*.[534] At a minimum, the accurizing of "mainstream" Euroamerican history—thereby replacing national/cultural hubris with the sort of humility accompanying all such admissions of criminal comportment—would undoubtedly go far towards dissipating the attitudes which gave rise to the residential school system and related atrocities while giving no small measure of psychic comfort to surviving victims.[535]

How such things are to be accomplished is not readily apparent. Codifications of law and the existence of appropriate judicial fora are one thing, enforcement of the law another thing entirely. As has been observed, governments inclined to perpetrate genocide and associated crimes, as well as the constituents endorsing them, tend not to be susceptible to moral suasion.[536] Instead, they are apt to turn with utmost viciousness upon those mounting anything resembling an effective challenge to their prerogatives, maintaining for such purposes highly developed police and military establishments.[537] Because of this, genocidal states determine to a considerable extent the methods necessary to bring them to heel. With regard to nazi Germany, for example, a world war was required to accomplish the task. In the aftermath of that catastrophe, and with an eye towards preventing the recurrence of anything so cataclysmic, the community of nations, prefiguring Malcolm X, vested the citizenry of every state with not only the right but the obligation to utilize *whatever* means might prove necessary to ensure the compliance of their governments with international law.[538] One firm indication of what was meant by this not-really-so-ambiguous mandate will be found in the postwar valorization of the group of German army officers who in 1944 attempted to forcibly disband the nazi government.[539]

The task is daunting. There is nothing comfortable or convenient about its doing, no petition that can be signed or electoral campaign that can be conducted, no manifesto nor protest song that can be written, no rally or candle-lit prayer vigil that can be held, no mass demonstration or peace march, no switch to an exotic diet, clothing and/or hair style, no "consciousness expanding" pills that can be taken to compel the requisite changes in the status quo.[540] Such change cannot be attained through tax-deductible cash contributions or the building of better bike paths, the banning of ashtrays in public spaces, or by teaching "our kids" to play soccer rather than baseball.[541] No, the process will be painful, unavoidably and exceedingly so, and it will not be over in a hurry. While its form will no doubt be decisively different, both its duration and the deprivations experienced by participants will likely surpass those evidenced in China during the Long March.[542]

Yet, should those among North America's settler societies who manage to see things clearly nonetheless shirk their responsibility to do that which is necessary, the agony of the Others who are their countries' victims will continue, incrementally worsening to the point of their long-prophesied extinction.[543] Somewhere between this point and that, those relegated to the excruciation of nullified existence will seize upon a moment of cumulative anguish and do the job themselves—or try to—in a manner both natural and far more horrific than if the defaulters had done it themselves.[544]

> Maintained at the level of animals by an oppressive system, they are not [allowed] any rights, not even the right to live, and their condition worsens day by day: when a people's only remaining option is in choosing how to die, when they have received from their oppressors only one gift—despair—what have they got to lose? Their misery will become their courage; they will turn the eternal rejection that colonization presents them with into an absolute rejection of colonization.[545]

If the resulting monumentality of violence would be redeemed by the fact that it was "no less than man reconstructing himself,"[546] far better that significant sectors of the colonizing populace joined hands with the colonized before the fact, eliminating colonialism in a common project that had the effect of reducing the magnitude of violence experienced by *all* concerned. Surely, such a project is worthy by any and all conceivable moral, ethical and legal standards. Equally surely, we owe it to the survivors of the ongoing process of genocide embodied in the residential schools—and to their children, their grandchildren, and to our own humanity, if ever it is to be reclaimed—that we shoulder the burden, *whatever* it may entail, of ensuring that the order of colonialism at last is shattered, never to be restored. Most importantly, we owe it, all of us, to our coming generations, seven deep into the future, to bequeath unto them lives free of the nightmarish reality in which we ourselves remain so mired. Should that prove to be the legacy of the little ones who suffered so long and so terribly in the schools, then perhaps their spirits may finally be at peace.

Notes

1. The late Lucy S. Dawidowicz offers a perfect illustration of such preoccupations in her *The Holocaust and the Historians* (Cambridge, MA: Harvard University Press, 1981) esp. pp. 13-7. For critique, see David E. Stannard, "Uniqueness as Denial: The Politics of Holocaust Scholarship," in Alan S. Rosenbaum, ed., *Is the Holocaust Unique? Perspectives on Comparative Genocide* (Boulder, CO: Westview Press, 1996) pp. 163-208, esp. pp. 169-71.

2. As was finally asked in connection with such studies, "Does it really matter so much if millions are gassed according to Eichmann's timetables, rather than slowly, crudely starved to death as in Stalin's regime, or marched around by ragged teenage Khmer Rouge soldiers and then beheaded or clubbed? Does the family mourning the loved one hacked to pieces by a spontaneous mob of Indonesian vigilantes care that much about abuses of science and technology? Does neatness count, finally, so damn much?"; Phillip Lopate, "Resistance to the Holocaust," in Peter Hayes, ed., *Testimony: Contemporary Writers Make the Holocaust Personal* (New York: Times Books, 1989) p. 292.

3. Probably the strongest theorization of the functionalist perspective will be found in Zygmunt Bauman's *Modernity and the Holocaust* (Cambridge, UK: Polity Press, 1989). Perhaps the best application of such principles is Götz Ally's *"Final Solution": Nazi Population Policy and the Murder of European Jews* (London: Arnold, 1999).

4. See, e.g., Steven T. Katz, "The 'Unique' Intentionality of the Holocaust," in his *Post-Holocaust Dialogues* (New York: New York University Press, 1983) pp. 287-318. For critique, see Alexander K.A. Greenawalt, "Rethinking Genocidal Intent: The Case for a Knowledge-Based Interpretation," *Columbia Law Review*, Dec. 1999.

5. The claim of rigor has been broadly advanced. See, as examples, Vahakn N. Dadrian, "A Typology of Genocide," *International Review of Modern Sociology*, No. 5, Fall 1975; Helen Fein, "Scenarios of Genocide: Models of Genocide and Critical Responses," in Israel W. Charny, ed., *Towards the Understanding and Prevention of Genocide: Proceedings of the International Conference on Holocaust and Genocide* (Boulder, CO: Westview Press, 1984) pp. 3-31; Roger W. Smith, "Human Destructiveness and Politics: The Twentieth Century as an Age of Genocide," and Barbara Harff, "The Etiology of Genocides," both in Isidor Wallimann and Michael N. Dobkowski, eds., *Genocide and the Modern Age: Etiology and Case Studies of Mass Death* (Westport, CT: Greenwood Press, 1987) pp. 21-39, 41-59; Henry Huttenbach, "Locating the Holocaust on the Genocide Spectrum: Towards a Methodology of Definition and Categorization," *Holocaust and Genocide Studies*, Vol. 3, No. 3, 1988; Barbara Harff and Ted Gurr, "Toward an Empirical Theory of Genocide and Politicide: Identification and Measurement of Cases Since 1945," *International Studies Quarterly*, Vol. 32, No. 3, Sept. 1988.

6. Such definitions have been "deliberately restrictive," as Frank Chalk and Kurt Jonassohn observe of the one advanced in their own book, *The History and Sociology of Genocide: Analyses and Case Studies* (New Haven, CT: Yale University Press, 1990) pp. 23-7, quote at p. 23. For the descriptor employed, see Roger Manvell and Heinrich Fraenkel, *Incomparable Crime: Mass Extermination in the 20th Century* (London: Hinemann, 1967). For the claim to "phenomenological uniqueness," see Steven T. Katz, *The Holocaust in Historical Context, Vol. 1: The Holocaust and Mass Death before the Modern Age* (New York: Oxford University Press, 1994) pp. 27-8.

7. Yehuda Bauer, *The Holocaust in Historical Perspective* (Seattle: University of Washington Press, 1978) p. 38.

8. See Ian Hancock, "Responses to the Porrajmos: The Romani Holocaust," in Rosenbaum, *Is the Holocaust Unique?* pp. 39-64. Further background will be found in Donald Kendrick, and Grattan Paxton, *Gypsies Under the Swastika* (Hartfield, UK: Hertfordshire University Press, 1995); Guenter Lewy, *The Nazi Persecution of the Gypsies* (New York: Oxford University Press, 2000).

9. For a good overview of those excluded by such "rigorous" Holocaust scholarship, see Michael Berenbaum, ed., *A Mosaic of Victims: Non-Jews Persecuted and Murdered by the Nazis* (New York: New York University Press, 1990).

10. Edward Alexander, *The Holocaust and the War of Ideas* (New Brunswick, NJ: Transaction, 1994) p. 195. Elsewhere, the same author has contended that *any* other group claiming to have suffered genocide is, on that basis alone, engaged in an "anti-Semitic" effort to "plunder the moral capital which the Jewish people [has accumulated] through its unparalleled suffering in World War II"; Edward Alexander, "Stealing

the Holocaust," *Midstream*, Vol. 26, No. 9, Nov. 1980, p. 47. A superb little critique of such posturing appears in Pierre Papazian's "A 'Unique Uniqueness'?" *Midstream*, Vol. 30, No. 4, 1984. Also see Norman G. Finkelstein, *The Holocaust Industry: Reflections on the Exploitation of Jewish Suffering* (London: Verso, 2000).

11. Consider, for example, the response of Paraguay's defense minister to charges filed with the United Nations Secretariat by the International League for the Rights of Man and several other organizations in March 1974 that his troops were engaged in genocidal actions against the Aché Indians. "Although there are victims and victimizer," he stated, "there is not the third element necessary to establish the crime of genocide—that is 'intent.' As there is no 'intent,' one cannot speak of 'genocide' "; quoted in Norman Lewis, "The Camp at Cecilio Baez," in Richard Arens, ed., *Genocide in Paraguay* (Philadelphia: Temple University Press, 1976) pp. 62-3. Similarly, when confronted with allegations that genocide was being perpetrated against the Yanomami and other peoples indigenous to the Amazon Basin during the late 1960s, Brazil's official response was that, "The crimes against the Brazilian indigenous population cannot be characterized as genocide, since the criminal parties involved never eliminated the Indians as an ethnic or cultural group. Hence there was lacking the special malice or motivation necessary to characterize the occurrence of genocide. The crimes in question were committed for exclusively economic reasons, the perpetrators having acted solely to take possession of the lands of their victims"; quoted in Leo Kuper, *Genocide: Its Political Use in the Twentieth Century* (New Haven, CT: Yale University Press, 1982) p. 34.

12. For a still excellent analysis of the intellectual dynamic at issue, see Noam Chomsky, "Objectivity and Liberal Scholarship," in his *American Power and the New Mandarins* (New York: Pantheon, 1967) pp. 23-158.

13. Consider, as but one striking example, the 1995 vote of the U.S. Senate to "cut funds to the Smithsonian Institution if a film it was partially funding used that word [genocide], even in passing, to describe the destruction of the Western Hemisphere's indigenous peoples"; Stannard, "Uniqueness as Denial," p. 165.

14. Denial of the judeocide is of course "indefensible, [but no less so than the] routine genocide denials that result from taking the Holocaust as unique and/or prototypical"; David Moshman, "Conceptual Restraints on Thinking About Genocide," *Journal of Genocide Research*, Vol. 3, No. 3, 2001, p. 436. On application of the French statute—primarily against the notorious "revisionist" Robert Faurisson—see Jeffrey Mehlman's foreword to Pierre Vidal-Naquet, *Assassins of Memory: Essays on Denial of the Holocaust* (New York: Columbia University Press, 1992) esp. pp. xiii, xx-xxi. On application of the Canadian statute, see Alan T. Davies, "The Queen Versus James Keegstra: Reflections on Christian Antisemitism in Canada," *American Journal of Theology and Philosophy*, Vol. 9, Nos. 1-2, 1988; Leonidas E. Hill, "The Trial of Ernst Zundel: Revisionism and the Law in Canada," *Simon Wiesenthal Annual, 1989* (Los Angeles: Simon Wiesenthal Institute, 1989); Alan T. Davies, "A Tale of Two Trials: Antisemitism in Canada," *Holocaust and Genocide Studies*, Vol. 4, 1989. There have been related cases in the U.S. and England, albeit a civil rather than criminal nature. On the U.S., see *Mel Mermelstein v. Institute for Historical Review, et al.* (Cal. St. Sup. Ct., Civ. No. 356542 (1985)). On the English counterpart, see Richard J. Evans, *Lying About Hitler: History, Holocaust, and the David Irving Trial* (New York: Basic Books, 2001); D.D. Guttenplan, *The Holocaust on Trial* (New York: W.W. Norton, 2001).

15. On Turkey's adamant and ongoing refusal to admit that genocide was perpetrated against the Armenians, as well as Israel's reinforcement of the lie, see Roger W. Smith, "Denial of the Armenian Genocide," in Israel W. Charny, ed., *Genocide: A Critical Bibliographic Review* (London: Mansell, 1991) Vol. 2, pp. 63-85. On the genocide itself, see Vahakn N. Dadrian, *The History of the Armenian Genocide: Ethnic Conflict from the Balkans to Anatolia to the Caucasus* (Oxford, UK: Berghahn Books, [3rd ed.] 1997).

16. Roger W. Smith, Eric Markusen, and Robert Jay Lifton, "Professional Ethics and the Denial of the Armenian Genocide," *Holocaust and Genocide Studies*, No. 9, 1995.

17. Leo Kuper, *The Prevention of Genocide* (New Haven, CT: Yale University Press, 1985); Charny, *Understanding and Prevention of Genocide*; Israel W. Charny, *How Can We Commit the Unthinkable? Genocide, the Human Cancer* (Boulder, CO, Westview Press, 1982).

18. Irving Louis Horowitz, *Genocide: State Power and Mass Murder* (New Brunswick, NJ: Transaction Books, 1976) p. 39. Newton is quoted in Eldridge Cleaver, "Cleaver on Cleaver," *Ramparts*, Dec. 14-28, 1969, p. 10.

19. Raphaël Lemkin, *Axis Rule in Occupied Europe: Laws of Occupation, Analysis of Government, Proposals for Redress* (Washington, D.C.: Carnegie Endowment for International Peace, 1944) pp. 79-95.

20. Ibid., p. 79.

21. Ibid.

22. Lebanese delegate to the United Nations ad hoc committee on genocide, 1946; quoted in Robert Davis and Mark Zannis, *The Genocide Machine in Canada: The Pacification of the North* (Montréal: Black Rose Books, 1973) p. 20.

23. Lemkin, *Axis Rule*, p. 79.

24. Bauman, *Modernity and the Holocaust*, p. 119.

25. Ibid.

26. Lemkin, *Axis Rule*, 79-80.

27. Ibid.

28. Ibid., pp. 86-7.

29. Ibid., p. 86.

30. Ibid., pp. 86-7. For further details on "Genocide Legislation" in Croatia, p. 601; in France, see pp. 399-401; in Luxemburg, pp. 440-2; in Norway, p. 504; in Poland, pp. 552-3; in Serbia, pp. 625-6; in Slovakia, p. 143.

31. This resolution, passed on Mar. 28, 1947, was itself pursuant to General Assembly Resolution 96(I) of Dec. 11, 1946, which proclaimed genocide to be "shock[ing to] the conscience of mankind," posited "punishment of the crime of genocide to be a matter of international concern," and charged ECOSOC with developing for General Assembly ratification the draft of a Convention formally defining and prohibiting it. By mid-1946, Lemkin had already been retained by the Secretariat as a consultant in such matters; M. Lippman, "The Drafting of the 1948 Convention on the Prevention and Punishment of Genocide," *Boston University International Law Journal*, No. 3, 1984.

32. The draft Convention is catalogued as U.N. Doc. A/362, 1947.

33. Davis and Zannis, *Genocide Machine*, pp. 19-20. Yitzak Arad, Shmuel Krakowski and Schmuel Spector, eds., *The Einsatzgruppen Reports: Selections from the Nazi Death Squads' Campaign Against the Jews in Occupied Territories of the Soviet Union, July 1941-January 1943* (New York: Holocaust Library, 1989).

34. Davis and Zannis, *Genocide Machine*, p. 20.

35. Ibid.

36. Robert Jay Lifton and Eric Markusen, *The Genocidal Mentality: Nazi Holocaust and Nuclear Threat* (New York: Basic Books, 1988).

37. Davis and Zannis, *Genocide Machine*, p. 20.

38. A very solid case study of exactly these effects will be found in Thayer Scudder, et al., *No Place To Go: Effects of Compulsory Relocation on Navajos* (Philadelphia: Institute for the Study of Human Issues, 1982).

39. Pieter N. Drost, in his book *The Crime of State* (Leyden: A.W. Sythoff, 1959), seems to have been the first to popularize the idea that ethnocide, a term he erroneously — or misleadingly — attributes to "French scholarship" rather than Lemkin, might refer to something other than genocide. Chalk and Jonassohn, among many others, have replicated Drost's error — see their *History and Sociology of Genocide* at p. 9 — in an effort to constrain the definition of genocide itself to certain types of mass killing.

40. "Another term could be used for the same idea, namely, *ethnocide*, consisting of the Greek word 'ethnos'—nation—and the Latin word 'cide' "; Lemkin, *Axis Rule*, p. 79n1.

41. There "may be no difference between Holocaust and genocide for the victims of either [but] there are gradations of evil, unfortunately. Holocaust was the policy of total, sacral Nazi act of mass murder of all Jews they could lay their hands on. Genocide [is] horrible enough, but it [does] not entail *total* murder [emphasis original]"; Bauer, *Holocaust in Historical Perspective*, p. 36.

42. Lippman, "Drafting the 1948 Convention." Also see Lawrence J. LeBlanc, *The United States and the Genocide Convention* (Durham, NC: Duke University Press, 1991) pp. 25-8.

43. On the Soviet maneuver; ibid., pp. 61-2. On that of the U.S.; Davis and Zannis, *Genocide Machine*, pp. 20-1.

44. It would take another half-century—until 1998—before the international community was prepared for Lemkin's proposal for an International Criminal Court. At that point, 120 countries endorsed

the idea. At present, only seven countries—Iraq, Libya, Sudan, China, Qatar, Israel and the U.S.—have refused to accept its jurisdiction; Phyllis Bennis, *Calling the Shots: How Washington Dominates Today's UN* (New York: Olive Branch Press, 2000) p. 277. For further background, see LeBlanc, *U.S. and the Genocide Convention*, pp. 151-174.

45. Davis and Zannis, *Genocide Machine*, pp. 17-8.

46. The full text of the Convention (U.N. GAOR Res. 260A(III)) will be found in Ian Brownlie, ed., *Basic Documents on Human Rights* (Oxford, UL: Clarendon Press, [3rd ed.] 1992) pp. 31-4.

47. The meaning of the Convention's "incitement" provision has been a source of much controversy and confusion. It is thus worth quoting the Secretariat's Draft, which defines it as including "all forms of public propaganda tending by their systematic and hateful character to provoke genocide, or tending to make it appear as a necessary, legitimate, or excusable act." Such an interpretation is entirely consistent with the case brought against nazi propagandist Julius Streicher at Nuremberg; Bradley F. Smith, *Reaching Judgment at Nuremberg* (New York: Basic Books, 1977) pp. 200-3.

48. Davis and Zannis, *Genocide Machine*, p. 24.

49. R.S.C. 1985, c. C-46.

50. *Daishowa Inc. v. Friends of the Lubicon* (Ontario Court of Justice (Gen. Div.), File No. 95-CQ-59707, Verdict of Judge J. MacPherson (Apr. 14, 1998)). For analysis, see the essay entitled "Forbidding the G-Word in Canada: Holocaust Denial as Judicial Doctrine in Canada," in my *Perversions of Justice: Indigenous Peoples and Angloamerican Law* (San Francisco: City Lights, 2003) pp. 247-61.

51. House of Commons, Canada, *Report of the Special Committee on Hate Propaganda in Canada* (also known as the *Cohen Report*; Ottawa: Supplies and Services, 1952) p. 61.

52. Canadian Civil Liberties Association, *Brief to the Senate Standing Committee on Civil and Constitutional Affairs on Hate Propaganda* (Ottawa: Supplies and Services, Apr. 22, 1952) p. 6.

53. *Cohen Report*, p. 61.

54. It should be noted that Canada was complicit in the U.S. initiative, having "reserved [its] right . . . during the general debate at the Economic and Social Council . . . to move deletion of Article III (on cultural genocide) at the third session of the General Assembly"; Dept. of External Affairs, *Canada and the United Nations* (Ottawa: Supplies and Services, 1948) p. 191.

55. The full text of the Sovereignty Package (S. Exec. Rep. 2, 99th Cong., 1st Sess., 1985) will be found in LeBlanc, *U.S. and the Genocide Convention*, pp. 253-4. The full text of the U.S. Genocide Convention Implementation Act ("Proxmire Act;" Title 18, Pt. I, Chap. 50A § 1091-1093 (1988)) will be found at pp. 255-6.

56. I have in mind here the notion of "the prerogative state" explained by émigré German scholar Ernst Fraenkel as being a "governmental system which exercises unlimited arbitrariness and violence unchecked by legal guarantees"; Ernst Fraenkel, *The Dual State: A Contribution to the Theory of Dictatorship* (New York: Oxford University Press, 1941) p. xiii. The idea is implicit to the work of preeminent nazi legal theorist Carl Schmitt; see, e.g., Carl Schmitt, *The Crisis of Parliamentary Democracy* (Cambridge, MA: MIT Press, 1985). More broadly, see Gopal Balakishnan, *The Enemy: An Intellectual Biography of Carl Schmitt* (London: Verso, 2000).

57. U.N. Secretariat, *Multilateral Treaties Deposited with the Secretary General: Status as of 31 December 1989* (St/Leg/Ser. E/8 97-98 (1990)) pp. 102-4.

58. This interpretation is consistent with that of the International Court of Justice; "Reservations to the Convention on Punishment and Prevention of Genocide," in *ICJ Reports of Judgments, Advisory Opinions and Orders* (The Hague: ICJ, 1951) pp. 15-69. The U.S. itself has expressed awareness that it is bound by customary law and that the genocide convention falls within this domain; *Restatement (Third) of the Foreign Relations Law of the United States* (Washington, D.C.: U.S. Dept. of State, 1987) pp. 153, 161-3. For broader contextualization, see Michael Byers, *Custom, Power and the Power of Rules: International Relations and Customary International Law* (Cambridge, UK: Cambridge University Press, 1999).

59. "Among other things . . . critics argued that the phrase would make the Convention applicable to racially motivated lynchings, thus perhaps opening the way for it to become an important tool in the civil rights struggle within the United States"; LeBlanc, *U.S. and the Genocide Convention*, p. 34. For background, see Stewart E. Tolnay and E.M. Beck, *A Festival of Violence: An Analysis of Southern Lynchings, 1882-1930* (Urbana: University of Illinois Press, 1955); W. Fitzhugh Brundage, *Lynching in the New South,*

1880-1930 (Urbana: University of Illinois Press, 1993). On the Klan, see Wyn Craig Wade, *The Fiery Cross: The Ku Klux Klan in America* (New York: Simon and Schuster, 1987). On the SS, see Heinz Höhne, *The Order of the Death's Head: The Story of Hitler's S.S.* (New York: Coward-McCann, 1969). On the Nuremberg declaration of the SS as a criminal organization, see Smith, *Reaching Judgment at Nuremberg*, pp.143-70.

60. See note 47. "Critics of the Convention . . . have questioned whether the [incitement] clause would undermine First Amendment guarantees" that rationalization of genocide should be considered legally permissible activities; LeBlanc, *U.S. and the Genocide Convention*, p. 147. For further details, see Randall L. Bytwerk, *Julius Streicher: The Man Who Persuaded a Nation to Hate Jews* (New York: Dorset Press, 1983).

61. "The "concept of 'mental harm' has often been cited in debates over ratification of the Convention by the United States. When the Senate Committee on Foreign Relations held its first hearings in 1950, opponents of ratification argued that the words 'mental harm' might be used, especially by civil rights groups, to denounce segregation laws in the United States"; Leblanc, *U.S. and the Genocide Convention*, p. 101. That they were correct was shortly confirmed by the 1951 submission by the Civil Rights Congress to the U.N. Secretariat of a complaint entitled *We Charge Genocide: The Crime of the Government Against the Negro People* citing chapter and verse how the Convention was applicable to U.S. domestic race policy; William L. Patterson, *The Man Who Cried Genocide: An Autobiography* (New York: New World, 1971) p. 11. For what is generally considered the definitive study of the structure of U.S. race relations at the time, see C. Vann Woodward, *The Strange Career of Jim Crow* (New York: Oxford University Press, [3rd ed.] 1974).

62. On scalp bounties, see my *A Little Matter of Genocide: Holocaust and Denial in the Americas, 1492 to the Present* (San Francisco: City Lights, 1997) pp. 178-88. On extermination campaigns, see pp. 208-45.

63. *Lone Wolf v. Hitchcock* (187 U.S. 553 (1903)). For background, see Blue Clark, Lone Wolf v. Hitchcock: *Treaty Rights and Indian Law at the End of the Nineteenth Century* (Lincoln: University of Nebraska Press, 1999).

64. On royalty rates, see Marjane Ambler, *Breaking the Iron Bonds: Indian Control of Energy Development* (Lawrence: University Press of Kansas, 1990) pp. 56, 66, 78, 140-41.

65. J. Michael Kennedy, "Truth and Consequences on the Reservation," *Los Angeles Times Magazine*, July 7, 2002; Joel Brinkley, "American Indians Say Government Has Cheated Them Out of Billions," *New York Times*, Jan. 7, 2003.

66. See, e.g., Paul Harrison, *Inside the Third World: The Classic Account of Poverty in the Developing Countries* (New York: Penguin Books, [3rd ed.] 1993).

67. For citations on this and related information, see Rennard Strickland, "Indian Law and the Miner's Canary: The Signs of Poison Gas," *Cleveland State Law Review*, No. 39, 1991, pp. 486-9. Additional background will be found in Alan L. Sorkin, "The Economic and Social Status of the American Indian, 1940-1970," *Nebraska Journal of Economics*, No. 22, Spring 1974. For further background concerning the conditions on Pine Ridge specifically, see Cheryl McCall, "Life on Pine Ridge Bleak," *Colorado Daily*, May 16, 1975; Edward Lazarus, *Black Hills, White Justice: The Sioux Nation versus the United States, 1775 to the Present* (New York: HarperCollins, 1991) p. 163.

68. Rennard Strickland, *Tonto's Revenge: Reflections on American Indian Culture and Policy* (Albuquerque: University of New Mexico Press, 1997) p. 53. On Canada, see James B. Waldram, D. Ann Herring and T. Kue Young, *Aboriginal Health in Canada: Historical, Cultural, and Epidemiological Perspectives* (Toronto: University of Toronto Press, 1995) esp. pp. 65-96.

69. Strickland, *Tonto's Revenge*, p. 53; Waldram, Herring and Young, *Aboriginal Health*, p. 66.

70. Relocation programs have been conducted in both a generalized fashion and, on occasion, with a focus on specific groups. On the generalized approach, see Donald L. Fixico, *Termination and Relocation: Federal Indian Policy, 1945-1960* (Albuquerque: University of New Mexico Press, 1986). With respect to a particular group, the Big Mountain Diné (Navajos), see Anita Parlow, *Cry, Sacred Ground: Big Mountain, USA* (Washington, D.C.: Christic Institute, 1988). Overall, see the essay entitled "Like Sand in the Wind: The Making of an American Indian Diaspora in the United States," in my *Acts of Rebellion: The Ward Churchill Reader* (New York: Routledge, 2003) pp. 141-62.

71. For data, see Russell Thornton, *American Indian Holocaust and Survival: A Population History Since 1492* (Norman: University of Oklahoma Press, 1987) p. 227. Various aspects of the cultural backdrop are

presented in Susan Lobo and Kurt Peters, eds., *American Indians and the Urban Experience* (Walnut Creek, CA: AltaMira Press, 2001).

72. By 1970, approximately two-thirds of the marriages of those on the tribal rolls were to people who were not, with the result that only 59 percent of births reflected a situation in which both parents registered themselves as possessing any Indian blood at all; U.S. Dept. of Health, Education and Welfare, *A Study of Selected Socio-Economic Characteristics of Ethnic Minorities Based on the 1970 Census, Vol. 3: American Indians* (Washington, D.C.: U.S. Government Printing Office, 1974) pp. 74, 78. For effects in terms of the "blood quantum" criteria by which native identity is officially defined in the U.S., see Thornton, *American Indian Holocaust and Survival*, pp. 174-5. The implications are clear: "Set the blood quantum at one-quarter, hold to it as a rigid definition of Indians, let intermarriage proceed as it [has] and eventually Indians will be defined out of existence"; Patricia Nelson Limerick, *The Legacy of Conquest: The Unbroken Past of the American West* (New York: W.W. Norton, 1987) p. 338.

73. Brint Dillingham, "Indian Women and IHS Sterilization Practices," *American Indian Journal*, Vol. 3, No. 1, Jan. 1977; Janet Larson, "And Then There Were None," *Christian Century*, Jan. 26, 1977. Also see "Women and Children First: The Forced Sterilization of American Indian Women," an excellent but unpublished undergraduate honors thesis prepared by Wellesley College student Robin Jerrill in 1988.

74. For a seminal articulation of the "settler state" concept and the especially virulent form of colonialism inherent to such entities, see A. Grenfell Price, *White Settlers and Native Peoples* (Cambridge, UK: Cambridge University Press, 1949). Much less liberal views will be found in Maxime Rodinson, *Israel: A Colonial-Settler State?* (New York: Pathfinder Press, 1973); J. Sakai, *Settlers: The Mythology of the White Proletariat* (Chicago: Morningstar Press, [2nd ed.] 1983); Donald Harmon Atkinson, *God's Peoples: Covenant and Land in South Africa, Israel and Ulster* (Ithaca: Cornell University Press, 1992); Patrick Wolf, *Settler State Colonialism and the Transformation of Anthropology: The Politics and Poetics of an Ethnographic Event* (London: Cassell, 1999).

75. Credible estimates of Native North American population, *circa* 1492, range from 12.5 on the low end to 18.5 million on the high. Based on 1890 census data showing fewer than 240,000 Indians surviving in the U.S., and a third that in Canada, a population reduction in the 95th to 99th percentile range is indicated. For the low-end estimate, see Russell Thornton, "American Indian Historical Demography: A Review Essay with Suggestions for the Future," *American Indian Culture and Research Journal*, No. 3, 1979 (Thornton revises his figures somewhat downward in *American Indian Holocaust and Survival*, pp. xvii, 242). For the high-end estimate, see Henry F. Dobyns, *Their Number Become Thinned: Native American Population Dynamics in Eastern North America* (Knoxville: University of Tennessee Press, 1983) p. 42. For 1890 figures, see U.S. Bureau of the Census, *Fifteenth Census of the United States, 1930: The Indian Population of the United States and Alaska* (Washington, D.C.: U.S. Government Printing Office, 1937), esp. "Table II: Indian Population by Divisions and States, 1890-1930" at p. 3; James M. Mooney, *The Aboriginal Population of America North of Mexico* (Washington, D.C.: Smithsonian Misc. Collections LXXX, No. 7, 1928) p. 33.

76. Much is made in Canada of that country's record of interaction with native peoples being far less bloody than that of the U.S. This is true, as far as it goes, but should not be taken as meaning that Canadian history is free of such things. The opposite is evidenced by the extermination of the Beothuks; L.F.S. Lupton, "The Extermination of the Beothuks of Newfoundland," *Canadian Historical Review*, Vol. 58, No. 2, 1977. It is also documented that extermination by bacteriological means was carried out during the late 19th century against the Carriers and other peoples of British Columbia; Peter McNair, Alan Hoover and Kevin Neary, *The Legacy: Tradition and Innovation in Northwest Coast Indian Art* (Seattle: University of Washington Press, 1984) p. 24.

77. Francis E. Leupp, *The Indian and His Problem* (New York: Scribner's, 1910) p. 93.

78. See generally, Frederick E. Hoxie, *A Final Promise: The Campaign to Assimilate the Indians, 1880-1920* (Lincoln: University of Nebraska Press, 1985).

79. This was done pursuant to the Major Crimes Act (ch. 341, 24 Stat. 362, 385 (1885), now codified at 18 U.S.C. 1153). For background, see Sidney L. Harring, *Crow Dog's Case: American Indian Sovereignty, Tribal Law, and United States Law in the Nineteenth Century* (Cambridge, UK: Cambridge University Press, 1994) esp. pp. 100-41.

80. Usurpation of native jurisdiction in Canada began with the 1803 Act for Extending

Jurisdiction of the Courts of Justice in the Provinces of Upper and Lower Canada, to the Trial and Punishment of Persons Guilty of Crimes and Offenses within Certain Parts of North America Adjoining to Said Provinces (43 Geo. III, c. 138), amplified and extended into the civil domain by the 1821 Act for Regulating the Fur Trade and Establishing a Criminal and Civil Jurisdiction within Certain Parts of North America (1 & 2 Geo. IV, c. 66); Bruce Clark, *Native Liberty, Crown Sovereignty: The Existing Aboriginal Right of Self-Government in Canada* (Montréal: McGill-Queens University Press, 1990) pp. 124-7.

81. This was done pursuant to the General Allotment Act (ch. 119, 24 Stat. 388 (1887), now codified as amended at 25 U.S.C. 331 et seq.; also known as the "Dawes Act," after its primary sponsor, Massachusetts Senator Henry M. Dawes). American Indians' reserved landbase was reduced from approximately 150 million acres in 1887 to about 50 million in 1934; for background, see D.S. Otis, *The Dawes Act and the Allotment of Indian Land* (Norman: University of Oklahoma Press, 1973); Janet A. McDonnell, *The Dispossession of the American Indian, 1887-1934* (Bloomington: Indiana University Press, 1991). On the heirship problem in particular, see Ethel J. Williams, "Too Little Land, Too Many Heirs: The Indian Heirship Land Problem," *Washington Law Review*, No. 46, 1971; Wilcomb E. Washburn, *Red Man's Land, White Man's Law* (Norman: University of Oklahoma Press, [2nd ed.] 1995) pp. 150-2.

82. See my essay, "The Crucible of American Indian Identity: Native Tradition versus Colonial Imposition in Postconquest North America," in *Perversions of Justice*, pp. 201-45. Although Canada does not employ a blood quantum system, per se, it has imposed its own methods of distinguishing "status" from "non-status" Indians; see B. Morris and R. Groves, "Canada's Forgotten Peoples: The Aboriginal Rights of Metis and Non-Status Peoples," *Law & Anthropology*, No. 2, 1987; Bill Wilson, "Aboriginal Rights: A Non-Status Indian View," in Menno Boldt and J. Anthony Long, eds., *The Quest for Justice: Aboriginal People and Aboriginal Rights* (Toronto: University of Toronto Press, 1985) pp. 62-70.

83. "Federal policy dictated a repression of Indian religious practices simply because religion was part of a larger cultural complex that federal officials thought necessary to eliminate in order to assimilate Indians into the larger society . . . The ceremonial Sun Dance ritual, the controversial Ghost Dance, the religious use of feathers, and the use of peyote have [all] been banned by federal and state officials"; Vine Deloria, Jr., and Clifford M. Lytle, *American Indians, American Justice* (Austin: University of Texas Press, 1983) pp. 231-2. Concerning compulsory Christianity, see Vine Deloria, Jr., and David E. Wilkins, *Tribes, Treaties, and Constitutional Tribulations* (Austin: University of Texas Press, 1999) pp. 102-5. On Canada, see Douglas Cole and Ira Chaikan, *An Iron Hand Upon the People: The Law Against the Potlatch on the Northwest Coast* (Vancouver: Douglas & McIntire, 1990); Katherine Pettitpas, *Severing the Ties That Bind: Government Repression of Indigenous Religious Ceremonies on the Prairies* (Winnipeg: University of Manitoba Press, 1994).

84. This was done pursuant to the Indian Reorganization Act (ch. 576, 48 Stat. 948 (1934), now codified at 25 U.S.C. 461-279). For background see Vine Deloria, Jr., and Clifford M. Lytle, *The Nations Within: The Past and Future of American Indian Sovereignty* (New York: Pantheon, 1984). In Canada, a series of statutes, beginning with the 1876 Act to Amend and Consolidate the Laws Respecting Indians (SC 1876, c. 18) and its 1880 sequel (SC 1880, c. 29), and extending through the 1884 Indian Advancement Act (SC 1884, c. 28) to the 1920 amendment to the 1906 Indian Act (SC 1919-1920, c. 50) accomplished essentially the same result; for texts, see Dept. of Indian and Northern Affairs Canada, *Indian Acts and Amendments, 1868-1950* (Ottawa: Treaties and Historical Research Center, 1981); *Report of the Special Committee of the House of Commons on Indian Self-Government* (Ottawa: Supplies and Services, 1983).

85. Fixico, *Relocation and Termination*; Also see James H. Gundlach, Nelson P. Reid and Alden E. Roberts, "Native American Migration and Relocation," *Pacific Sociological Review*, No. 21, 1978; Ray Moisa, "The BIA Relocation Program," in Susan Lobo and Steve Talbot, eds., *Native American Voices: A Reader* (New York: Longman, 1998) pp. 154-8. On Canada, see Boyce Richardson, *The People of* Terra Nullius: *Betrayal and Rebirth in Aboriginal Canada* (Vancouver/Seattle: Douglas & McIntyre/University of Washington Press, 1993) pp. 227-49.

86. All told, 109 indigenous nations, or portions of them, were terminated between 1953 and 1958, and several more during the early 1960s. This was done through a sequence of statutes, pursuant to House Concurrent Resolution 108 (Aug. 1, 1953); see generally, Fixico, *Termination and Relocation*; Larry M. Burt, *Tribalism in Crisis: Federal Indian Policy, 1953-1961* (Albuquerque: University of New Mexico Press, 1982). It is noteworthy that the individual selected as Indian Commissioner to implement federal termination/relocation policies was the same man who'd presided over the mass internment of Japanese-

Americans during World War II: Richard Drinnon, *Keeper of Concentration Camps: Dillon S. Myer and American Racism* (Berkeley: University of California Press, 1987).

87. The plenary power doctrine in the U.S. was first enunciated in the 1824 *Gibbons v. Ogden* opinion of the Supreme Court (22 U.S. [9 Wheat.] 1), first applied to Indians in *U.S. v. Kagama* (18 U.S. 375 (1886)), and consolidated in the latter regard in the *Lone Wolf* opinion (see note 63). For an examination of the doctrine as an assertion of "unlimited and absolute power," see David E. Wilkins and K. Tsianina Lomawaima, *Uneven Ground: American Indian Sovereignty and Federal Law* (Norman: University of Oklahoma Press, 2001) pp. 106-14. For analysis of the doctrine as applied in a related context, see Christina Duffy Burnett and Burke Marshall, eds., *Foreign in a Domestic Sense: Puerto Rico, American Expansion, and the Constitution* (Chapel Hill, NC: Duke University Press, 2001).

88. Useful overviews will be found in Michael C. Coleman, *American Indian Children at School, 1850-1930* (Jackson: University of Mississippi Press, 1993); Margaret Connell Szasz, *Education and the American Indian: The Road to Self-Determination Since 1928* (Albuquerque: University of New Mexico Press, [3rd ed.] 1999); J.R. Miller, *Shingwauk's Vision: A History of the Indian Residential Schools* (Toronto: University of Toronto Press, 1996).

89. Szasz, *Education and the Indian*, pp. 18-20; Miller, *Shingwauk's Vision*, pp. 126-7.

90. As of 1928, fewer than half of all native children were attending public or reservation day schools in the U.S. 27 percent—21,053—were in government-run boarding schools, and the balance in residential facilities administered by various Christian religious denominations; Szasz, *Education and the Indian*, p. 18. In Canada, where the population was much smaller, residential schools accommodated 6,641 of approximately 14,000 native students in 1927; Miller, *Shingwauk's Vision*, p. 142. At their respective peaks, the U.S. system boasted 154 facilities, the Canadian system 80.

91. For the phrases used, see John S. Milloy, *"A National Crime": The Canadian Government and the Residential School System, 1879 to 1986* (Winnipeg: University of Manitoba Press, 1999); David Wallace Adams, *Education for Extinction: American Indians and the Boarding School Experience, 1875-1928* (Lawrence: University Press of Kansas, 1995).

92. Richard Henry Pratt, "The Advantages of Mingling Indians with Whites," *Proceedings and Addresses of the National Education Association, 1895* (Washington, D.C.: National Educational Association, 1895) pp. 761-2.

93. Quoted in Coleman, *Indian Children at School*, p. 46.

94. Sheridan's actual statement was that "the only good Indians I ever saw were dead"; quoted in Paul Andrew Hutton, *Phil Sheridan and His Army* (Lincoln: University of Nebraska Press, 1985) p. 180.

95. For background on Chivington and the event in question, see Stan Hoig, *The Sand Creek Massacre* (Norman: University of Oklahoma Press, 1961). A an excellent compendium of similar utterances will be found in David Svaldi's *Sand Creek and the Rhetoric of Extermination: A Case Study in Indian-White Relations* (Lanham, MD: University Press of America, 1989).

96. For Pratt's prideful recounting of his "accomplishments," see his autobiography *Battlefield and Classroom: Four Decades with the American Indian, 1867-1904* (New Haven, CT: Yale University Press, 1967 reprint of 1906 original) esp. Chaps. 10-17. For critical analysis, see Richard J. Stephon, "Richard Henry Pratt and His Indians," *Journal of Ethnic Studies*, No. 15, Summer 1987. On Fort Marion in particular, see Pamela Holco Oestreicher, *On the White Man's Road? Acculturation and the Fort Marion Southern Plains Prisoners* (Lansing: Ph.D. dissertation, Michigan State University, 1981).

97. This was referred to as an "incapacitation mode" by the director of the federal Bureau of Prisons in 1988; quoted in Fukoka Sano, "BoP Overseer: A Glimpse of J. Michael Quinlan," in my and J.J. Vander Wall's coedited *Cages of Steel: The Politics of Imprisonment in the United States* (Washington, D.C.: Maisonneuve Press, 1992) p. 110. Also see notes 469 and 470, below, and accompanying text.

98. See the chapter entitled "Big Bucks from the Big House: The Prison-Industrial Complex and Beyond," in Christian Parenti, *Lockdown America: Police and Prisons in the Age of Crisis* (London: Verso, 1999) pp. 211-44. For further historical backdrop, see Alex Lichtenstein, *Twice the Work of Free Labor: The Political Economy of Convict Labor in the New South* (London: Verso, 1996); David M. Oshinsky, *"Worse Than Slavery": Parchman Farm and the Ordeal of Jim Crow Justice* (New York: Free Press, 1996).

99. On Scott, see E. Brian Titley, *A Narrow Vision: Duncan Campbell Scott and the Administration of Indian Affairs in Canada* (Vancouver: University of British Columbia Press, 1986). On U.S. influence, see

Nicholas F. Davin, *Report on Industrial Schools for Indians and Halfbreeds* (Ottawa: Dept. of Indian Affairs, Mar. 14, 1879) p. 12.

100. S. Prov. C. 1857, c. 26.

101. SC 1884, c. 28.

102. Malloy, *"National Crime"*, p. 19.

103. Quoted in David A. Nock, *A Victorian Missionary and Canadian Indian Policy: Cultural Synthesis vs. Cultural Replacement* (Waterloo, Ont.: Wilfred Laurier University Press, 1988) p. 4.

104. Quoted in Titley, *Narrow Vision*, p. 50.

105. "Report of the Deputy Superintendent General," in *Canada, Sessional Papers (No. 27), 1901: Report of the Department of Indian Affairs for 1900*; quoted in Miller, *Shingwauk's Vision*, p. 121.

106. Alternately, we are left with what some analysts have called the "Standard Account" which "disposes neatly of all problems associated with Indian Residential Schooling" under the premise that they were "unintentional" or even "well-intended"; Roland Chrisjohn and Sherri Young with Michael Maraun, *The Circle Game: Shadows and Substance in the Indian Residential School Experience in Canada* (Penticton, B.C.: Theytus Books, 1997) pp. 2-3.

107. For contextualization of the issue of redress, see Roy L. Brooks, ed., *When Sorry Isn't Enough: The Controversy Over Apologies for Human Injustice* (New York: New York University Press, 1999).

108. My thinking here extends from that referenced in note 18, and borrows heavily from Marcuse's observation that we are speaking here of a breach in false consciousness and that any such "break through . . . may provide the Archimedean point for a larger emancipation—at an infinitesimally small spot, to be sure, but it is in the enlargement of such small spots that the chance of change depends"; Herbert Marcuse, "Repressive Tolerance," in Robert Paul Wolf, Barrington Moore, Jr., and Herbert Marcuse, *A Critique of Pure Tolerance* (Boston: Beacon Press, 1965) p. 111. For consideration of the proposition that certain aspects of genocide remain "unthinkable" because of their suppression by false consciousness, see Charny, *How Can We Commit the Unthinkable?*

109. I use the term "denial" in both its clinical and political senses. On the clinical, see Donald L. Nathanson, "Denial, Projection and the Empathic Wall"; on the political, see Léon Wurmser, "Cultural Paradigms of Denial," and Rafael Moses, "Denial in the Political Process"; all three in E.L. Edelstein, Donald L. Nathanson and Andrew M. Stone, eds., *Denial: A Clarification of Concepts and Research* (New York: Plenum Press, 1989) pp. 37-60, 277-86, 287-98. Also see Stanley Cohen, *States of Denial: Knowing About Atrocities and Suffering* (Cambridge, UK: Polity Press, 2001).

110. *Statutes at Large of the United States*, Vol. 26, p. 1014.

111. *Statutes at Large of the United States*, Vol. 27, p. 635. Also see U.S. Dept. of Interior, Bureau of Indian Affairs, *Education Circular No. 130* (Washington, D.C.: Office of Indian Affairs, Jan. 15, 1906).

112. An Act to Further Amend the Indian Act (c. 32, 57-58 Vict.). It should be noted that compulsory education provisions were further reinforced by amendments to the Indian Act made in 1920 (c. 50 . . . 157) which authorized the imposition of "penalties or fines or imprisonment for non-compliance." In any event, Canada's efforts focused on children as young as six in the belief, voiced by the Archbishop of St. Boniface in 1912, that they must be "caught young to be saved from what is on the whole the degenerating influence of their home environment"; quoted in Milloy, *"National Crime"*, p. 27.

113. Brenda J. Child, *Boarding School Seasons: American Indian Families, 1900-1940* (Lincoln: University of Nebraska Press, 1998) pp. 13, 90. For further details on Hopi resistance, see Harry C. James, *Pages from Hopi History* (Tucson: University of Arizona Press, 1988) pp. 76-83.

114. Adams, *Education for Extinction*, p. 211.

115. *Annual Report of the Commissioner of Indian Affairs* (Washington, D.C.: 49th Cong., 1st Sess., 1886) p. 417.

116. Quoted in Adams, *Education for Extinction*, p. 216.

117. Ibid., pp. 216-22. For the threats to "kill and scalp" resisters, see the *Pocatello Tribune*, Sept. 29, 1897.

118. As examples, see Helen Sekaquaptewa as told to Louise Udall, *Me and Mine: The Life Story of Helen Sekaquaptewa* (Tucson: University of Arizona Press, 1962) pp. 8-12; James Kaywaykla, *In the Days of Victorio: Recollections of a Warm Springs Apache* (Tucson: University of Arizona Press, 1970) pp. 199-200; Lame Deer (John Fire) and Richard Erdoes, *Lame Deer, Seeker of Visions: The Life of a Sioux Medicine Man*

(New York: Simon & Schuster, 1972) p. 33; Fred Kabotie, *Fred Kabotie, Hopi Indian Artist: An Autobiography told with Bill Belknap* (Flagstaff: Museum of Northern Arizona/Northland Press, 1977) pp. 8-10.

119. Miller, *Shingwauk's Vision*, p. 128.

120. Suzanna Fournier and Ernie Crey, *Stolen From Our Embrace: The Abduction of First Nations Children and the Restoration of Aboriginal Communities* (Vancouver: Douglas & McIntyre, 1997) p. 56; Basil Johnson, *Indian School Days* (Norman: University of Oklahoma Press, 1989) p. 6.

121. Miller, *Shingwauk's Vision*, p. 128.

122. Milloy, *"National Crime"*, pp. 69-70.

123. Paraphrasing Fournier and Crey, *Stolen From Our Embrace.*

124. Milloy, *"National Crime"*, p. 19.

125. Quoted in ibid., p. 19.

126. Adams, *Education for Extinction*, p. 212.

127. Allan G. Harper, "Canada's Indian Administration: Basic Concepts and Objectives," *American Indigena*, Vol. 5, No. 2, 1945, p. 127.

128. A leading expert on the topic lists concentration camps, labor camps, prisons, mental hospitals and army barracks as salient examples of "total institutions"; Erving Goffman, "The Characteristics of Total Institutions," in Amitai Etzioni, ed., *Complex Organizations: A Sociological Reader* (Chicago: Aldine, 1961) pp. 313-4. Although adding Indian boarding schools to the list is usually decried as an overstatement, it is worth noting that in 1891, U.S. Indian Commissioner Thomas J. Morgan himself proudly compared the schools to "asylums" and "houses of correction"; *Annual Report of the Commissioner of Indian Affairs* (Washington, D.C.: 51st Cong., 2nd Sess., 1891) pp. 62-3. On Canada, see Chrisjohn and Young with Maraun, *Circle Game*, pp. 68-76.

129. Miller, *Shingwauk's Vision*, p. 204; Mary Crow Dog with Richard Erdoes, "Civilize Them with a Stick," in Lobo and Talbot, *Native American Voices*, p. 245.

130. Such denigration, both of the students personally and of their heritage, was standard practice; Chrisjohn and Young with Maraun, *Circle Game*, p. 32.

131. Many former students recall weeping as their hair was shorn; see, e.g., Luther Standing Bear, *My People, the Sioux* (Lincoln: University of Nebraska Press, 1975 reprint of 1928 original) pp. 140-1. Others were afterwards "too ashamed to eat"; see, e.g. James McCarthy, *Papago Traveler: The Memoirs of James McCarthy* (Tucson: Sun Tracks/University of Arizona Press, 1985) pp. 28-9.

132. Coleman, *Indian Children at School*, p. 83.

133. Adams, *Education for Extinction*, p. 101.

134. Milloy, *"National Crime"*, p. 124. It is noteworthy that in 1938 a joint delegation of Canadian clergy enthusiastically embraced the requirement of uniforms because of the success thus achieved by "modern Dictators" like Hitler and Mussolini in "implanting political doctrines and even racial and theological ideas"; quoted at p. 125. A good, and very succinct, study of how these principles were imposed in the U.S. will be found in Michael L. Cooper, *Indian School: Teaching the White Man's Way* (New York: Clarion Books, 1999).

135. Adams, *Education for Extinction*, pp. 108-10. An especially insidious variant reported by Francis La Flesche at pp. 74-5 of his autobiographical *The Middle Five: Indian Schoolboys of the Omaha Tribe* (Madison: University Press, 1963) was to have older students select Anglicized names for each newcomer, thereby implicating the children themselves in the undermining of their own cultures; Coleman, *Indian Children at School*, p. 84.

136. See, as examples, Ah-nen-la-de-ni (Daniel LaFrance), "An Indian Boy's Story," *The Independent*, July 30, 1903, p. 1783; Albert Yava, *Big Falling Snow: A Tewa-Hopi Indian's Life and Times and the History and Traditions of His People* (Albuquerque: University of New Mexico Press, 1978) p. 3; Asa Daklugie, *Indeh: An Apache Odyssey* (Norman: University of Oklahoma Press, 1988) p. 144.

137. Inspector of Indian Schools J.A. Macrae, Dec. 18, 1886; quoted in Milloy, *"National Crime"*, p. 27.

138. Convention of the Catholic Principals of Indian Residential Schools, Aug. 29, 1924; quoted in Milloy, *"National Crime"*, p. 38.

139. Presbyterian Women's Missionary Society, quoted in Dept. of Indian Affairs, *Annual Reports* (Ottawa: Supplies and Services, 1915) p. 59.

140. Indian Commissioner Thomas J. Morgan, quoted in Coleman, *Indian Children at School*, p. 42.

141. Chrisjohn and Young with Maraun, *Circle Game*, p. 32.

142. "Taking children in for short terms and letting them go again is worse than useless [because the] effect of allowing the children to visit their Reserves is bad"; Superintendent General for Indian Affairs Edgar Dewdney, Apr. 1891; quoted in Milloy, *"National Crime"*, p. 30. Also see Dewdney's commentary on "deleterious home influences" in Dept. of Indian Affairs, *Annual Report* (Ottawa: Supplies and Services, 1889) p. xi.

143. *Annual Report of the Commissioner of Indian Affairs* (Washington, D.C.: 37th Cong., 3rd Sess., 1863) p. 172.

144. "Report of the School at Lawrence, Kansas," attached to the *Annual Report of the Commissioner of Indian Affairs* (Washington, D.C.: 50th Cong., 1st Sess., 1888) p. 262.

145. *Annual Report of the Commissioner of Indian Affairs* (Washington, D.C.: 43rd Cong., 1st Sess., 1873) p. 376-7. A good case study in this regard will be found in Clyde Ellis, *To Change Them Forever: Indian Education at the Rainy Mountain Boarding School, 1893-1920* (Norman: University of Oklahoma Press, 1996).

146. By 1886, according to Indian Commissioner J.D.C. Atkins, there was "not an Indian pupil whose tuition and maintenance is paid for by the United States Government who is permitted to study in any language other than our own vernacular—the language of the greatest, most powerful, and enterprising nationalities under the sun"; *Annual Report of the Commissioner of Indian Affairs* (Washington, D.C.: 49th Cong., 2nd Sess., 1886) p. xxiii.

147. Adams, *Education for Extinction*, p. 140.

148. "So long as . . . an Aboriginal person . . . keeps his native tongue, he will remain a community apart [and] be permanently disabled"; Dept. of Indian Affairs, *Annual Report* (Ottawa: Supplies and Services, 1895) pp. xxii-xxiii. On the effectiveness of the prohibition in eventually destroying the proficiency of students who'd arrived at school fluent in their own languages, see, e.g., Adams, *Education for Extinction*, p. 142.

149. Milloy, *"National Crime"*, p. 39.

150. "Whether at work or at play, we were continuously watched"; Ah-nen-la-de-ni, "Indian Boy's Story," p. 1783. Also see Chrisjohn and Young with Maraun, *Circle Game*, p. 69; Coleman, *Indian Children at School*, p. 88.

151. Miller, *Shingwauk's Vision*, p. 204.

152. See generally, Assembly of First Nations, *Breaking the Silence: An Interpretive Study of Residential School Impact and Healing as Illustrated by the Stories of First Nations Individuals* (Ottawa: Assembly of First Nations, 1994). For a more particularized study, see Isabelle Knockwood, *Out of the Depths: The Experiences of Mi'kmaw Children at the Residential School at Shubenacadie, Nova Scotia* (Lockeport, NS: Roseway, 1992). A framing of my use of the word "survivor" in this connection will be found in Celia Haig-Brown, *Resistance and Renewal: Surviving the Indian Residential School* (Vancouver: Tillacum Library, 1988).

153. Miller, *Shingwauk's Vision*, p, 204.

154. Ibid.

155. Ibid., p. 205.

156. Ibid.

157. Ibid.

158. Linda F. Witmer, *The Indian School: Carlisle, Pennsylvania, 1879-1918* (Carlisle, PA: Cumberland County Historical Society, [2nd ed.] 2000) p. 11.

159. For histories of two of the schools mentioned, see K. Tsianina Lomawaima, *They Called It Prairie Light: The Story of the Chilocco Boarding School* (Lincoln: University of Nebraska Press, 1994); Robert A. Trennert, Jr., *The Phoenix Indian School: Forced Assimilation in Arizona, 1891-1935* (Norman: University of Oklahoma Press, 1988).

160. An excellent illustration of what is meant is offered by the photo of the "dormitory" at the Shingwauk Residential School (Ontario) included in Milloy, *"National Crime"*, between pp. 128 and 129.

161. See, e.g., the photo of the Phoenix Indian School campus in Adams, *Education for Extinction*, p. 114.

162. See the examples in Witmer, *Indian School*.

163. Adams, *Education for Extinction*, p. 117.

164. Szasz, *Education and the Indian*, pp. 20-1.

165. Coleman, *Indian Children at School*, p. 87; quoting Sekaquaptewa, *Me and Mine*, pp. 134-8, 105.

166. Thomas Wildcat Alford, as told to Florence Drake, *Civilization, and the Story of the Absentee Shawnees* (Norman: University of Oklahoma Press, 1936) pp. 99-100.

167. Coleman, *Indian Children at School*, p. 88.

168. See, e.g., Lucille Winnie, *Sah-gan-de-oh: The Chief's Daughter* (New York: Vantage Press, 1969) Chap. 1.

169. *Annual Report of the Commissioner of Indian Affairs* (Washington, D.C.: 55th Cong., 2nd Sess., 1898) p. 541.

170. See. e.g., E.P. Grinstead, "The Value of Military Drills," *Native American*, Mar. 21, 1914, p. 153.

171. *Sherman Bulletin*, Dec. 21, 1910.

172. For overviews of academic instruction in the U.S. and the intent underlying it, see Adams, *Education for Extinction*, pp. 136-49; Coleman, *Indian Children at School*, pp. 105-12. On Canada, see Miller, *Shingwauk's Vision*, pp. 151-82; Milloy, *"National Crime"*, pp. 155-86.

173. Horace E. Scudder, *A History of the United States of America* (Philadelphia: J.W. Butler, 1884). For a broad overview of such materials, see Ruth M. Elson, *Guardians of Tradition: American Schoolbooks of the Nineteenth Century* (Lincoln: University of Nebraska Press, 1964) esp. pp. 71-81, 166-85. Also see Laurence Hauptman, "Mythologizing Westward Expansion: Schoolbooks and the Image of the American Frontier Before Turner," *Western Historical Quarterly*, No. 8, July 1977; "Westward Course of Expansion: Geography Schoolbooks and Manifest Destiny," *Historian*, No. 40, May 1978.

174. Scudder, *History of the U.S.*, p. iv.

175. Ibid., pp. 18, 21, 93, 94, 95, 418.

176. The degree to which this was true by the 1950s is attested in the phenomenon of Indian children enthusiastically cheering the cinematic cowboys' and cavalrymen's ritualized slaughter of Indians during Saturday matinées; Strickland, *Tonto's Revenge*, p. 18. Elsewhere, I have compared this to Jewish children being indoctrinated to applaud the nazi extermination of *their* ancestors; see the cover quotation on the first edition of my *Fantasies of the Master Race: Literature, Cinema and the Colonization of American Indians* (Monroe, ME: Common Courage Press, 1992).

177. "Christian proselytization suffused the educational effort"; Coleman, *Indian Children at School*, p. 115.

178. The imposition of Christianity upon all Indians in the U.S. was formally enunciated as a national priority under the "Peace Policy" of President Ulysses S. Grant in the Act of April 10, 1869 (16 Stat. 40). For an itemization of which native peoples were thereupon assigned to be administered by which Christian denominations, see Francis Paul Prucha, *The Great Father: The United States Government and the American Indian* (Lincoln: University of Nebraska Press, 1984) pp. 517-9.

179. "The first known boarding-school arrangement for Indian youths in Canada began in 1620 under the auspices of the Récollets, an order of Franciscans, who took a number of boys into what they referred to grandly as their 'seminary' "; Miller, *Shingwauk's Vision*, p. 39. In the U.S. portion of North America, the first significant experiment seems to have been conducted by the Protestant missionary Eleazar Wheelock, founder of Dartmouth College, when in 1754 he established Moor's Charity School, a residential facility housing about 90 children; Margaret Connell Szasz, *Indian Education in the American Colonies, 1607-1783* (Albuquerque: University of New Mexico Press, 1988) p. 191. In both the U.S. and Canada, the establishment of boarding schools formed an important part of missionary efforts by the early 19th century; see generally, Robert J. Berkhofer, Jr., *Salvation and the Savage: An Analysis of Protestant Missions and American Indian Response, 1787-1862* (New York: Atheneum, 1972); Jean Barman, Yves Hébert and D. McCaskall, eds., *Indian Education in Canada, Vol. 1: The Legacy* (Vancouver: Nakota Institute/ University of British Columbia Press, 1986).

180. See note 178. Also see Francis Paul Prucha, *American Indian Policy in Crisis: Christian Reformers and the Indian, 1865-1900* (Norman: University of Oklahoma Press, 1976).

181. Consider, e.g., the roles played by Bishop Grandin, representing the Catholic Church, and John McGougall, representing the Methodists, in negotiating the educational provisions of Canada's Treaty 6 with the Plains Cree. The "treaty promises in the area of education gave the churches a lever to

move the government to provide funds for [their] schools and teachers. They did not hesitate to use it"; Milloy, *"National Crime"*, p. 54. On the U.S., see R. Pierce Beaver, *Church, State and the American Indian: Two and a Half Centuries of Partnership in Missions Between Protestant Missions and the Government* (St. Louis, MO: Concordia University Press, 1966).

182. Milloy, *"National Crime"*, p. xiii.

183. Coleman, *Indian Children at School*, p.115.

184. Crow Dog and Erdoes, "Civilize with a Stick," p. 245.

185. As is well known, the Euroamerican/Eurocanadian racism of the 19th/early-20th centuries claimed a "scientific" basis; for background, see William Stanton, *The Leopard's Spots: Scientific Attitudes Toward Race in America, 1815-59* (Chicago: University of Chicago Press, 1960); Steven Jay Gould, *The Mismeasure of Man* (New York: W.W. Norton, 1981). For insight into the intractable nature of the attitudinal legacy generated by the tradition of "scientific racism," see Michael Omi and Howard Winant, *Racial Formation in the United States: From the 1960s to the 1990s* (New York: Routledge, 1994); William H. Tucker, *The Science and Politics of Racial Research* (Urbana: University of Illinois Press, 1994) esp. pp. 138-79.

186. As this "disturbing situation" was politely described in an official Canadian study undertaken during the mid-60s, "graduates" (i.e., survivors) were trapped between the "conflicting pulls of two cultures" while being fully accepted by neither, and few, if any, were "equipped to handle this struggle on their own"; George Caldwell, *Indian Residential Schools: A Research Study of the Child Care Programmes for Nine Residential Schools in Saskatchewan* (Ottawa: Canadian Welfare Council, 1967) pp. 151, 61. This is again a theme running like a river through survivor literature; see those autobiographical works already cited, as well as Polingaysi Qoyawayma (Elizabeth Q. White), as told to Vada S. Carlson, *No Turning Back: A Hopi Indian Girl's Struggle to Bridge the Gap Between the World of Her People and the World of the White Man* (Albuquerque: University of New Mexico Press, 1964).

187. Milloy, *"National Crime"*, p. 115.

188. A.B. Simes to Dir. of Indian Affairs H. McGill, Oct. 19, 1944 (N.A.C. RG 10, Vol. 6262, File 578-1 (4-5), MR C 8653). The document is usually referred to as the "Simes Report."

189. Milloy, *"National Crime"*, pp. 118, 332n101.

190. Ibid., pp. 62-6.

191. Ibid., p. 73.

192. Ibid., pp. 75, 103.

193. This was certainly the view of Canada's Committee of Churches Cooperating with the Department of Indian Affairs which, in early 1938, claimed that declining buying power had cost the churches $840,000 over the preceding five years alone; Committee memo dated Feb. 8, 1938 (United Church Archives, WMS Fonds, Accession 83.058C, File 3).

194. Among those who have advanced this shameless rewriting of history was the accountant-turned-top-bureaucrat, Duncan Campbell Scott; Titley, *Narrow Vision*, p. 22.

195. Quoted in Milloy, *"National Crime"*, p. 103.

196. R.A. Hoey to Dir. of Indian Affairs H. McGill, Nov. 4, 1938 (N.A.C. RG 10, Vol. 7185, File 1/25-1-7-1). The situation in the U.S. was even worse. In 1928, the average per capita allocation to support an Indian residential student was $167 per year, while that allotted a white child in a state-run residential institution was $610, and $700 per white child was expended in private facilities; Lewis Meriam, et al., *Problem of Indian Administration* (Baltimore: Johns Hopkins University Press, 1928) pp. 348-50.

197. Ibid.

198. The specific facility at issue was the Rice Indian Boarding School (Arizona), where "the diet of the children consisted of bread, black coffee and syrup for breakfast, bread and boiled potatoes for [lunch], more bread and boiled potatoes for dinner." The average daily expenditure in all such institutions was 11¢ ($40.15 per student/year); Meriam, et al., *Problem of Indian Administration*, pp. 12, 327-31.

199. In actuality, the additional expense probably came nearer to doubling than tripling the per capita expenditure for food; Ray Lyman Wilbur and William A. DuPuy, *Conservation in the Department of Interior* (Washington, D.C.: U.S. Dept. of Interior, 1931) p. 126.

200. Szasz, *Education and the Indian*, p. 19.

201. Loring Benson Priest, *Uncle Sam's Stepchildren: The Reformation of United States Indian Policy, 1865-1887* (Lincoln: University of Nebraska Press, 1975 reprint of 1942 original).

202. Milloy, *"National Crime"*, p. 115.

203. Ibid., p. 118

204. Ibid., p. 126.

205. Quoted in Milloy, *"National Crime"*, p. 109.

206. D.C. Scott to F. Mears, Jan. 11, 1924 (N.A.C. RG 10, Vol. 6320, File 658-1, MR C 9802). One can hardly avoid comparison to the nazi posture of denial concerning conditions in the camps; see Walter Laqueur, *The Terrible Secret: Suppression of the Truth about Hitler's "Final Solution"* (Boston: Little, Brown, 1981).

207. Milloy, *"National Crime"*, p. 121.

208. Ibid., p. 117.

209. Ibid.

210. "At no time did the department make any sustained attempt to ensure 'that an arrangement might be made to get a good weekly allowance' of food to the children"; ibid., p. 122; quoting an Indian Department bureaucrat named Halliday who was among the several who by 1926 had pointed out to Scott that the diet in the schools was radically deficient. It is thus fair to say that Scott knew what was going on, and that he either didn't care or condoned it.

211. Child, *Boarding School Seasons*, p. 32.

212. Edna Groves, "Report on the Flandreau Indian School" (Washington, D.C.: Bureau of Indian Affairs [NA, RG 75], May 12, 1925).

213. Child, *Boarding School Seasons*, p. 32.

214. The available documentation can be extremely misleading. In 1915, for example, the superintendent at Haskell claimed that purchases of "fish, sausage, meats, chicken [and] raisins" were made to supplement the "pupils' mess." In his annual report the same year, however, he proudly announced that average "upkeep" per student had come to only $4.16 per month. If this last were true, the one can only wonder who was eating all the supplements he was supposedly buying. The specter of the Regina School's purchasing pattern is unavoidable.

215. Miller, *Shingwauk's Vision*, p. 293.

216. Ibid. The damage inflicted by such bias was in some respects and for obvious reasons as much emotional as nutritional. Consider the poignant story of a man who in 1965—the year it was runner up in the Saskatchewan championship—was an 11-year-old player on the Lestock School's peewee hockey team. Arriving back at school after the big game, the team was rewarded with a "victory feast" consisting of cocoa and baloney sandwiches. The youngsters, he remembers, were quite excited by this rare "treat," until, passing by the staff dining hall on the way to their dormitory, they realized the adults were celebrating with steaks and chicken; John PeeAce, "We Almost Won," in Jack Funk and Gordon Lobe, eds., *". . . and They Told Us Their Stories": A Book of Indian Stories* (Saskatoon, Sask.: Saskatoon District Tribal Council, 1991) p. 68.

217. Milloy, *"National Crime"*, p. 284.

218. Miller, *Shingwauk's Vision*, p. 294.

219. Ibid. For background on Kamloops, see Haig-Brown, *Resistance and Renewal*.

220. Marilyn Millward, "Clean Behind the Ears: Micmac Parents, Micmac Children, and the Shubenacadie Residential School," *New Maritimes*, Mar./Apr. 1992, p. 11.

221. Miller, *Shingwauk's Vision*, pp. 325-6; Millward, "Clean Behind the Ears," p. 14.

222. This is one of the reasons, perhaps, that administrators regularly filed "menus" that had nothing at all to do with what the children were actually fed; Milloy, *"National Crime"*, p. 118.

223. On foraging for cats and raw wheat, see the text accompanying note 205. There are many other such accounts, especially of boys engaging in the forbidden activity of snaring rabbits; see, e.g., Miller, *Shingwauk's Vision*, p. 296. Recollections of pilfering food when and wherever possible are almost universal among survivors; for representative samples, see Knockwood, *Out of the Depths*, esp. pp. 35-6; Haig-Brown, *Resistance and Renewal*, pp. 98-101.

224. Miller, *Shingwauk's Vision*, p. 296.

225. Ibid., pp. 296-7.

226. Ibid., p. 297.

227. Milloy, *"National Crime"*, pp. 78, 112.

228. Amherst's action has been treated in a number of studies. For one of the earliest, see E. Wagner Stearn and Allen E. Stearn, *The Effects of Smallpox on the Destiny of the Amerindian* (Boston: Bruce Humphries, 1945) pp. 44-50.

229. On British Columbia, see note 76. On Fort Clark, see Thornton, *American Indian Holocaust and Survival*, pp. 94-5. On California, see Robert F. Heizer, ed., *The Destruction of California Indians* (Lincoln: University of Nebraska Press, 1993 reprint of 1974 Peregrine Smith ed.) p. 251.

230. Roberto Mario Salmon, "The Disease Complaint at Bosque Redondo (1864–1868)," *Indian Historian*, No. 9, 1976. For broader background, see Gerald Thompson, *The Army and the Navajo: The Bosque Redondo Reservation Experiment, 1863-1868* (Tucson: University of Arizona Press, 1982).

231. "What was the death rate in Indian schools generally? This is surely an important question, but unfortunately an impossible one to answer . . . [M]ost superintendents only reported the deaths of those students who were actually attending school; it was common practice to dismiss the sickly students. Although this occasionally could be justified on the basis of removing contagious students . . . as necessary to the overall health of the school, it also had the practical effect of [appearing to lower] the death rate"; Adams, *Education for Extinction*, p. 130. "School records do not count the number of students sent home to their families gravely ill or who died in tuberculosis sanatoriums"; Child, *Boarding School Seasons*, p. 67.

232. D.C. Scott, "Indian Affairs, 1867-1912," in A. Shortt and A.G. Doughty, eds., *Canada and Its Provinces* (Toronto: University of Edinburgh Press, 1913) p. 615.

233. Michael Burleigh, *Ethics and Extermination: Reflections on the Nazi Genocide* (Cambridge, UK: Cambridge University Press, 1997) p. 211. One should be careful not to conflate concentration camps with outright "death camps" or "extermination centers" like Auschwitz. The latter were much rarer—there were in fact only a half-dozen of them—and served a different purpose than did camps like Mauthausen and Dachau, of which there were well over a thousand. A useful explication of the distinction between the two types of camp will be found in Lucy S. Dawidowicz, *The War Against the Jews, 1933-1945* (New York: Holt, Rinehart & Winston, 1975) esp. Chapter 7, "The Annihilation Camps: Kingdom of Death," pp. 129-49. In this connection, it is noteworthy that *no* prisoner is known to have survived a 10-year sentence under the conditions prevailing in Mississippi's convict leasing system from 1866 inception to formal abolition in1890; Oshinsky, *"Worse Than Slavery"*, p. 46.

234. Adams, *Education for Extinction*, p. 125.

235. Child, *Boarding School Seasons*, p. 57.

236. Ibid., p. 66.

237. Ibid.

238. The overall death rate among Indians from tuberculosis during the first third of the 20th century was 6.5 times that of the U.S. general population, and far higher in the boarding schools; Szasz, *Education and the Indian*, p. 20. On influenza and smallpox, see Child, *Boarding School Seasons*, p. 55.

239. Quoted in Adams, *Education for Extinction*, p. 130.

240. Ales Hrdlicka, *Tuberculosis Among Certain Indian Tribes of the United States* (Washington, D.C.: Smithsonian Institution, 1909) esp. pp. 25, 32. Also see Joseph Murphy, "Health Problems of the Indians," *Annals of the Academy of Political Science*, No. 37, Mar. 1911, esp. pp. 106-7.

241. U.S. Public Health Service, *Contagious and Infectious Diseases Among the Indians* (Washington, D.C.: 63rd Cong., 1st Sess., [Senate Doc. 1038] 1913); on trachoma, see esp. pp. 16-9. Also see Diane Putney's superb doctoral dissertation, *Fighting the Scourge: American Indian Morbidity and Federal Policy, 1897-1928* (Marquette, MI: Marquette University, 1980) pp. 141-3.

242. Adams, *Education for Extinction*, p. 130. Also see Putney, *Fighting the Scourge*, pp. 23-8.

243. Szasz, *Education and the Indian*, p. 19.

244. William McConnell to Sec. of Interior Ethan Hitchcock, Oct. 31, 1899; excerpted in Putney, *Fighting the Scourge*, pp. 10-1.

245. "Burke buried the report, and it never saw the light of day until 1928"; Adams, *Education for Extinction*, p. 135. The document, entitled "A Study of the Need for Public Health Nursing on Indian Reservations," was prepared by Florence Patterson, an experienced public health care practitioner. It finally surfaced during congressional hearings conducted in 1928; U.S. Senate, Committee on Indian Affairs, *Survey of Conditions of the Indian in the United States* (Washington, D.C.: 71st Cong., 1st Sess., 1929) Pt. 3; see esp. pp. 960-76. Further background will be found in Prucha, *Great Father*, pp. 852-5.

246. Child, *Boarding School Seasons*, p. 63.

247. Peairs produced an 11-page rebuttal to a muckraking article by Vera L. Connelly, "The Cry of a Broken People," which was published in the Feb. 1929 issue of *Good Housekeeping* and provided the first broad public exposure to conditions in the schools. Among other falsehoods, Peairs' paper argued that the children lodged therein were provided "perfectly adequate" diets and that there were only "occasionally a few who have tuberculosis"; Child, *Boarding School Seasons*, pp. 33-4. So thoroughly at odds were his glowing assertions with official data that he was finally forced to resign in July 1930, after 42 years of controlling the lives—and deaths—of American Indian children; Szasz, *Education and the Indian*, p. 29.

248. As of 1890, 9,865 American Indian children had been placed in boarding schools, a number that grew to 17,708 by 1900. By 1910, there were 19,628 children in BIA-run residential facilities, another 5,150 in church-run and private contract schools, for a total of 24,778. In 1920, the numbers were about the same in federal boarding schools—19,631—but had grown to 6,546 in church/private facilities, for a total of 26,177; Adams, *Education for Extinction*, pp. 58, 320. Meanwhile, as the number of children in the schools rose by more than 250%, the overall native population in the U.S. *declined* slightly, from 248,253 in 1890 to 244,437 in 1920; *Fifteenth U.S. Census*, Table 3. Hence, not only were children replaced at a rate faster than they died in the schools—although the proportion of students dying can be presumed to have remained relatively constant—the proportional impact on Native North America rose both steadily and sharply. The bottom line is that calling such facilities "death mills" is no overstatement.

249. For statistics, see Szasz, *Education and the Indian*, p. 60. For health data, see, e.g., Rosemary Wood, "Health Problems Facing American Indian Women," National Institute of Education, *Conference on the Educational and Occupational Needs of American Indian Women, October 1976* (Washington, D.C.: U.S. Dept. of Education, Off. of Educational Research and Improvement, 1980) esp. pp. 179-80. Also see Gail Marks-Jarvis, "The Fate of the Indian," *National Catholic Reporter*, May 27, 1977.

250. All but a handful of the boarding schools were closed in 1982, during President Ronald Reagan's first round of major budget cuts. Several of the old facilities—Chemawa, Flandreau, the Sherman Institute, Riverside Indian School (Anadarko, OK), Sequoia School (Tahlequah, OK) and the Santa Fe Indian School—remain open, but are run on a contract basis by the Indians themselves; Szasz, *Education and the Indian*, pp. 216-7. For background on the Chemawa facility, see Sonciray Bonnell, *Chemawa Indian Boarding School: The First One Hundred Years, 1880-1980* (Hanover, NH: MA thesis, Dartmouth College, 1997).

251. P.H. Bryce, *Report on the Indian Schools of Manitoba and the Northwest Territories* (Ottawa: Government Printing Bureau, 1907) pp. 17-20. The study is usually referred to simply as the "Bryce Report".

252. Ibid.

253. Milloy, *"National Crime"*, p. 92.

254. Ibid., p. 93. For background on the Kuper Island facility, see Sylvia Olsen with Rita Morris and Ann Sam, *No Time to Say Goodbye: Children's Stories of the Kuper Island Residential School* (Victoria, BC: Sono Nis Press, 2001).

255. Ibid., pp. 87-8.

256. Ibid., p. 92.

257. The document, usually referred to as the "Paget Report," was submitted on Nov. 25, 1908 (N.A.C. RG 10, Vol. 4041, File 334503, MR C 10178).

258. Milloy, *"National Crime"*, pp. 82-3.

259. Ibid., p. 79.

260. Ibid., p. 85.

261. M. Benson to J.D. McLean, July 15, 1895 (N.A.C. RG 10, Vol. 6039, File 160-1, MR C 8152).

262. Dr. J.P. Rice to C. Sifton, Aug. 3, 1903 (N.A.C. RG 10, Vol. 3920, File 116818, MR C 10161).

263. On infection/death rates, see George Jasper Wherrett, *The Miracle of Empty Beds: A History of Tuberculosis in Canada* (Toronto: University of Toronto Press, 1977) p. 110.

264. Milloy, *"National Crime"*, p. 85.

265. The quotes are assembled from articles in *Saturday Night*, (Nov. 23, 1907) and *Montreal Star*

(Nov. 15, 1907), as well as a banner story titled "Schools Aid White Plague—Startling Death Rolls Revealed Among Indians" appearing in the *Ottawa Citizen* on Nov. 16, 1907.

266. Blake self-published his allegations and the arguments sustaining them in the form of a pamphlet entitled *Can You Hear the Red Man Calling?* in 1908.

267. *Ottawa Citizen*, Nov. 16, 1907.

268. To be fair, it may be that Duncan Campbell Scott, the accountant who took over as director of the Indian Service in 1913 and held the position until 1932, was willing to consider a shift of emphasis from residential facilities to day schools (in the name of "cost efficiency," if nothing else). If so, he was stymied by powerful political forces. "The Roman Catholic bishops and the Oblates who [ran] most of the Catholic schools were opposed to [any] plan to de-emphasize residential schooling [and] insisted that *more* residential facilities were needed [emphasis added]"; Miller, *Shingwauk's Vision*, p. 139.

269. By 1927, the number of students in residential facilities at the time of the *Bryce Report*—3,755—had grown considerably, to 6,641; ibid., p. 142. Meanwhile, the number of schools actually declined from 77 in 1907 to 72 in 1923—a matter which obviously exacerbated overcrowding tremendously—before a construction spurt took the number of schools up to its peak of 80 in 1931. Thereafter, the number of facilities began to decline again—only 75 remained by 1943—while the number of students continued to climb, not peaking until 1948, when there were 9,368 Indian residential students in Canada (60% of the school-age population); Milloy, *"National Crime"*, pp. 55, 102, 208.

270. S. Swinford, Dec. 4, 1907 (N.A.C. RG 10, Vol. 4037, File 317021, MR C 10177).

271. Manitoba Indian Commissioner David Laird, quoted in Milloy, *"National Crime"*, p. 92. The evidence is solid that efforts were periodically made to create a false impression of reality during on-site visits to the schools by independent inspectors; ibid., pp. 114-5. 118. It should be noted that such statements and related techniques are not dissimilar from those employed by nazi officials who claimed, in the face of mounting international criticism of conditions in Dachau and other concentration camps in 1933, "that 'for the mass [of camp inmates] hailing from the proletarian milieux, their material standard of living is higher than they knew in civilian life.' A Swiss International Committee [of the Red Cross] inspection team concurred with this view after a sanitized tour of Dachau"; Michael Burleigh, *The Third Reich: A New History* (New York: Hill and Wang, 2000) p. 225.

272. Milloy, *"National Crime"*, p. 95.

273. P.H. Bryce, *The Story of a National Crime being an Appeal for Justice for the Indians of Canada* (Ottawa: James Hope & Sons, 1922).

274. F.A. Corbett to Hon. Sir James Lougheed, Dec. 1, 1920 (N.A.C. RG 10, Vol. 4092, File 546898, MR C 10187); F.A. Corbett to W. Graham, Dec. 7, 1920 (N.A.C. RG 10, Vol. 546898, MR C 10187).

275. Milloy, *"National Crime"*, pp. 98-9.

276. Ibid., p. 99.

277. Corbett to Graham, Dec. 7, 1920.

278. Ibid.

279. Ibid.

280. Memo from W. Ditchburn, Oct. 12, 1920 (N.A.C. RG 10, Vol. 7182, File 1/25-1-1-1, MR C 9695); Rev. J. Woodsworth to Sec., Nov. 25, 1918 (N.A.C. RG 10, Vol. 3921, File 116818-1B, MR C 10161).

281. Woodsworth to Sec., Nov. 25, 1918.

282. Titley, *Narrow Vision*, p. 87.

283. "Total [annual] expenditures for the system fell by thirty-three percent, from $811,764 to $542, 568" per year, between 1914 and 1918; Milloy, *"National Crime"*, p. 330n63. On student enrollment, see note 269, above.

284. *Saturday Night*, Nov. 23, 1907.

285. D.C. Scott to A. Meighan, Jan. 1918 (N.A.C. RG 10, Vol. 6001, File 1-1-1 (1), MR C 8134).

286. Wherrett, *Miracle of Empty Beds*, pp. 107, 111-4.

287. "St. John's, Chapleau, a school that had a difficult record in Scott's day, was not greatly improved" by 1944. "The Red Cross found that 'the standard of all food preparation was very low and the meals [were] distinctly unpalatable' . . . Everything about the kitchen and dining room was dirty and

there was a 'lack of cleanliness and sanitary care in the handling of food.' The place was full of flies: 'It was not uncommon to see the food particularly black with them . . . Cockroaches were everywhere' "; Milloy *"National Crime"*, pp. 263, quoting Mrs. A. Stevenson, Red Cross Survey, Oct. 1944 (N.A.C. RG 6033, File 150-44 (2), MR C 8149). Such examples abound, right on into the mid-1950s. The 1957 reforms, not fully implemented until 1961, mainly replaced the per capita system of subsidy with a centralized "controlled cost" structure; ibid., pp. 270-2; Miller, *Shingwauk's Vision*, pp. 393-4.

288. Food, as always, provides a convenient lens through which to view the whole. In 1969, Agnes L. Campbell, another nutritionist, reported that at least some schools were allotting less than 3 oz. of "minced meat" (hamburger) per child at dinner, that macaroni or spaghetti was being served as dinner 4 times per week and bologna 5 times on average; Report of Regional Nutritionist, Apr. 30, 1969 (INAC File 1/35-1-4-1. Vol. 2).

289. Fournier and Crey, *Stolen From Our Embrace*, p. 61. As in the U.S., several of the old schools— 7, to be exact, all in Alberta and Saskatchewan—continue to operate, but are now under the direct control of native people. The Shingwauk Home in Sault St. Marie, Ontario, has also been converted into the Indian-controlled Algoma University College; Miller, *Shingwauk's Vision*, pp. 402-5.

290. Milloy, *"National Crime"*, p. 99.

291. Ibid., p. 102.

292. Ibid. "Most historians . . . believe that the majority [of Germans] had some vague knowledge [of what was being done to the Jews and others] and were indifferent or acquiescent . . . Hitler's racial politics were simply not important to most Germans"; Sarah Gordon, *Hitler, Germans, and the "Jewish Question"* (Princeton, NJ: Princeton University Press, 1984) pp. 166, 208.

293. The mentality at issue is described as a complex blend of dissociation, psychic numbing, brutalization and doubling. In a passage resonating well with the observable sensibility among the settler populations of both Canada and the U.S. vis-à-vis Native North Americans, Lifton and Markusen explain that with regard to "Nazi cruelties toward Jews and others," most "Germans . . . could maintain a workable psychological equilibrium, combining feelings of [national] vitality and an activated sense of immortality (via the Thousand Year Reich), on the one hand, and an array of dissociative defenses on the other. Even in the midst of killing . . . those dissociative defenses could block out the horror of the enterprise. And there were parallel patterns of dissociation in less extreme environments—[those] far removed from the killing . . . would [later] claim to have been ignorant or helpless concerning what was happening . . . Here, the dissociation included patterns of denial or psychic numbing, each entailing withdrawal of empathy from designated victims. The withdrawal was highly selective: [Good Germans] were perfectly capable of retaining fellow feeling toward other 'Aryans'—that is toward everyone but a few [officially targeted] groups"; Lifton and Markusen, *Genocidal Mentality*, pp. 13, 195.

294. Szasz, *Education and the Indian*, p. 10; Miller, *"National Crime"*, p. 55.

295. As Duncan Campbell Scott put it, the schools were "divided into two classes, industrial and boarding, but the work carried on in each is in all essentials the same"; quoted in Miller, *Shingwauk's Vision*, p. 140.

296. Oliver LaFarge, "Revolution with Reservations," *New Republic*, Oct. 9, 1935, p. 233. In Canada, Métis organizer Malcolm Norris later adapted LaFarge's description to his own purposes, referring to the residential schools as "penitentiaries . . . that [native] children are compelled to attend FOR THE CRIME OF BEING INDIAN"; *Indian Speaking Leaf*, May/June 1940; quoted in Milloy, *"National Crime"*, p. 191.

297. Quoted in Fournier and Crey, *Stolen From Our Embrace*, p. 61.

298. Quoted in Miller, *Shingwauk's Vision*, p. 387.

299. Meriam, et al., *Problem of Indian Administration*, p. 13.

300. For overviews, see Adams, *Education for Extinction*, pp. 149-56; Miller, *Shingwauk's Vision*, pp. 251-68.

301. See the chapter entitled "Working for the School," in Child, *Boarding School Seasons*, pp. 69-86. On girls specifically, see Robert A. Trennert, Jr., "Educating Indian Girls at Nonreservation Boarding Schools, 1878-1920," *Western Historical Quarterly*, Vol. 13, No. 3, 1982.

302. "The student was expected to contribute his [*sic*] labor to the upkeep and operation of a run-down plant, and anything he learned by this haphazard method was incidental"; William Kizer, "History

of the Flandreau Indian School, Flandreau, South Dakota" (MA thesis, University of South Dakota, 1940) p. 69. Also see Trennert, *Phoenix Indian School*, p. 47; Miller, *Shingwauk's Vision*, pp. 257, 268.

303. Child, *Boarding School Seasons*, p. 36.

304. Meriam, et al., *Problem of Indian Administration*, p. 13.

305. For a broader explication of this rationale, see Paul W. Bennett, "Turning 'Bad Boys' into 'Good Citizens': The Reforming Impulse of Toronto's Industrial Schools Movement, 1883-1920," *Ontario History*, Vol. 78, No. 3, 1986. Also see Trennert, *Phoenix Indian School*, pp. 68-9, 123-4; Lomawaima, *Prairie Light*, pp. 68-80.

306. Child, *Boarding School Seasons*, pp. 75-6.

307. Adams, *Education for Extinction*, p. 150. On "treadmill tasks" in Canada, see Milloy *"National Crime"*, p. 170.

308. Kizer, "History of the Flandreau Indian School," p. 69. A counterpart observation in Canada, made in 1936 with regard to the Birtle Indian Residential School (Manitoba), was that the "farm should be operated for the school—not the school for the farm"; Milloy, *"National Crime"*, p. 169.

309. Adams, *Education for Extinction*, p. 149.

310. Ibid., p. 150. Probably the most poignant image conjured in this connect was that of "small girls from the kindergarten class daily darn[ing] socks for hours on end" in the Crow Creek Boarding School, South Dakota; Estelle Aubrey Brown, *Stubborn Fool: A Narrative* (Caldwell, ID: Claxton, 1952) pp. 45-6.

311. Adams, *Education for Extinction*, p. 149.

312. Child, *Boarding School Seasons*, p. 35.

313. Lomawaima, *Prairie Light*, p. 77.

314. Ibid., p. 68.

315. Meriam, et al., *Problem of Indian Administration*, p. 327.

316. A total of $235,745 was allocated to Chilocco in 1927, while actual operating expenses at the school that year came to $309,999. Proceeds from student labor made up the difference; Lomawaima, *Prairie Light*, p. 77.

317. Uniforms notwithstanding, the quality of clothing allowed residential school students was always "scandalous" and often deeply embarrassing to the children, especially in Canada. There, garments sent from home or by charitable groups were commonly impounded by staff and either sold or given over to charities serving white communities; Miller, *Shingwauk's Vision*, pp. 298-300.

318. Quoted in Milloy, *"National Crime"*, pp. 169, 171. It is impossible to avoid the eerie similarity between these circumstances—not to mention the beastly logic shaping them—and those of the modern "prison-industrial complex" remarked in note 98 and accompanying text. Another analogous context is, of course, the employment of concentration camp labor described by Helmut Krausnick, Hans Buchheim, Martin Broszat and Hans-Adolf Jacobson in their *Anatomy of the SS State* (New York: Walker, 1965) pp. 483-93. Still another is that of the Soviet "Empire of the Camps," depicted quite succinctly by Stéphane Courtois, et al., in *The Black Book of Communism: Crimes, Terror, Repression* (Cambridge, MA: Harvard University Press, 2000) pp. 203-15. Those who would argue that such comparisons are "overstated" should realize that their objections devolve upon differences in scale and/or intensity, not of kind. It should be noted as well that none of the ugly examples mentioned took—or take—*children* as a primary target.

319. In Canada, there was talk at least as early as 1884 of "making the school[s] in the near future self-supporting by the labour of [their] pupils"; quoted in Milloy, *"National Crime"*, p. 169. In effect, the extraction of labor from students was from the outset calculated into federal budgets as a "hidden grant" or subsidy extracted from the native populace to support an assimilative apparatus they in the main strongly opposed; Miller, *Shingwauk's Vision*, p. 252. An example of an institution actually turning a profit is the Kamloops School, where, among other things, students collected 300-350 eggs each day from the facility's hen house but were served only one egg per child every second Thursday—the staff ate eggs daily, while the remainder were sold—and the superintendent, a priest named O'Grady, reported in 1954 that the institution's "finances are sound and a large surplus is sent annually to the Province"; Haig-Brown, *Resistance and Renewal*, p. 69. The pervasiveness of such realities in the U.S. is witnessed in a query posed by federally commissioned investigators in 1928 as to the propriety of "supporting Indian boarding schools . . . through the labor of the children"; Meriam, et al., *Problem of Indian Administration*, p. 13.

320. *Annual Report of the Commissioner of Indian Affairs* (Washington, D.C.: 54th Cong., 2nd Sess., 1897) p. 324.

321. Child, *Boarding School Seasons*, p. 75. Theoretically, each individual could withdraw these monies when s/he graduated (or otherwise left school). Several former boarding school students have recounted to me how all or part of the money in their accounts "disappeared" when it came time to claim it, suggesting a pattern of embezzlement on the part of at least some administrators and/or that student earnings were treated more like administrative slush funds. The disposition of monies accrued by students who died at school is also unclear in many instances.

322. Adams, *Education for Extinction*, pp. 156-63.

323. Miller, *Shingwauk's Vision*, p. 253.

324. Adams, *Education for Extinction*, pp. 163, 366-7n65. On convict leasing, see Lichtenstein, *Twice the Work of Free Labor*; Matthew L. Mancini, *One Dies, Get Another: Convict Leasing in the American South, 1866-1928* (Columbia: University of South Carolina Press, 1996).

325. Miller, *Shingwauk's Vision*, p. 255.

326. Adams, *Education for Extinction*, p. 151.

327. The caloric content of an average residential student diet was computed in 1951 by an Indian Service nursing supervisor named Anna Swaile; Milloy, *"National Crime"*, pp. 266-7. The daily intake of calories per student in 1886, the year from which the Fort Stevenson labor example is drawn, was likely lower than 1,500. The average daily caloric requirement for an adolescent male *not* engaged in hard labor is generally estimated at 2,500. When hard labor is involved, upwards of 4,000 calories is considered a minimum daily requirement. For data and relevant comparisons, see David E. Stannard, *American Holocaust: Columbus and the Conquest of the New World* (New York: Oxford University Press, 1992) pp. 138-9.

328. See all survivor literature cited thus far. Also see Irene Stewart, *A Voice in Her Tribe: A Navajo Woman's Own Story* (Socorro, NM: Ballena Press, 1980) esp. p. 17.

329. Proportional comparisons are again instructive. "[O]f the 3.1 million Jewish deaths that took place in the concentration and death camps, at least 1.6 million resulted from 'natural' causes, added to 800,000 Jews outside the camps who died of . . . 'ghettoization and privation.' This makes a total of more than 2.4 million of the 5.1 million Jewish deaths during the Holocaust, at a bare minimum, directly attributable to the same so-called natural phenomena—disease, exploitation, malnutrition, and the like—that were also the immediate cause of death for many of the Americas' indigenous people," including the residential school victims; Stannard, "Uniqueness as Denial," p. 178, relying on Raul Hilberg, *The Destruction of European Jews*, 3 vols. (New York: Holmes and Meier, [rev. ed.] 1985) Vol. 3, pp. 1047-8, 1201-20; Arno J. Mayer, *Why Did the Heavens Not Darken? The "Final Solution" in History* (New York: Pantheon, 1990) pp. 365, 462.

330. Stannard, "Uniqueness as Denial," p. 177.

331. Quoted in Adams, *Education for Extinction*, p. 153.

332. Quoted in Miller, *Shingwauk's Vision*, p. 158.

333. "By evening, I was too tired to play and just fell asleep wherever I sat down . . . [This is] why it was so hard to learn. We were too tired to study"; Stewart, *Voice in Her Tribe*, p. 17. Such accounts are too numerous to cite.

334. Milloy, *"National Crime"*, p. 171.

335. Child, *Boarding School Seasons*, p. 77.

336. Milloy, *"National Crime"*, p. 171.

337. Ibid.; referring to Barman, Hébert and McCaskill, *Indian Education in Canada, Vol. 1*, esp. p. 9.

338. Canada's Western Interior Minister, Clifford Sifton, 1897; quoted in Miller, *Shingwauk's Vision*, p. 158.

339. Child, *Boarding School Seasons*, p. 81; Kizer, "Flandreau Indian School," p. 84.

340. *Flandreau Student Handbook, 1938-39*; quoted in Child, *Boarding School Seasons*, p. 71.

341. For a reasonably broad overview, see Alice Littlefield and Martha C. Knack, *Native Americans and Wage Labor: Ethnohistorical Perspectives* (Norman: University of Oklahoma Press, 1996).

342. For overviews, see Coleman, *Indian Children at School*, pp. 146-61; Adams, *Education for Extinction*, pp. 209-38; Miller, *Shingwauk's Vision*, pp. 343-74.

343. These prohibitions, which are constitutional in both the U.S. and Canada, are also reflected

in international customary law, as codified in the United Nations Standard Minimum Rules for the Treatment of Prisoners (U.N. Doc. A/CONF/6/1, Annex I, A (1956); E.S.C. Res. 663 (XXIV) C, 24 U.N. ESCOR, Supp. (No. 1) 11, U.N. Doc. E/3048 (1957)). For text, see Burns H. Weston, Richard A. Falk and Anthony D'Amato, eds., *Basic Documents in International Law and World Order* (Minneapolis: West, 1990) pp. 322-34.

344. Most specifically at issue are the United Nations Declaration on Protection from Torture (U.N.G.A. Res. 3452 (XXX), 9 Dec. 1975), the United Nations Convention against Torture and Other Cruel, Inhuman or Degrading Treatment or Punishment (U.N.G.A. Res. 39/46 Annex, 39 U.N. GAOR, Supp. (No. 51) 197, U.N. Doc. E/CN.4/1984/72, Annex (1984), *reprinted in* 23 I.L.M. 1027 (1984)), and the Inter-American Convention to Prevent and Punish Torture (O.A.S. Treaty Ser. No. 67, O.A.S. Doc. OEA/Ser. P, AG/doc. 2023/85 rev. 1, at 46, *reprinted in* 25 I.L.M. 519 (1986)). For texts, see Brownlie, *Basic Documents on Human Rights*, pp. 35-7, 38-51, 531-8.

345. Office of Indian Affairs, *Rules for the Indian School Service* (Washington, D.C.: U.S. Dept. of Interior, 1898) p. 31.

346. Annual Report of the Commissioner of Indian Affairs (Washington, D.C.: 56th Cong., 1st Sess., 1900) p. clii.

347. Adams, *Education for Extinction*, p. 121.

348. As Indian Commissioner Morgan put it at the time, native children were "brutish . . . their higher nature undeveloped . . . and can be reached apparently in no other way than by corporal punishment, confinement, deprivation of privileges, or restriction of diet"; *Annual Report of the Commissioner of Indian Affairs* (Washington, D.C.: 52nd Cong., 1st Sess., 1892) p. 617.

349. Adams, *Education for Extinction*, p. 122; quoting Sekaquaptewa, *Me and Mine*, pp. 136-7; "Myrtle Begay," in Broderick H. Johnson, ed., *Stories of Traditional Navajo Life and Culture* (Tsaile, AZ: Navajo Community College Press, 1977) p. 63; unidentified Comanche quoted in Sally J. McBeth, *Ethnic Identity and the Boarding School Experience of West-Central Oklahoma Indians* (Washington, D.C.: University Press of America, 1983) p. 106. For comparable examples, see Don Talayesva, *Sun Chief: The Autobiography of a Hopi Indian* (New Haven, CT: Yale University Press, 1942) p. 130; Frank Mitchell, *Navajo Blessingway Singer: The Autobiography of Frank Mitchell* (Tucson: University of Arizona Press, 1978) p.67; Zitkala-Sa (Gertrude Bonnin), *American Indian Stories* (Lincoln: University of Nebraska Press, 1985 reprint of 1921 original) pp. 57-9; Qoyawayma, *No Turning Back*, pp. 27-8; Lame Deer and Crow Dog, *Lame Deer*, p. 25; Winnie, *Sah-gan-de-oh*, p. 50; Crow Dog and Erdoes, "Civilize with a Stick," p. 244; "Paul Blatchford," in Johnson, *Stories of Traditional Navajo Life*, p. 175.

350. In Oklahoma's 31 Indian residential schools, "whipping with a rubber hose and the 'belt line' were fairly common punishments"; McBeth, *Identity and the Boarding School*, p. 106. At the Phoenix Indian School, "head disciplinarian Jacob Duran and his assistants regularly struck children with their fists, beat them with leather straps, knocked them down and kicked them . . . beating some boys with baseball bats"; Trennert, *Phoenix Indian School*, pp. 193, 171. Such accounts are far too numerous to be discounted or ignored; see, e.g., U.S. Senate, Committee on Indian Affairs, *Survey of Conditions of the Indians of the United States* (Washington, D.C.: U.S. GPO. 1928-31) Part 8, esp. pp. 3015-23.

351. Adams, *Education for Extinction*, p. 123; quoting the Indian Rights Association Report for 1912 at p. 57. In his autobiographical *Middle Five*, at pp. 46, 121, Francis La Flesche also recounts an episode in which a teacher referred to as "Grey Beard" beat a "dull pupil almost into unconsciousness"; Coleman, *Indian Children at School*, p. 90. An even worse story concerns a boy who ran away after being beaten into unconsciousness at the Phoenix Indian School in 1922, and was then beaten *to death* after being captured and returned; Trennert, *Phoenix Indian School*, p. 193.

352. Adams, *Education for Extinction*, p. 123; quoting the Indian Rights Association Report for 1914 at p. 34. For a broader sampling of such atrocities in U.S. schools, see Robert A. Trennert, Jr., "Corporal Punishment and the Politics of Indian Reform," *History of Education Quarterly*, Vol. 29, No. 4, 1989.

353. Meriam, et al., *Problem of Indian Administration*, pp. 11-2, 332, 392-3, 577-9.

354. McBeth, *Identity and the Boarding School*, p. 106.

355. Adams, *Education for Extinction*, p. 123; relying on McBeth, *Identity and the Boarding School*, p. 105; Jo Ann Ruckman, "Indian Schooling in New Mexico in the 1890s: Letters of a Teacher in the Indian Services," *New Mexico Historical Review*, Vol. 56, No. 1, 1981, p. 45. For comparable examples, see Coleman,

Indian Children at School, pp. 89-90; Lomawaima, *Prairie Light*, pp. 106-121. Representative personal recollections of such things will be found in Jim Whitewolf, *Jim Whitewolf: The Life of a Kiowa Apache Indian* (New York: Dover, 1969) p. 89; Sekaquaptewa, *Me and Mine*, p. 137; Mitchell, *Blessingway*, p. 67; Lame Deer and Erdoes, *Lame Deer*, p. 23; "Jeanette Blake" and "Ernest Nelson," both in Johnson, *Stories of Traditional Navajo Life*, pp. 204, 241.

356. Trennert, *Phoenix Indian School*, p. 188; Lawrence C. Kelly, "Charles Henry Burke," in Robert M. Kvasnicka and Herman J. Viola, eds., *The Commissioners of Indian Affairs, 1824-1977* (Lincoln: University of Nebraska Press, 1979) p. 260

357. Rhodes' partial lifting of Burke's prohibition was promulgated in BIA Circular 2666, Mar. 20, 1930; see Trennert, *Phoenix Indian School*, p. 192.

358. A case in point is that of John B. Brown, superintendent of the Phoenix Indian School, who was documented in Senate hearings conducted in May 1930 to have disregarded the supposed ban on corporal punishment—nine significant incidents were documented as having occurred after Burke's pronouncement, including "the severe beating of a boy who took a bath in violation of the rules"—but was left in his position without so much as an official letter of reprimand. Having held his job since 1917, Brown finally retired with full pension on July 1, 1931; Trennert, *Phoenix Indian School*, pp. 192-8.

359. Ibid., p. 210; Crow Dog and Erdoes, "Civilize with a Stick," p. 245.

360. Milloy, *"National Crime"*, p. 138. As in the U.S., such measures were ostensibly prohibited by Indian Service rules put forth in 1889 and 1895, but these were ignored with impunity.

361. Ibid., p. 143. For more on this particular facility, see Elizabeth M. Furniss, *Victims of Benevolence: Discipline and Death at the Williams Lake Indian Residential School, 1891-1920* (Williams Lake, B.C.: Cariboo Tribal Council, 1992).

362. Ibid., p. 139; quoting W. Graham to D.C. Scott, Dec. 3, 1921 (N.A.C. RG 10, Vol. 6348, File 752-1, MR C 8705).

363. Haig-Brown, *Resistance and Renewal*, p. 83.

364. Miller, *Shingwauk's Vision*, pp. 326-7.

365. C.S. Gould to D.C. Scott, Jan. 26, 1920 (N.A.C. RG 10, Vol. 6358, File 758 (1-2) MR C 8713).

366. For another such account, see Milloy, *"National Crime"*, p. 143.

367. Ibid., p.150. For more on the Spanish Indian Boys School—there was also a girls school—see Johnson, *Indian School Days*.

368. "My father, who attended the Alberni Indian Residential School for four years in the twenties, was physically tortured by his teachers for speaking Tseshaht: they pushed sewing needles through his tongue, a routine punishment for language offenders"; Randy Fred, "Foreword," in Haig-Brown, *Resistance and Renewal*, pp. 15-6.

369. Chrisjohn and Young with Maraun, *Circle Game*, p. 32.

370. There are cases on record of adolescent females at least planning such things, perhaps most notably a young woman at Shubenacadie who stole a knife with the apparent intent to attack an especially abusive nun; Miller, *Shingwauk's Vision*, p. 327.

371. Milloy, *"National Crime"*, p. 147.

372. Skinner is also known to have battered female students with his fists on several occasions; ibid., p. 141.

373. "I wish to state that the Department will not countenance such corrective measures as chaining pupils to benches and corporal punishment that leaves a boy or girl marked. Treatment that might be considered pitiless or jail-like in character will not be permitted"; D.C. Scott to Rev. J. Rioui, O.M.I., Dec. 12, 1921 (N.A.C. RG 10, Vol. 6348, File 752-1, MR C 8705).

374. For samples of such reports, see the correspondence referenced in notes 362 and 365. There are *many* similar missives in the archives.

375. Miller, *Shingwauk's Vision*, p. 327.

376. Chrisjohn and Young with Maraun, *Circle Game*, p. 32.

377. Milloy, *"National Crime"*, p. 284; Miller, *Shingwauk's Vision*, p. 325. Variations with the younger children included placing the wet sheets over their heads while spanking them and/or locking them in closets or cupboards; Haig-Brown, *Resistance and Renewal*, pp. 83-4.

378. In 1886, for instance, the superintendent of the school at Ft. Stevenson, in the U.S., reported that his facility's enrollment was low because of the students' "pernicious habit of running away," a phenomenon already ongoing for several years; quoted in Adams, *Education for Extinction*, p. 224.

379. See, as examples: ibid, pp. 224-9; Coleman, *Indian Children at School*, pp. 162-5; Child, *Boarding School Seasons*, pp. 87-95; Milloy, *"National Crime"*, pp. 142-7, 282-7; Miller, *Shingwauk's Vision*, pp. 366-81; Haig-Brown, *Resistance and Renewal*, pp. 109-10. Virtually all the survivor narratives cited also contain accounts of runaways.

380. Milloy, *"National Crime"*, p. 144.

381. Ibid., p. 146.

382. Ibid., p. 147.

383. Ibid., p. 288.

384. Miller, *Shingwauk's Vision*, p. 326.

385. Ibid., p. 327.

386. Milloy, *"National Crime"*, p. 139.

387. Ibid., p. 142.

388. Ibid.

389. Ibid., p. 285.

390. Ibid., pp. 285-6.

391. Haig-Brown, *Resistance and Renewal*, p. 110.

392. Milloy, *"National Crime"*, p. 286.

393. Ibid., pp. 286-7.

394. Ibid., p. 286; quoting Ian Adams, "The Lonely Death of Charlie Wenjack," *Maclean's Magazine*, Feb. 1967.

395. Adams, *Education for Extinction*, pp. 225, 224.

396. Ibid., p. 228.

397. Coleman, *Indian Children at School*, p. 164.

398. Adams, *Education for Extinction*, p. 228.

399. "Considering the strains they faced at school, it is possible that many of the children who died at, or in flight from, the schools . . . committed suicide or acted so recklessly that death was likely"; Coleman, *Indian Children at School*, pp. 164-5. For a corroborating view by a former student, see "James Henley," in Johnson, *Stories of Traditional Navajo Life*, p. 32. Several others have conceded this possibility in personal discussions with me.

400. Trennert, *Phoenix Indian School*, p. 50.

401. Milloy, *"National Crime"*, pp. 148, 153-4. An earlier (1903) Canadian case involves a young girl at the Regina Industrial School (Saskatchewan) who, when she confided in a teacher her desire to commit suicide—an obvious plea for help—was handed a revolver and told to pull the trigger. "She did—but the gun was empty" (p. 153).

402. Ibid., p. 288.

403. Ibid.

404. David Lester, *Suicide in American Indians* (New York: Nova Science, 2001) p. 19; describing the conclusions drawn in Robert J. Havighurst's "The Extent and Significance of Suicide among American Indians Today," *Mental Health*, No. 55, 1971. Lester notes that most scholars who've studied the schools—which Havighurst did not—have drawn the opposite conclusion, finding the institutional experience to have served as a major "suicidogenic stressor."

405. This comes under the heading of "Necessary Illusions," a concept applied by Noam Chomsky in other connections, notably in the book of the same title published by South End Press in 1989. Analogously, witness the care taken by the nazis to create the misimpression that the "Final Solution" was something other than it was. "Those in charge" of the Third Reich "made a determined effort to spread misleading information about the fate of the Jews [and many others] . . . Jews were not executed, let alone killed or murdered; they were 'resettled', 'evacuated', 'removed', 'deported', or at worst given 'special treatment' "; Laqueur, *Terrible Secret*, p. 17.

406. Chrisjohn, Young and Maraun do an excellent job of summarizing and disposing of such defensive polemics in their *Circle Game*, pp. 7-25.

407. One can search, but the search will be in vain, for evidence of a nonwhite presence in jobs other than kitchen help among those employed by either U.S. or Canadian residential schools prior to the 1970s.

408. Fred, "Foreword," p. 21.

409. In the alternative, as Chrisjohn, Young and Maraun point out, we are expected to believe that "the [system] did bad by doing good"; *Circle Game*, p. 23.

410. To offer but one example from a myriad in Canada: in 1919, W.M. Graham, a senior western department official of the Indian Service, reported a case in which a staff member at Old Sun's School had admitted using shackles and a horse quirt to "discipline" a returned runaway, recommending that the man be "relieved of his duties." Duncan Campbell Scott took no action in this or any similar instance, and "Graham's frustrations [steadily] increased as he dealt with more cases and failed each time to bring the Department to initiate corrective measures." By 1924, even the RCMP was submitting comparable reports, but Scott "would not be moved"; Milloy, *"National Crime"*, p. 146. For a U.S. counterpart example, see note 358.

411. Szasz, *Education and the Indian*, p. 21.

412. Trennert, *Phoenix Indian School*, pp. 192-5.

413. See notes 350 and 358.

414. See generally, Kenneth R. Philp, *John Collier's Crusade for Indian Reform, 1920-1954* (Tucson: University of Arizona Press, 1977); Lawrence C. Kelly, *Assault on Assimilation: John Collier and the Origins of Indian Policy Reform* (Albuquerque: University of New Mexico Press, 1983).

415. Ian Adams, "The Indians: An Abandoned and Dispossessed People," *Weekend Magazine*, July 31, 1965. For further details, see Milloy, *"National Crime"*, pp. 288-9.

416. Both the U.S. and Canada have formally endorsed the United Nations Affirmation of the Principles of International Law Recognized by the Charter of the Nuremberg Tribunal (U.N.G.A. Res. 95(I), U.N. Doc. A/236 (1946), at 1144); for text, see Weston, Falk and D'Amato, *Basic Documents in International Law*, p. 140. For explication of the principle at issue herein, see Quincy Wright, "The Law of the Nuremberg Tribunal, Part II," in Jay W. Baird, ed., *From Nuremberg to My Lai* (Lexington, MA: D.C. Heath, 1972) pp. 41-3.

417. 18 USCS § 1961-1968 (1970). For background, William G. Ross, "RICO," in Kermit L. Hall, ed., *The Oxford Companion to American Law* (New York: Oxford University Press, 2002) pp. 706-7.

418. In truth, there is no order or other such clearcut statement of intent linking Adolf Hitler to the extermination of European Jews; Gerald Fleming, *Hitler and the Final Solution* (Berkeley: University of California Press, 1982). So much for arguments of the sort discussed in notes 4, 11, and accompanying text.

419. Quoted in Agnes Grant, *No End of Grief: Indian Residential Schools in Canada* (Winnipeg, Man: Pemmican Press, 1996) p. 229.

420. As the Indian Department's director of education for British Columbia put it in 1990, "The sad thing is that we didn't know it was happening . . . [Departmental] staff have no recollection of records or reports—either verbal or written"; quoted in Milloy, *"National Crime"*, p. 297.

421. Ibid., p. 149; quoting W. Ditchburn to Sec., Oct. 31, 1912 (N.A.C. RG 10, Vol. 6455, File 885-1 (1-2), MR C 8152).

422. Milloy, *"National Crime"*, p. 145; citing D.C. Scott to A. Grant, Sept. 19, 1914 (N.A.C. RG 10, Vol. 6027, File 117-1-1, MR C 8147). For further background on this facility, see Elizabeth M. Furniss, *Conspiracy of Silence: The Case of the Native Students at St. Joseph's Residential School, 1891-1920* (Williams Lake, B.C.: Cariboo Tribal Council, 1991).

423. Miller, *Shingwauk's Vision*, p. 329.

424. Ibid., pp. 329-30.

425. Far more than sexual predation was covered by this procedure. As early as 1892, a missionary named Tims, serving as principal of the Anglican boarding school on the Blackfeet Reserve (Alberta), refused to allow a father to remove his daughter from the facility during a tuberculosis epidemic. When the little girl shortly died of TB, her father and uncles set upon revenge. Tims fled, and was immediately promoted, despite—or because of—his callous disregard for the child's wellbeing, to the position of directing all Anglican missions in the region; ibid., pp. 129-30.

426. Recounted by former student Mike Cachagee on CBC radio program *Sunday Morning*, Oct. 1991.

427. Roy MacGregor, *Chief: The Fearless Vision of Billy Diamond* (Toronto: Penguin, 1988) p. 24.

428. Miller, *Shingwauk's Vision*, p. 333.

429. Rix Rogers, Special Advisor to the Minister of National Health and Welfare on Child Sexual Abuse, quoted in "Reports of abuse may be low, expert says," *Toronto Globe and Mail*, June 1, 1990.

430. Miller, *Shingwauk's Vision*, p. 334.

431. Fournier and Crey, *Stolen from Our Embrace*, p. 73.

432. Ibid.

433. Ibid.; Miller, *Shingwauk's Vision*, p. 331.

434. Fournier and Crey, *Stolen from Our Embrace*, pp. 73-4, 71.

435. Ibid., p. 71.

436. See note 428.

437. Aboriginal Rights Coalition to the Hon. Tom Siddon, Aug. 1992 (INAC File E6757-18-2, Vol. 4).

438. Quoted in Milloy, *"National Crime"*, p. 301.

439. Ibid., pp. 299, 301. On the Presbyterians, see Miller, *Shingwauk's Vision*, p. 340.

440. The expression of regret was made by Ass't. Min. Bill Van Iterson in June 1991, and that was as far as the Indian Service would go. The most important thing, in Siddon's view, was not justice for the victims, but that the department "respond to incidents of abuse and the resultant effect on Indian communities . . . in a way that liability [was] not admitted"; internal document stamped "PROTECTED"; quoted in Milloy, *"National Crime"*, p. 301.

441. Dept. of Indian and Northern Affairs, "Communications Strategy: Child Sexual Abuse in Residential Schools," 1990 draft (INAC FileE6575-18, Vol. 10).

442. Ibid.

443. These were two of the men, Cyril Paul and Simon Danes, who testified during the 1996 Dougherty case. "A week after the trial, Danes was dead, by his own hand. Tragically, a little more than a year [later], Paul too would take his own life"; Fournier and Grey, *Stolen From Our Embrace*, p. 75.

444. There is indication that DIAND officials were more actively than collaterally protecting predators, given the parameters established internally for being "as open as possible" with file material, without "compromising" former staffers' "privacy rights [as] individuals"; see note 440.

445. Fournier and Crey, *Stolen From Our Embrace*, p. 77. A similar arrangement was reached in 1997 in British Columbia when two plaintiffs reached a "confidential financial settlement" with regard to an action brought against the Salvation Army, employer of the "infamous pedophile William Gareth Douglas, who had sexually abused every boy between the ages of six and eleven while he was preacher to the tiny B.C. reserve of Canyon City, known today as Gitwinsihlkw . . . The Army apologized [but the] federal government, although it [paid] part of the compensation . . . [did] so 'without prejudice'— or apology"; ibid., pp. 77-8.

446. Assembly of First Nations, *Breaking the Silence*.

447. It will be noted that the great majority of the books/articles on Canadian residential schools cited herein were published after 1990; see, additionally, Roland Chrisjohn, *Faith Misplaced: Lasting Effects of Abuse in a First Nations Community* (Williams Lake, B.C.: Cariboo Tribal Council, 1991). Notwithstanding the occasional efforts of Bryce, Blake and a few others, there is a pronounced dearth of readily accessible literature on the topic dating from earlier periods.

448. On Oka, see Geoffrey York and Loreen Pindera, *People of the Pines: The Warriors and the Legacy of Oka* (Boston: Little, Brown, 1991). On establishment of the Royal Commission, Milloy, *"National Crime"*, pp. 302-3.

449. This was described as an issue "affecting virtually every aspect of Aboriginal people's lives"; Royal Commission on Aboriginal Peoples, *Renewal: A Twenty Year Commitment: Report of the Royal Commission on Aboriginal Peoples, Vol. 5* (Ottawa: Canada Communications Group, 1996) p. 1.

450. Royal Commission on Aboriginal Peoples, *Looking Forward, Looking Back: Report of the Royal Commission on Aboriginal Peoples, Vol. 1* (Ottawa: Canada Communications Group, 1997) p. 383.

451. Jane Stewart, *Gathering Strength: Canada's Aboriginal Action Plan* (Ottawa: Dept. of Indian and Northern Affairs, 1998).

452. Stewart's plan overlaps decisively with recommendations advanced by the Canadian Council of Catholic Bishops in their *Let Justice Flow Like a Mighty River* (Ottawa: Catholic Church of Canada, 1995).

453. Chrisjohn and Young with Maraun, *Circle Game*, pp. 104-6; relying on Andrew Polsky, *The Rise of the Therapeutic State* (Princeton, NJ: Princeton University Press, 1991).

454. Miller, *"National Crime"*, p. 305.

455. This is not at all to say that psychological counseling was not needed by/useful to those who survived the nazi camps, just that the régime that created/maintained the camp system was the last entity on earth entitled to preside over such therapy. A very close second would be the society from whence the perpetrator régime had arisen, and which had benefited, materially, from the camps' existence. For explication, see the essays collected in Joel E. Dimsdale, ed., *Survivors, Victims, and Perpetrators: Essays on the Nazi Holocaust* (New York: Hemisphere, 1980).

456. Cecelia Kitzinger and Rachel Perkins have referred to this strategy in another connection, rather astutely, as adding up to "psychology's colonization of our political terrain"; see their *Changing Our Minds: Lesbian Feminism and Psychology* (New York: New York University Press, 1993) p. 72.

457. The process falls within the scope of what Gramsci described as formation of an "hegemonic bloc" precluding the proper understanding of sociohistorical realities; see Walter L. Adamson, *Hegemony and Revolution: A Study of Antonio Gramsci's Political and Cultural Theory* (Berkeley: University of California Press, 1980) esp. pp. 170-9.

458. The titles of certain books already cited—notably Assembly of First Nations, *Breaking the Silence*, and Furniss, *Conspiracy of Silence*—says it all.

459. By mid-January 2003, 1,205 U.S. priests had been accused of child molestation, and numerous higher Catholic officials of participating in a massive and sustained coverup of their subordinates' predations. As in Canada, only a relative handful of the accused clergymen had at that point been criminally convicted, but more than 400 had resigned or taken early retirement in the face of multiple allegations, the Church had reached out of court settlements in an undisclosed number of cases (estimated at more than 100), and more than 1,000 lawsuits remained pending; "1,200 Priests in Sex Abuse Cases," AP Online, Jan. 11, 2003. Among the locations at which such priestly activity allegedly occurred was Boy's Town, a nonindian residential school in Nebraska; Karyn Spencer and David Hendee, "Boys Town, diocese will review new abuse suits," *Omaha World-Herald*, Feb. 1, 2003.

460. Witness, as but one striking example, Robert A. Trennert's strenuous efforts in the final chapter of his book on the Phoenix Indian School—containing as it does abundant information to the contrary (see, e.g., notes 350, 351 and 358, above)—that "there was nothing shameful" about what was done there and that the facility was therefore "not an evil place." Indeed, he professes to find it unfortunate that, in view of "its past history . . . one tribal official felt compelled to call the school a place of 'cultural genocide'"; Trennert, *Phoenix Indian School*, pp. 206, 207, 212. The "reasoning" here, if it may be called that, is of a piece with the variety of pathological denial most commonly associated with alcoholics; see William H. Chrisman, *The Opposite of Everything is True: Reflections on Denial in Alcoholic Families* (New York: William Morrow, 1991).

461. INAC File 6575-18-2, Vol. 01 (protected).

462. The term "Residential School Syndrome" seems to have been coined by the Royal Commission on Aboriginal Peoples. For a good summary of what is encompassed by the term in common usage, see Grant, *No End of Grief*, pp. 247-65. Also see Roland Chrisjohn, et al., "Faith Misplaced: The Lasting Effects of Abuse on a First Nations Community," *Canadian Journal of Native Education*, No. 18, 1991.

463. That trauma is transmissible from parents to children has been well established in studies of survivors of the nazi camps. See, as examples, Axel Russel, "Late Effects: Influence on the Children of the Concentration Camp Survivor," in Dimsdale, *Survivors, Victims, Perpetrators*; Helen Epstein, *Children of the Holocaust: Conversations with Sons and Daughters of Survivors* (New York: Bantam, 1979). William Neiderland, "The Clinical Aftereffects of the Holocaust on Survivors and Their Offspring," and Janice Bistritz, "Transgenerational Pathology in Families of Holocaust Survivors," both in Randolph Braham, ed., *Psychological Perspectives on the Holocaust and Its Aftermath* (New York: Columbia University Press, 1988); Norman Solkoff, "The Holocaust: Survivors and Their Children," in Metin Basoglu, ed., *Torture*

and Its Consequences: Current Treatment Approaches (Cambridge, UK: Cambridge University Press, 1992). Relatedly, see Sarah Haley, "The Vietnam Veteran and His Preschool Child: Child-Rearing as a Delayed Stress in Combat Veterans," *Journal of Psychotherapy*, No. 4, 1983.

464. To reiterate an earlier point, "approximately 50% of all Indian [people over 50 years of age] attended Residential School"; Chrisjohn and Young with Maraun, *Circle Game*, p. 121n42.

465. The symptomotologies square almost perfectly with those exhibited by victims of severe child abuse in more conventional settings; Judith Herman, *Trauma and Recovery* (New York: Basic Books, [2nd ed.] 1997) pp. 122-3.

466. Chrisjohn, Young and Maraun do an excellent job with this point in their *Circle Game* at pp. 79-80.

467. See, as examples, Ann W. Burgess and Lynda L. Holmstrom, "Rape Trauma Syndrome," *American Journal of Psychiatry*, No. 131, 1974; 1986; Basoglu, *Torture and Its Consequences*; Dee L. Graham, Edna Rawlings and Nelly Rumini, "Survivors of Terror: Battered Women, Hostages, and the Stockholm Syndrome," in Kersti Yllo and Michele Bograd, *Feminist Perspectives in Wife Abuse* (Beverly Hills, CA: Sage, 1988) pp. 217-33; Jeffrey Bryer, et al., "Childhood Sexual and Physical Abuse as Factors in Adult Psychiatric Illness," *American Journal of Psychiatry*, No. 148, 1987.

468. See R.S. Laufer, E. Brett and M.S. Gallops, "Symptom Patterns Associated with Post-Traumatic Stress Disorder among Vietnam War Veterans Exposed to War Trauma," *American Journal of Psychiatry*, No. 142, 1985; Herbert Hendin and Ann P. Haas, *Wounds of War: The Psychological Aftermath of Combat in Vietnam* (New York: Basic Books, 1984); Eva Kahana, Boaz Kahana, Zev Harel, et al., "Coping with Extreme Trauma," in John P. Wilson, Zev Harel and Boaz Kahana, eds., *Human Adaptation to Extreme Stress: From the Holocaust to Vietnam* (New York: Plenum, 1988) pp. 55-80.

469. See, as examples, Joel E. Dimsdale, "The Coping Behavior of Nazi Concentration Camp Survivors," in Dimsdale, *Survivors, Victims, Perpetrators*, pp. 163-74; Ruth Jaffe, "Dissociative Phenomena in Former Concentration Camp Inmates," *International Journal of Psycho-Analysis*, No. 49, 1968; J.D. Kinzie, R.H. Frederickson, R. Ben, et al., "PTSD Among Survivors of Cambodian Concentration Camps," *American Journal of Psychiatry*, No. 141, 1984. Also see the essays collected in Braham, *Psychological Perspectives on the Holocaust and Its Aftermath*.

470. See Mike Ryan, "Solitude as Counterinsurgency: The U.S. Isolation Model of Political Incarceration," and Fay Dowker and Glenn Good, "From Alcatraz to Marion to Florence: Control Unit Prisons in the United States," both in Churchill and Vander Wall, *Cages of Steel*, pp. 83-109, 131-51.

471. Dr. Richard Korn, "Effects of Confinement in the HSU" (hereinafter, "Korn Report"), appended to National Prison Project, *Report on the High Security Unit for Women, Federal Correctional Institution, Lexington, Kentucky* (New York: American Civil Liberties Union, Aug. 27, 1987). For further background, see note 97.

472. The classic case of Stockholm Syndrome in the U.S. was that of Patty Hearst, the newspaper heiress who came so completely to identify with the terrorist cell that kidnapped her that in the end she appeared to willingly join it. An excellent popular description is given in Shana Alexander's *Anyone's Daughter* (New York: Bantam Books, 1979) pp. 562-3. In more technical parlance, this is referred to as "traumatic bonding," a process by which hostages "come to view their captors as saviors," a battered woman her abuser as the "source of strength, guidance, and life itself." The key in any such scenario is that the victimizer be positioned to exercise total control over the victim. The more complete the domination, the more likely the victim will come to define his/her wellbeing—or survival—in terms of pleasing her/his victimizer, even to point of "entering a kind of . . . delusional world, embracing the grandiose belief system of [their tormentors] and voluntarily suppressing their own doubts as proof of loyalty and submission"; Herman, *Trauma*, p. 92. The condition, depending on the intensity and duration of the precipitating experience, often continues long after the victim escapes or is released. Obviously, children are the most susceptible of all victims to being permanently reduced to this state of "psychological infantilism"; Martin Symonds, "Victim Responses to Terror: Understanding and Treatment," in Frank M. Ochberg and David A. Soskis, *Victims of Terrorism* (Boulder, CO: Westview Press, 1982) p. 99. Also see Graham, Rawlings and Rumini, "Survivors of Terror"; Thomas Strentz, "The Stockholm Syndrome: Law Enforcement Policy and Victim Behavior," in Ochberg and Soskis, *Victims*, pp. 149-63.

473. The term "broker class" is borrowed from Rodolfo Acuña; see his *Occupied America: A History of the Chicanos* (New York: HarperCollins, [3rd ed] 1988) pp. 377-86. For additional background, see Margaret Connell Szasz, ed., *The Cultural Broker: Link Between American Indian and White Worlds, 1690s-1990s* (Norman: University of Oklahoma Press, 1994). Among the better analyses of the psychology bound up this positioning are Albert Memmi's *The Colonizer and the Colonized* (Boston: Beacon Press, 1965); Frantz Fanon's *Black Skins, White Masks: The Experiences of a Black Man in a White World* (New York: Grove Press, 1967); Thomas Gladwin's *Slaves of the White Myth: The Psychology of Neocolonialism* (Atlantic Highlands, NJ: Humanities Press, 1980); and Ashis Nandy's *The Intimate Enemy: Loss and Recovery of Self Under Colonialism* (New York: Oxford University Press, 1983).

474. "Whole families leave the reserves to escape the cronyism and elitism of . . . chiefs and band councils"; Fournier and Crey, *Stolen From Our Embrace*, p. 213. For several unintended expositions on precisely this dynamic in the U.S., see L.G. Moses and Raymond Wilson, eds., *Indian Lives: Essays on Nineteenth- and Twentieth Century Native American Leaders* (Albuquerque: University of New Mexico Press, 1985).

475. Much of the survivor literature already cited takes up this theme. See esp. Qoyawayma, *No Turning Back*. Also see John F. Bryde, *The Indian Student: A Study of Scholastic Failure and Personality Conflict* (Vermillion: University of South Dakota Press, 1970); Linda R. Bull, "Indian Residential Schooling: The Native Perspective," *Canadian Journal of Native Education*, No. 18 (supplement), 1991; Grant, *No End of Grief*, pp. 245-65.

476. "Today, there is a problem with alcoholism, depression, family violence, and [other] destructive behavior" in a great many, perhaps most, indigenous home settings; analyst N. Roselyn Ing, quoted in Vicki Hormack, "Residential schools planted seed of violence, instructor says," *Opasquia Times*, Nov. 23, 1990, p. 4. Also see Ing's "The Effects of Boarding Schools on Native Child-Rearing Practices," *Canadian Journal of Native Education*, No. 18 (supplement), 1991.

477. Many "people, torn from their families as little children, literally don't know what a family is. What, really, is a father? What does he do? How should he act? For me, these are not rhetorical questions"; male survivor, quoted in Fournier and Crey, *Stolen From Our Embrace*, p. 151. "I expected perfection from my two children. Everything had to be done at a certain time, and done in a certain way . . . Everything had to be orderly . . . This was how I was trained at the Residential School, with the constant yelling. I remember always yelling at my daughter . . . who later became anorexic [but] I was only doing what I'd learned . . . at the Residential School"; female survivor, quoted in Ing, "Effects of Boarding Schools," p. 99. "I was a single parent and an alcoholic. It was very tough. I always felt so unloved, so used and abused . . . I had this uncontrollable anger. I just hit and hit and kicked and kicked. I would punch my son. Once when I was feeding [my baby daughter] in a high chair, I told her to eat and she wouldn't, so I smacked her right off the chair and onto the floor. I never learned any parenting skills, not at residential school, not with the childhood I had"; female survivor, quoted in Fournier and Crey, *Stolen From Our Embrace*, p. 131. Similar recountings are legion; see Assembly of First Nations, *Breaking the Silence*, for analysis.

478. Lester, *Suicide in American Indians*, pp. 19-41. Comparison is again useful. German Jews, for example, when subjected to a harsh régime of discrimination, dispossession and disemployment by the nazis during the 1930s, shortly came to evidence a suicide rate some three times that of the German public as a whole. During the early 1940s, as they were being relocated to Poland and concentrated there in reservations and urban ghettos—they were not yet aware of being slated for outright extermination—the Jewish suicide rate rose to a level approximately *fifty* times higher than that of non-Jews; Raul Hilberg, *Perpetrators, Victims, Bystanders: The Jewish Catastrophe, 1944-1945* (New York: HarperCollins, 1992) pp. 170-2. Among Gypsies, the same general tendency prevailed; Kendrick and Paxton, *Gypsies under the Swastika*, p. 101. For that matter, the suicide rate among *Germans* followed much the same trajectory during the first years of postwar occupation; Richard Grunberger, *The 12-Year Reich: A Social History of Nazi Germany, 1933-1945* (New York: Holt, Rinehart and Winston, 1971) p. 89.

479. The implications are brought forth with stark clarity in a range of literature. See, as examples, A.H. Green, "Dimensions of Psychological Trauma in Abused Children," *Journal of the American Association of Child Psychiatry*, No. 22, 1983; Judith L. Herman, Diana E.H. Russell and Karen Trocki, "Long-Term Effects of Incestuous Abuse in Childhood," *American Journal of Psychiatry*, No. 143, 1986; Bryer, et al.,

"Childhood Physical and Sexual Abuse" ; V.E. Pollack, J. Briere and L. Schneider, et al., "Childhood Antecedents of Antisocial Behavior: Parental Alcoholism and Physical Abuse," *American Journal of Psychiatry*, No. 147, 1990; Lenore C. Terr, "Childhood Traumas: An Overview and Outline," *American Journal of Psychiatry*, No. 148, 1991. Additional background will be found in Lenore C. Terr, *Too Scared to Cry: How Trauma Affects Children and Ultimately Us All* (New York: Basic Books, 1990). For an explicitly native orientation to these data, see Fournier and Crey, *Stolen From Our Embrace*, pp. 143-72.

480. "One could always hear boys crying from loneliness after lights out in the dormitory"; Miller, *Shingwauk's Vision*, p. 338. Also see Haig-Brown, *Resistance and Renewal*, p. 57; Child, *Boarding School Seasons*, pp. 43-54.

481. Another dimension of this problem is that although native people comprise less than 10% of the overall population in Canada, over half the children taken into care by federal and state authorities each year are native, and over 80% of *these* are "placed with non-native caregivers." As a result, "homeless shelters, courtrooms, youth detention centres and prisons are full of aboriginal [young] people who grew up in non-native substitute care . . . Vancouver's Urban Native Youth Association estimates that half to three-quarters of all . . . habituated native street kids [and] 95 percent of the prisoners in Prince Albert penitentiary . . . are 'graduates of foster care or non-native adoptions that didn't work out. They're looking for a sense of identity and belonging with other aboriginal street kids . . . that they never got [at] home' "; Fournier and Crey, *Stolen From Our Embrace*, pp. 90, 92.

482. On Grassy Narrows, see Anastasia M. Shkilnyk, *A Poison Stronger than Love:The Destruction of an Ojibwa Community* (New Haven, CT: Yale University Press, 1985); on the others, Geoffrey York, *The Dispossessed: Life and Death in Native Canada* (Boston: Little, Brown, 1992) pp. 175-200.

483. For surveys of the supposed genetic "findings," see the booklet entitled *Alcoholism:An Inherited Disease* (Rockville, MD: National Institute on Substance Abuse and Alcoholism, 1985) and the special 1987 issue of *Progress in Clinical and Biological Research*, edited by H. Warner Goedde and Dharam P. Agrawal under the title "Genetics and Alcoholism." Adding in the cultural dimension, one encounters a whole mythology of "drunken Indians." For both exposition and critique, see. Joseph Westermeyer, "The Drunken Indian: Myths and Realities," *Psychiatric Annals*, No. 4, 1974; Joy Leland, *Firewater Myths: North American Indian Drinking and Alcohol Addiction* (New Brunswick: Rutgers University Center for Alcohol Studies No. 11, 1976); Brian Maracle, *Crazywater: Native Voices on Addiction and Recovery* (New York: Penguin, 1993); Frederick A. May, "The Epidemiology of Alcohol Abuse among American Indians: Mythical and Real Properties," *American Indian Culture and Research Journal*, Vol. 18, No. 2, 1994.

484. On Irish-American drinking patterns and high rates of diagnosed "schizophrenia" and other forms of "insanity," see Kerby A. Miller, *Emigrants and Exiles: Ireland and the Irish Exodus to North America* (New York: Oxford University Press, 1985) pp. 112, 319-20, 506.

485. On Canada, see Gary Remington and Brian Hoffman, "Gas Sniffing as Substance Abuse," *Canadian Journal of Psychiatry*, No. 29, 1984; Fournier and Crey, *Stolen From Our Embrace*, pp. 209-10. The same pattern prevails on at least some reservations in the U.S.; see, e.g., Arthur Kaufman, "Gasoline Sniffing among Children in a Pueblo Village," *Pediatrics*, No. 51, 1973.

486. On Manitoba, see York, *Dispossessed*, p. 10; on Labrador, see Mary Rogan, "Please Take Our Children Away," *New York Times Magazine*, Mar. 4, 2001.

487. As Canada's Royal Commission put it in 1996, the "blunt and shocking message is that a significant number of aboriginal [children] in this country believe they have more reasons to die than to live"; quoted in Fournier and Crey, *Stolen From Our Embrace*, p. 210. On the U.S., see Strickland, *Tonto's Revenge*, p. 53. On suicide clusters or "epidemics" and their implications in the U.S., see Lester, *Suicide in American Indians*, pp. 33-7; on Canada, see J.A. Ward and Joseph Fox, "A Suicide Epidemic on an Indian Reserve," *Canadian Psychiatric Association Journal*, Mo. 22, 1977.

488. Herman, *Trauma and Recovery*, pp. 120-2.

489. Ibid., p. 123.

490. Caroline C. Fish-Murray, Elizabeth V. Koby and Bessel A. van der Kolk, "Evolving Ideas: The Effect of Abuse on Children's Thought," in Bessel A. van der Kolk, ed., *Psychological Trauma* (Washington, D.C.: American Psychiatric Press, 1987) pp. 89-95.

491. Bessel A. van der Kolk, "The Body Keeps Score: Approaches to the Psychobiology of Post Traumatic Stress Disorder," in Bessel A. van der Kolk, Alexander C. McFarlane, and Lars Weisaeth, eds.,

Traumatic Stress: The Effects Overwhelming Experience on Mind, Body, and Society (New York: Guilford Press, 1996) pp. 214-41.

492. This is precisely the distinction made by Hendin and Haas in their *Wounds of War*. The connotations are not insignificant.

493. Indeed, as "one psychiatrist candidly confesses, 'As a resident, I recalled asking my supervisor how to treat patients with borderline personality disorder, and he answered sardonically, "You refer them'"; Herman, *Trauma and Recovery*, p. 123.

494. This phenomenon is both covered and contextualized by Deborah Lipstadt in her *Denying the Holocaust: The Growing Assault on Truth and Memory* (New York: Free Press, 1993). Also see Vidal-Niquet, *Assassins of Memory*.

495. Although more sophisticated than outright denial, this, too, is a neonazi ploy, developed by such propagandists as the British pseudohistorian David Irving. For background, see Evans, *Lying About Hitler*.

496. Herman, *Trauma and Recovery*, pp. 67, 69; Alison M. Jaggar, *Feminist Politics and Human Nature* (Totawa, NJ: Rowman & Littlefield, 1983) pp. 262-3.

497. The issue is covered in the essays entitled "Let's Spread the 'Fun' Around: The Issue of Sports Team Names and Mascots" and "In the Matter of Julius Streicher: Applying Nuremberg Standards in the United States," in my *From a Native Son: Selected Essays in Indigenism, 1985-1995* (Boston: South End Press, 1996) pp. 439-44, 445-54. Also see Carol Spindel, *Dancing at Halftime: Sports and the Controversy over American Indian Mascots* (New York: New York University Press, 2000); C. Richard King and Charles Frueling Springwood, eds., *Team Spirits: The Native American Mascots* Controversy (Lincoln: University of Nebraska Press, 2001).

498. "Squaw" is a corruption of the Mohawk word for female genitalia, analogous, when used as slang, to the term "cunt"; Barbara Alice Mann, *Iroquoian Women: The Gantowisas* (New York: Peter Lang, 2000) p. 364. There are currently about a thousand officially designated place names including the word—"Squaw Valley," "Squaw Peak," "Squaw Creek," and so on—in North America. The effect on native women—not to mention six-year-old little girls—of being referred to in this fashion is anything but "harmless"; see, e.g., Rayna Green, "The Pocahontas Perplex: The Image of Indian Women in American Culture," *Massachusetts Review*, Vol. 16, No. 4, 1975.

499. See the title essay in my *Fantasies of the Master Race: Literature, Cinema, and the Colonization of American Indians* (San Francisco: City Lights, [2nd ed.] 1998) pp. 157-224.

500. See Laurie Anne Whitt, "Cultural Imperialism and the Marketing of Native America," in Duane Champagne, ed., *Contemporary Native American Cultural Issues* (Walnut Creek, CA: AltaMira Press, 1999) pp. 169-92.

501. This is, of course, standard rightwing rhetoric, emblematized in Ronald Reagan's "pensive" 1988 reflection—delivered during a state visit to the Soviet Union—upon whether "allowing" American Indians to retain *any* property or sense of identity distinct from that of the settler society hadn't been an "error in national policy"; quoted in the *Los Angeles Times*, June 1, 1988.

502. See Anna Haebich, *For Their Own Good: Aborigines and the Government in the Southwest of Western Australia, 1900-1940* (Nedlands: University of Western Australia Press, 1988) pp. 188-221; Andrew Armitage, *Comparing the Policy of Aboriginal Assimilation: Australia, Canada, and New Zealand* (Vancouver: University of British Columbia Press, 1995) pp. 42-4, 236-7.

503. Peter Read, *A Rape of the Soul So Profound: The Return of the Stolen Generations* (St. Leonard's: Allen & Unwin, 1999); Andrew Marcus, "Genocide in Australia," *Aboriginal History*, Vol. 25, 2001.

504. Miller, *Emigrants and Exiles*, pp. 75-9. Also see Mary Raftery and Eoin O'Sullivan, *Suffer the Little Children: The Inside Story of Ireland's Industrial Schools* (New York: Continuum, 2001).

505. Martin Carnoy, *Education as Cultural Imperialism* (New York: David McKay, 1974) pp. 78-143.

506. Chrisjohn and Young with Maraun, *Circle Game*, p. 139n173. Also see Kenneth Bagnell, *The Little Immigrants: The Orphans Who Came to Canada* (Toronto: Macmillan, 1989);Phillip Bean and Joy Melville, *Lost Children of the Empire: The Untold Story of Britain's Child Migrants* (London: Unwin Hyman, 1989). On the U.S., see Marilyn Holt, *The Orphan Trains: Placing Out in America* (Lincoln: University of Nebraska Press, 1992).

507. See, e.g., Jean-Paul Sartre, "Colonialism is a System," in his *Colonialism and Neocolonialism* (New York: Routledge, 2001) pp. 30-47.

508. "Conquest was achieved by violence, over-exploitation and domination demand the maintenance of violence"; Jean-Paul Sartre, "Albert Memmi's *The Colonizer and the Colonized*," in *Colonialism and Neocolonialism*, p. 50. For the phrase quoted in the text, see "*The Wretched of the Earth*," in *Colonialism and Neocolonialism*, p. 145; original translation in Sartre's "Preface" to Fanon's *The Wretched of the Earth* (New York: Grove Press, 1966) p. 15.

509. Sartre, "*Wretched of the Earth*", pp. 142-3; "Preface," p. 13.

510. Jean-Paul Sartre, "A Victory," in *Colonialism and Neocolonialism*, p. 76.

511. Jean-Paul Sartre, "On Genocide," in Jean-Paul Sartre and Arlette El Kaïm Sartre, *On Genocide and a Summary of the Evidence and the Judgments of the International War Crimes Tribunal* (Boston: Beacon Press, 1968) p-. 62-3. For a critique of Sartre's formulation, ending with the grudging concession that he was more correct than not, see Kuper, *Genocide*, pp. 44-5.

512. There are of course exceptions to this, notably Bauman in *The Holocaust and Modernity*, Davis and Zannis in *Genocide Machine*, and Israel Charny, in each of the works cited. Apart from her simplistic equation of genocide to killing, per se, another worthy addition to the roster is the typology and "sociological definition" offered by Helen Fein in "Genocide: A Sociological Perspective," *Current Sociology*, Vol. 38, No. 1, 1990.

513. "The most familiar usage of the term 'denial' refers to the maintenance of social worlds in which an undesirable situation (event, condition, phenomenon) is unrecognized, ignored or made to seem normal," a circumstance most often spawned by the fact that whatever is denied is objectively at odds with the sense of self-interest or -entitlement embraced by those in denial; Cohen, *States of Denial*, p. 51. Such refusal of inconvenient/unpleasant facts, a standard phase in early childhood development, is so common—although technically "abnormal"—among mainstream adults that it has been assigned its own heading in the clinical literature; Lawrence Weiskrantz, "Blindsight," in M.W. Eynsenck, *The Blackwell Dictionary of Cognitive Psychology* (Oxford, UK: Blackwell, 1994) pp. 44-6. Insofar as avoidance rather than active distortion of information is at issue, some analysts have elected to describe this sort of denial as being "innocent" or "benign," at least in the context of genocide and other crimes against humanity; see, e.g., Israel W. Charny, " 'Innocent Denials' of Known Genocides: A Further Contribution to a Psychology of Genocide Denial (Revisionism)," *Internet on the Holocaust and Genocide*, No. 46, Sept. 1993, pp. 23-5. Personally, I'm far less charitable in interpreting the phenomenon.

514. Denial of this sort is conscious, intentional and deliberately protective of the "right" of the perpetrator entity to engage in genocide. Given that it is by definition an intellectual exercise, it seldom involves anything so crude as a straightforward assertion that nothing happened. "The standard alternative to [acknowledging the obvious] is to admit the raw facts—yes, something *did* happen: people were killed, injured or detained without trial—but deny the interpretive framework placed on these events. No, what happened was *not* really torture, genocide or extrajudicial killing, but something else. The harm is cognitively reframed and then reallocated to another, less pejorative class of event [emphasis added]," of the sort usually referred to as "errors" or "excesses"; Cohen, *States of Denial*, pp. 105-6. For reference to a classic example of this sort of performance in conjunction with the residential schools, see note 460. For examples in other connections, see notes 2 and 11.

515. Smith, Markusen and Lifton, "Professional Ethics and the Denial of the Armenian Genocide," p. 16.

516. Ludwig Wittgenstein, *An Inquiry into Meaning and Truth* (New York: W.W. Norton, 1940) p. 9.

517. The notion that one should address truth to "power" rather than to people seems deeply ensconced among progressives. Among the dozen titles currently in print that employ some variation of this formulation, see Manning Marable, *Speaking Truth to Power: Essays in Race, Resistance and Radicalism* (Boulder, CO: Westview Press, 1998); Kerry Kennedy and Nan Richardson, eds., *Speak Truth to Power: Human Rights Defenders Who are Changing Our World* (New York: Crown, 2000).

518. See note 18.

519. Only a generation ago, this principle seemed well understood. Among the better framings of that period were those of the late Amilcar Cabral. See his *Revolution in Guinea: Selected Texts* (New York: Monthly Review Press, 1969); *Unity and Struggle: Speeches and Writings* (New York: Monthly Review Press, 1979).

520. As illustration, consider the following: "[Q]uite unlike formerly colonized third-world nations, Indians in Canada do not need to develop an indigenous economy to feed their people. They

live in the midst of a state that is already highly developed in economic terms. The problem they confront is to overcome the internal and external social, cultural, and political barriers that preclude and exclude them from full participation in the economy of one of the richest nations in the world. For this, they do not need sovereignty. In fact, sovereignty may serve merely to heighten the barriers to full participation in the mainstream Canadian economy"; Menno Boldt, *Surviving as Indians: The Challenge of Self-Government* (Toronto: University of Toronto Press, 1993) p. 239. If actualized, such an integrationist schema would embody both the final consolidation of Canada's internal colonial structure and consummate the longstanding assimilationist drive to merge native peoples with the "broader" settler society (i.e., "imposing the national pattern of the oppressor group"). Duncan Campbell Scott could not have said it better. For the same kind of argumentation vis-à-vis the U.S., see, e.g., Fergus M. Bordewich, *Killing the White Man's Indian: Reinventing Native Americans at the End of the Twentieth Century* (Garden City, NY: Doubleday, 1996).

521. Cleaver's formulation, which he actually attributed to his wife, Kathleen, was first articulated in a speech at Syracuse University during the fall of 1968, an excerpt from which was collected on an obscure spoken word LP entitled *Dig!* the following year. By then, it had also been adopted as the masthead slogan of *New Left Notes*, the organizational newspaper of Students for a Democratic Society (SDS).

522. See, as examples, the United Nations Declaration on the Granting of Independence to Colonial Countries and Peoples (U.N.G.A. Res. 1514 (XV), 15 U.N. GAOR, Supp. (No. 16) 66, U.N. Doc. A/4684 (1961) Pt. 2; the International Covenant on Economic, Social and Cultural Rights (U.N.G.A. Res. 2200 (XXI), 21 U.N. GAOR, Supp. (No. 16) 49, U.N. Doc. A/6316 (1967), *reprinted in* 6 I.L.M. 360 (1967)) Art. 1 (1); the International Covenant on Civil and Political Rights (U.N.G.A. Res. 2200 (XXI), 21 U.N. GAOR, Supp. (No. 16) 52, U.N. Doc. A/6316 (1967), *reprinted in* 6 I.L.M. 368 (1967)) Art. 1 (1); and the United Nations Declaration on the Right to Development (U.N.G.A. Res. 41/128, 41 U.N. GAOR, Supp. (No. 53) U.N. Doc. A/41/925 (1986)); Weston, Falk and D'Amato, *Basic Documents*, pp. 344, 371, 376, 485.

523. In its 1979 Final Report, the federal Indian Claims Commission concluded that the U.S. could make no pretense of acquiring legal title to approximately one-third of the gross territoriality of the 49 contiguous states. This estimate was made without considering the additive effects of such transparently fraudulent instruments of cession as the 1861 Treaty of Fort Wise. The situation is little different in Canada; see the essay entitled "Charades Anyone? The Indian Claims Commission in Context," in my *Perversions of Justice*, pp. 125-52. There are, moreover, compelling arguments to be made that indigenous nations are not the only internal colonies of which the North American megastates are comprised; see, as examples, Acuña, *Occupied America*; Imari Abubakari Obadele I, *Foundations of the Black Nation* (Detroit, MI: House of Songhay, 1975); Helen Matthews Lewis, Linda Johnson and Don Askins, eds., *Colonialism in Modern America: The Appalachian Case* (Boone, NC: Appalachian Consortium Press, 1978); Jane Jacobs, *The Question of Separatism: Quebec and the Struggle over Sovereignty* (New York: Random House, 1980).

524. It is well-established that such prerogatives are fundamental to the exercise of self-determining rights; see W. Ofuatey-Kodjoe, *The Principle of Self-Determination in International Law* (Hamden, CT: Archon Books, 1972); Antonio Rigo-Sureda, *The Evolution of the Right to Self-Determination: A Study of United Nations Practice* (Leiden, Netherlands: A.W. Sijhoff, 1973); Michla Pomerance, *Self-Determination in Law and Practice* (The Hague: Marinus Nijhoff, 1982); Hurst Nannum, *Autonomy, Sovereignty and Self-Determination* (Philadelphia: University of Pennsylvania Press, 1990).

525. The argument is made on the basis of the 1934 Indian Reorganization Act (ch. 576, 48 Stat. 948, now codified at 25 U.S.C. 461-279) and the 1975 Indian Self-Determination and Educational Assistance Act (88 Stat. 2203, codified at 25 U.S.C. 450a and elsewhere in Titles 25, 42 and 50, U.S.C.A.), both of which have the effect of *foreclosing* the right of self-determination as guaranteed in international law. For background, see Deloria and Lytle, *Nations Within*.

526. "[T]he U.S. understanding of the term 'internal self-determination' [is that it] is not necessarily synonymous with more general understandings of self-determination under international law [in that] it does not include a right of independence or permanent sovereignty over natural resources"; National Security Council Cable, Jan. 18, 2001; included as Appendix D in my *Perversions of Justice*, pp.

427-32. The formulation was advanced as part of a longstanding effort by the U.S. to gut a United Nations Draft Declaration of Indigenous Rights before its submission to the General Assembly. For background, see Isabelle Schulte-Tenckhoff, "The Irresistible Ascension of the UN Declaration of the Rights of Indigenous Peoples: Stopped Dead in Its Tracks?" *European Review of Native American Studies*, Vol. 9, No. 2, 1995.

527. For the texts of 371 treaties with Indians duly ratified by the U.S. Senate, see Charles J. Kappler, ed., *Indian Treaties, 1778-1883* (New York: Interland, 1973). For the remainder, as well as the texts of agreements and unratified treaties upon which the U.S. has predicated claims to land title/jurisdiction, see Vine Deloria, Jr., and Raymond J. DeMallie, *Documents of American Indian Diplomacy: Treaties, Agreements, and Conventions, 1775-1979*, 2 vols. (Norman: University of Oklahoma Press, 1999). On Canada, see *Canada: Indian Treaties and Surrenders from 1680 to 1890*, 3 vols. (Ottawa: Queen's Printer, 1891); George Brown and Ron McGuire, *Indian Treaties in Historical Perspective* (Ottawa: Indian and Northern Affairs Canada, 1979). Most U.S. interpretation doctrine concerning Indian treaties, most specifically the "last in line" doctrine—by which it is held that a more recent domestic statute has the effect of superceding and thereby nullifying the terms and provisions of a preexisting treaty—is invalid under international customary law, as codified in Article 27 of the Vienna Convention on the Law of Treaties (U.N. Doc. A/CONF.39/27 at 289 (1969), 1155 U.N.T.S. 331, *reprinted in* 8 I.L.M. 679 (1969)); Weston, Falk and D'Amato, *Basic Documents*, p. 98. For further background, see Sir Ian Sinclair, *The Vienna Convention on the Law of Treaties* (Manchester, UK: Manchester University Press, [2nd ed.] 1984).

528. United Nations Charter (59 Stat. 1031; T.S. No. 993, 3 Bevans 1153, 1976 Y.B.U.N. 1043 (1945)), Chapter XI: Declaration Regarding Non-Self-Governing Territories; Weston, Falk and D'Amato, *Basic Documents*, pp. 27-9.

529. Apart from the Genocide Convention and the items mentioned in note 522, see the Universal Declaration of Human Rights (U.N.G.A. Res. 217 A (III), U.N. Doc. A/810, at 71 (1949)); the American Declaration on the Rights and Duties of Man (O.A.S. Off. Rec. OEA/Ser. L/V/L4 Rev. (1965)); the International Convention on the Elimination of All Forms of Racial Discrimination (660 U.N.T.S. 195, *reprinted in* 5 I.L.M. 352 (1966))l the American Declaration on Human Rights (O.A.S. Treaty Ser. No. 36, O.A.S. Off. Rec. OEA/Ser. L/V/II.23 doc. 21 rev. 6 (1979), *reprinted in* 9 I.L.M. 673 (1970)); the Universal Declaration on the Eradication of Hunger and Malnutrition (U.N. Doc. E/Conf. 65/20, Ch. IV (1974)); the United Nations Declaration on the Elimination of All Forms of Intolerance and of Discrimination Based on Religion or Belief (U.N.G.A. Res. 36/55, 36 U.N. GAOR, Supp. (No. 51) 171, U.N. Doc. A/36/684 (1981), *reprinted in* 21 I.L.M. 205 (1982)); the Convention Against Torture and Other Cruel or Degrading Treatment or Punishment (U.N.G.A. Res. 39/46 Annex, 39 U.N. GAOR, Supp. (No. 51) 197, U.N. Doc. E/CN.4/1984/72, Annex (1984), *reprinted in* I.L.M. 1027 (1984)); the United Nations Declaration on the Right to Development (U.N.G.A. Res. 41/128, 41 U.N. GAOR, Supp. (No. 53) U.N. Doc. A/41/925 (1986)); and the Convention on the Rights of the Child (U.N.G.A. Res. 44/25, Annex, 44 U.N. GAOR, Supp. (No.49) at 167, U.N. Doc. A/RES/44/25 (1989), *reprinted in* 28 I.L.M. 1457 (1989)); Weston, Falk and D'Amato, *Basic Documents*, pp. 298-300, 293-6, 364-8, 398-412, 429-31, 459-61, 463-71, 485-8, 498-512. This listing is less than exhaustive.

530. On the matter of international torts, see Eduardo Jiminez de Arechaga, "International Responsibility," in M. Sorenson, ed., *Manual of Public International Law* (New York: St. Martin's Press, 1968) pp. 564-72. Also see Istvan Vasarhelyi, *Restitution in International Law* (Budapest: Hungary Academy of Science, 1964).

531. Roy L. Brooks, "What Form Redress?" in Brooks, *When Sorry Isn't Enough*, pp. 87-91. Also see Elazar Barkman, *The Guilt of Nations: Restitution and Negotiating Historical Injustices* (New York: W.W. Norton, 2000).

532. Statute of the International Court of Justice (59 Stat. 1031, T.S. No. 993, 3 Bevans 1153, 1976 Y.B.U.N. 1052 (1945); Weston, Falk and D'Amato, *Basic Documents*, pp. 33-8. For background, see Michla Pomerance, *The Advisory Function of the International Court in the League and U.N. Eras* (The Hague: Martinus Nijhoff, 1973).

533. For background on the U.S. posture regarding establishment of an International Criminal Court modeled based upon the Nuremberg precedent (which the U.S. itself was instrumental in creating), see LeBlanc, *U.S. and the Genocide Convention*, pp. 151-74. For more recent developments, see Geoffrey

Robertson, *Crimes Against Humanity: The Struggle for Global Justice* (New York: New Press, 2000) pp. 324–67.

534. Karl Jaspers, *The Question of German Guilt* (New York: Fordham University Press, 2002).

535. Eventually, the process of introspection and reconsideration called for by Jaspers led Germans to collectively embrace an "internationalization of [their] 'national' history" as an antidote to the "collective, narcissistic self-exaltation" enshrined in previous narratives of German identity; Daniel Jonah Goldhagen, "*Modell Bundesrepublik*: National History, Democracy, and Internationalization in Germany," in Robert R. Shandley, *Unwilling Germans? The Goldhagen Debate* (Minneapolis: University of Minnesota Press, 2000) pp. 275–6. As concerns the potential beneficial effect on survivors, a common theme among those suffering traumatic stress disorders, whether complex or "simple," is first to desire literal revenge, an impulse often transformed over time into "righteous indignation" and abiding "quest for justice." The end goal in many cases is to attain some sense of closure—that is, to finally be able to in some tangible sense "put the past in the behind me"—by "forgiving" the perpetrator(s). "Even divine forgiveness," however, "is not unconditional. True forgiveness cannot be granted until the perpetrator has sought and earned it through confession, repentance, and restitution." The problem is, of course, that "genuine contrition in a perpetrator is a rare miracle" to which American Indians are both fully entitled and, at present, all but completely denied; Herman, *Trauma and Recovery*, pp. 189–90.

536. See, e.g., Lucy Dawidowicz's rejoinder to Gandhi's vacuous recommendation that German Jews employ his "morally pure" *Satyagraha* method of passive resistance against the nazis in her *War Against the Jews* (New York: Free Press, 1986) p. 274. More broadly, see my and Mike Ryan's *Pacifism as Pathology: Reflections on the Role of Armed Struggle in North America* (Winnipeg: Arbiter Ring, 1998).

537. For an overview of such developments in the U.S., see my preface to the classics edition to my and Jim Vander Wall's *The COINTELPRO Papers: Documents from the FBI's Secret Wars Against Dissent in the United States* (Cambridge, MA: South End Press, [Classics ed.] 2002) pp. xxii–liv. On Canada, which has a significantly less lethal record thus far, see Gary Kinsman, Dieter K. Buse and Mercedes Steedman, eds., *Whose National Security? Canadian State Surveillance and the Creation of Enemies* (Toronto: Between the Lines, 2000).

538. For a general, but very constrained, articulation of the relevant doctrine, see Francis Anthony Boyle, *Defending Civil Resistance Under International Law* (Dobbs Ferry, NY: Transnational, 1988). On the thinking of Malcolm X in this connection, see George Breitman's well-edited collection of his speeches, *By Any Means Necessary* (New York: Pathfinder Press, 1970).

539. Peter Hoffmann, *The History of the German Resistance, 1933-1945* (Montréal: McGill-Queens University Press, [3rd ed.] 1996) esp. "Part VI: Assassination Attempts, 1933-1942" (pp. 251-62) and "Part VIII: Stauffenberg and the Replacement Army" (pp. 315-503).

540. For an excellent if unintended summary of exactly where arguments to the contrary end up in practical terms, see Terry H. Anderson, *The Movement and the Sixties: Protest in America from Greensboro to Wounded Knee* (New York: Oxford University Press, 1995) pp. 355–410.

541. Ibid., pp. 411-23.

542. See Dick Wilson, *The Long March, 1935: The Epic of Chinese Communist Survival* (New York: Viking, 1971). For a background on Americans who made the mistake of confusing the figurative with the literal in this connection, see Max Elbaum, *Revolution in the Air: Sixties Radicals and the turn to Lenin, Mao and Che* (London: Verso, 2002).

543. This was a persistent theme in American letters during the late nineteenth and early twentieth centuries. See, e.g., B.O. Flower, "An Interesting Representative of a Vanishing Race," *Arena*, July 1896; William R. Draper, "The Last of the Red Race," *Cosmopolitan*, Jan. 1902; Charles M. Harvey, "The Last Race Rally of Indians," *World's Work*, May 1904; E. S. Curtis, "Vanishing Indian Types: The Tribes of the Northwest Plains," *Scribner's*, June 1906; James Mooney, "The Passing of the Indian," *Proceedings of the Second Pan American Scientific Congress, Sec. 1: Anthropology* (Washington, D.C.: Smithsonian Institution, 1909-1910); Joseph K. Dixon, *The Vanishing Race: The Last Great Indian Council* (Garden City, NY: Doubleday, 1913); Stanton Elliot, "The End of the Trail," *Overland Monthly*, July 1915; Ella Higginson, "The Vanishing Race," *Red Man*, Feb. 1916; Ales Hrdlicka, "The Vanishing Indian," *Science*, No. 46, 1917; J.L. Hill, *The Passing of the Indian and the Buffalo* (Long Beach, CA: n.p., 1917); John Collier, "The Vanishing American," *Nation*, Jan. 11, 1928.

544. For contextualization of exactly this point, see my introduction, "On the Intersection of Justice and History" in *Acts of Rebellion: The Ward Churchill Reader* (New York: Routledge, 2003) pp. xi-xx. Also see the essay titled "The Ghosts of 9-1-1: Reflections on History, Justice and Roosting Chickens," in my *On the Justice of Roosting Chickens: Reflections on the Consequences of American Conquest and Carnage* (Oakland, CA: AK Press, 2003).

545. Sartre, "Memmi," p. 53.

546. Sartre, quoted by Azzedine Haddour in his introduction to *Colonialism and Neocolonialism*, p. 6.

Appendix

American Indian Residential Schools in the U.S.

1880-1980

Arizona

Chinle Indian Boarding School
Colorado River Indian School
Fort Apache Indian School
Fort Mojave Indian School
Keams Canyon Indian School
Leupp Indian Boarding School
Navajo Indian Boarding School
Pima Indian School
Rice Station Indian Boarding School
San Carlos Indian Boarding School
Truxton Canyon Indian School
Phoenix Indian Industrial School
Western Navajo Indian School

California

Fort Bidwell Indian Industrial School
Fort Yuma Indian Boarding School
Greenville Indian Boarding School
Hoopa Indian Boarding School
Sherman Institute (Perris Indian School)

Colorado

Fort Lewis Indian School
Grand Junction Indian School
Southern Ute Indian School

Idaho

Fort Hall Indian Boarding School
Fort Lapwai Indian Boarding School
Lemhi Indian Boarding School

Iowa

Sac & Fox Indian Boarding School

Kansas

Haskell Institute
Kickapoo Indian School
Pottawatomie Indian School

Michigan

Mount Pleasant Indian Boarding School

Minnesota

Cass Lake Indian School
Clontart Indian Boarding School
Cross Lake Indian School
Leech Lake Indian School
Morris Indian Boarding School
Pine Point Indian School
Pipestone Indian Industrial School
Red Lake Indian School
Vermillion Lake Indian School
White Earth Indian School
Wild Rice River Indian School

Montana

Blackfeet Indian Boarding School
Crow Agency Indian School
Fort Belknap Indian Boarding School
Fort Peck Indian Boarding School
Fort Shaw Indian Boarding School
Pryor Creek Indian School
Tongue River Indian School

Nebraska

Genoa Indian Industrial School
Omaha Indian Boarding School
Santee Sioux Indian School
Winnebago Indian School

Nevada

Carson Indian Boarding School

New Mexico

Albuquerque Indian School
Jicarilla Apache Indian School
Mescalero Apache Indian School
Pueblo Bonito Indian School
San Juan Indian Boarding School
Santa Fe Indian School
Tohatchi Indian Boarding School
Zuni Indian Boarding School

North Carolina

Eastern Cherokee Indian School

North Dakota

Bismark Indian School
Fort Berthold Indian School

Fort Totten Indian Boarding School
Standing Rock Indian Agricultural School
Standing Rock Indian Industrial School
Wahpeton Indian Agricultural School

Oklahoma

Absentee Shawnee Indian School
Anadarko Indian Boarding School
Armstrong Indian Boarding School
Bloomfield Indian Boarding School
Cantonment Indian Boarding School
Cherokee Indian Orphan School
Cheyenne & Arapaho Indian School
Chilocco Indian Agricultural School
Euchee Indian Boarding School
Eufaula Indian Boarding School
Fort Sill Indian Boarding School
Jones Indian Boarding School
Kaw Indian Boarding School
Mekusuky Indian Boarding School
Nuyaka Indian Boarding School
Osage Indian Boarding School
Otoe Indian Boarding School
Pawnee Indian Boarding School
Ponca Indian Boarding School
Rainy Mountain Indian School
Red Moon Indian Boarding School
Riverside Indian Boarding School
Sac & Fox Indian School
Seger Indian Boarding School
Seneca Indian Boarding School
Shawnee Indian Boarding School
Tuskahoma Indian Boarding School
Quapaw Indian Boarding School
Wheelock Indian School

Oregon

Grande Rondo Indian School
Klamath Indian School
Salem Indian Industrial School
Siletz Indian Boarding School
Umatilla Indian Boarding School
Warm Springs Indian School
Yaimax Indian Boarding School

South Dakota

Chamberlain Indian Boarding School
Cheyenne River Indian School
Crow Creek Indian Boarding School
Flandreau Indian Agricultural School
Grace Indian Boarding School
Grand River Indian School
Hope Indian Boarding School
Lower Brule Indian School
Pierre Indian Industrial School
Pine Ridge Indian Boarding School
Rapid City Indian Industrial School
Rosebud Sioux Indian School
Sisseton Sioux Indian School
Yankton Sioux Indian School

Utah

Uintah Indian Boarding School

Washington

Cushman Indian Boarding School
Puyallup Indian Boarding School
Tulalip Indian Boarding School
Yakima Indian Boarding School

Wisconsin

Keshena Indian Boarding School
Hayward Indian Industrial School
Lac de Flambeau Indian School
Menominee Indian School
Oneida Indian BoardingSchool
Tomah Indian Boarding School
Wittenberg Indian School

Wyoming

Shoshone Indian Boarding School

American Indian Residential Schools in Canada

1880–1980

Alberta

Brocket Indian School (Anglican)
Calgary Indian Residential School (Catholic)
Cardston Indian Residential School (Catholic)
Cluny Indian Residential School (Catholic)
Dunbow Indian Residential School (Catholic)
Edmonton Indian Residential School (Methodist)
Fort Chipewayan Indian School (Catholic)
Fort Vermillion Indian School (Catholic)
Grouard Indian School (Catholic)
Hobbema Indian School (Catholic)
Joussard Indian School (Catholic)
Lac La Biche Residential School (Catholic)
Morley Indian School (Methodist)
Onion Lake Indian School (Catholic)
Red Deer Indian School (Methodist)
St. Paul Indian Residential School (Catholic)
Wabasca Indian School (Catholic)

British Columbia

Ahousaht Indian School (Presbyterian)
Alberni Indian Residential School (Presbyterian)
Alert Bay Indian Residential School (Anglican)
Christie Indian Residential School (Catholic)
Coqueleetza Indian School (Methodist)

Cranbrook Indian Residential School (Catholic)
Fort Simpson Indian School (Methodist)
Kamloops Indian Residential School (Catholic)
Kitimaat Indian Residential School (Methodist)
Kuper Island Indian Industrial School (Catholic)
Lejac Indian Residential School (Catholic)
Lower Post Indian School (Catholic)
Lytton Indian School (Anglican)
Metlakatia Indian School (Anglican)
Mission City Indian School (Catholic)
North Vancouver Indian Industrial School (Catholic)
Secheit Indian Residential School (Catholic)
Williams Lake Indian Residential School (Catholic)
Yale Indian Residential School (Anglican)

Manitoba

Birtle Indian Residential School (Presbyterian)
Brandon Indian Residential School (Methodist)
Camperville Indian School (Catholic)
Cross Lake Indian School (Catholic)
Elhorn Indian School (Anglican)
Fort Alexander Indian School (Catholic)
Norway House Indian School (Catholic)
Portage La Prairie Indian School (Presbyterian)
Sandy Bay Indian School (Catholic)
The Pas Residential School (Anglican/Catholic)
Winnipeg Indian Residential School (Catholic)

Northwest Territories

Aklavik (Inuvik) Residential School (Catholic)
Chesterfield Inlet Youth Hostel (Catholic)
Fort Providence Indian School (Catholic)
Fort Resolution Indian School (Catholic)
Hay River Indian School (Anglican)

Nova Scotia

Schubenacadie Indian School (Catholic)

Ontario

Brantford Academy (Anglican)
Chapleau Indian School (Anglican)
Fort Albany Indian School (Catholic)
Fort Francis Indian School (Catholic)
Kenora Indian School (Presbyterian)
McIntosh Indian Residential School (Catholic)
Moose Factory Indian School (Anglican)
Mount Elgin Indian School (Methodist)
Sault Ste Marie Indian School (Anglican)
Sioux Lookout Indian School (Anglican)
Spanish Indian Boys School (Catholic)
Wikwemikong Indian School (Catholic)

Saskatchewan

Battleford Indian School (Anglican)
Beauval Indian School (Catholic)
Delmas Indian Residential school (Catholic)
Duck Lake Indian School (Catholic)
Gordon Indian Residential School (Anglican)
Île-à-la-Crosse Indian School (Catholic)
La Ronge Indian School (Anglican)
Lebret Indian School (Catholic)
Lestock Indian Residential School (Catholic)
Merieval Indian School (Catholic)
Prince Albert Indian Residential School (Anglican)
Regina Indian Residential School (Presbyterian)
Round Lake Indian School (Presbyterian)
St. Philip Indian School (Catholic)

Québec

Amos Indian Residential School (Catholic)
Fort George Indian School (Catholic)
La Tuque Indian School (Catholic)
Pointe-Bleue Indian School (Catholic)
Sept-Îles Indian Residential School (Catholic)

Yukon

Carcross Indian Residential School (Anglican)
Dawson City Indian Youth Hostel (Anglican)
Whitehorse Indian School (Baptist)

BIBLIOGRAPHY

Books

Abraham, K.C., and B. Mbuy-Beya, eds., *Spirituality in the Third World: A Cry for Life: Papers and Reflections from the Third Assembly of the Ecumenical Association of Third World Theologians, Nairobi, Kenya, January 1992* (Maryknoll, NY: Orbis Books, 1994).

Acuña, Rodolfo, *Occupied America: A History of the Chicanos* (New York: HarperCollins, [3ʳᵈ ed.] 1988).

Adams, David Wallace, *Education for Extinction: American Indians and the Boarding School Experience, 1875-1928* (Lawrence: University Press of Kansas, 1995).

Adamson, Walter L., *Hegemony and Revolution: A Study of Antonio Gramsci's Political and Cultural Theory* (Berkeley: University of California Press, 1980).

Alessandrini, Anthony C., ed., *Frantz Fanon: Critical Perspectives* (New York: Routledge, 1999).

Alexander, Edward, *The Holocaust and the War of Ideas* (New Brunswick, NJ: Transaction, 1994).

Alexander, Shana, *Anyone's Daughter* (New York: Bantam Books, 1979).

Alford, Thomas Wildcat, as told to Florence Drake, *Civilization, and the Story of the Absentee Shawnees* (Norman: University of Oklahoma Press, 1936).

Ally, Götz, *"Final Solution": Nazi Population Policy and the Murder of European Jews* (London: Arnold, 1999).

Alvineri, Shlomo, ed., *Karl Marx on Colonialism and Modernization* (Garden City, NY: Doubleday, 1968).

Ambler, Marjane, *Breaking the Iron Bonds: Indian Control of Energy Development* (Lawrence: University Press of Kansas, 1990).

Anderson, Terry H., *The Movement and the Sixties: Protest in America from Greensboro to Wounded Knee* (New York: Oxford University Press, 1995).

Arad, Yitzak, Shmuel Krakowski and Schmuel Spector, eds., *The Einsatzgruppen Reports: Selections from the Nazi Death Squads' Campaign Against the Jews in Occupied Territories of the Soviet Union, July 1941-January 1943* (New York: Holocaust Library, 1989).

Arden, Harvey, ed., *Noble Red Man: Lakota Wisdomkeeper Mathew King* (Hillsboro, OR: Beyond Words, 1994).

Arendt, Hannah, *Eichmann in Jerusalem: A Report on the Banality of Evil* (New York: Penguin, 1964).

Arens, Richard, ed., *Genocide in Paraguay* (Philadelphia: Temple University Press, 1976).

Armitage, Andrew, *Comparing the Policy of Aboriginal Assimilation: Australia, Canada, and New Zealand* (Vancouver: University of British Columbia Press, 1995).

Ashcroft, Bill, Gareth Griffiths and Helen Tifflin, eds., *The Post-Colonial Studies Reader* (New York: Routledge, 1995).

Assembly of First Nations, *Breaking the Silence: An Interpretive Study of Residential School Impact and Healing as Illustrated by the Stories of First Nations Individuals* (Ottawa: Assembly of First Nations, 1994).

Atkinson, Donald Harmon, *God's Peoples: Covenant and Land in South Africa, Israel and Ulster* (Ithaca: Cornell University Press, 1992).

Axtell, James, *Beyond 1492: Encounters in Colonial North America* (New York: Oxford University Press, 1992).

Battiste, Marie, ed., *Reclaiming Indigenous Voice and Vision* (Vancouver: UBC Press, 2000).

Bean, Phillip, and Joy Melville, *Lost Children of the Empire: The Untold Story of Britain's Child Migrants* (London: Unwin Hyman, 1989).

Bagnell, Kenneth, *The Little Immigrants: The Orphans Who Came to Canada* (Toronto: Macmillan, 1989).

Baird, Jay W., ed., *From Nuremberg to My Lai* (Lexington, MA: D.C. Heath, 1972).

Balakishnan, Gopal, *The Enemy: An Intellectual Biography of Carl Schmitt* (London: Verso, 2000).

Barkman, Elazar, *The Guilt of Nations: Restitution and Negotiating Historical Injustices* (New York: W.W. Norton, 2000).

Barman, Jean, Yves Hébert and D. McCaskall, eds., *Indian Education in Canada, Vol. 1: The Legacy* (Vancouver: Nakota Institute/ University of British Columbia Press, 1986).

Basoglu, Metin, ed., *Torture and Its Consequences: Current Treatment Approaches* (Cambridge, UK: Cambridge University Press, 1992).

Bauer, Yehuda, *The Holocaust in Historical Perspective* (Seattle: University of Washington Press, 1978).

Bauman, Zygmunt, *Modernity and the Holocaust* (Cambridge, UK: Polity Press, 1989).

Beaver, R. Pierce, *Church, State and the American Indian: Two and a Half Centuries of Partnership in Missions Between Protestant Missions and the Government* (St. Louis, MO: Concordia University Press, 1966).

Bennis, Phyllis, *Calling the Shots: How Washington Dominates Today's UN* (New York: Olive Branch Press, 2000).

Benson, Robert, ed., *Children of the Dragonfly: Native Voices on Child Custody and Education* (Tucson: University of Arizona Press, 2001).

Berenbaum, Michael, ed., *A Mosaic of Victims: Non-Jews Persecuted and Murdered by the Nazis* (New York: New York University Press, 1990).

Berkhofer, Robert J. Jr., *Salvation and the Savage: An Analysis of Protestant Missions and American Indian Response, 1787-1862* (New York: Atheneum, 1972).

Blum, William, *Rogue State: A Guide to the World's Only Superpower* (Monroe, ME: Common Courage Press, 2000).

Boldt, Menno, *Surviving as Indians: The Challenge of Self-Government* (Toronto: University of Toronto Press, 1993).

Boldt, Menno, and J. Anthony Long, eds., *The Quest for Justice: Aboriginal People and Aboriginal Rights* (Toronto: University of Toronto Press, 1985).

Bordewich, Fergus M., *Killing the White Man's Indian: Reinventing Native Americans at the End of the Twentieth Century* (Garden City, NY: Doubleday, 1996).

Boyle, Francis Anthony, *Defending Civil Resistance Under International Law* (Dobbs Ferry, NY: Transnational, 1988).

Braham, Randolph, ed., *Psychological Perspectives on the Holocaust and Its Aftermath* (New York: Columbia University Press, 1988).

Breitman, George, ed., *Malcolm X: By Any Means Necessary* (New York: Pathfinder Press, 1970).

Brooks, Roy L., ed., *When Sorry Isn't Enough: The Controversy Over Apologies for Human Injustice* (New York: New York University Press, 1999).

Brown, Estelle Aubrey, *Stubborn Fool: A Narrative* (Caldwell, ID: Claxton, 1952).

Brown, George, and Ron McGuire, *Indian Treaties in Historical Perspective* (Ottawa: Indian and Northern Affairs Canada, 1979).

Brownlie, Ian, ed., *Basic Documents on Human Rights* (Oxford, UL: Clarendon Press, [3rd ed.] 1992).

Brownmiller, Susan, *Against Our Will: Men, Women and Rape* (New York: Simon and Schuster, 1975).

Brundage, W. Fitzhugh, *Lynching in the New South, 1880-1930* (Urbana: University of Illinois Press, 1993).

Bryce, P.H., *The Story of a National Crime being an Appeal for Justice for the Indians of Canada* (Ottawa: James Hope & Sons, 1922).

Bryde, John F., *The Indian Student: A Study of Scholastic Failure and Personality Conflict* (Vermillion: University of South Dakota Press, 1970).

Bulhan, Hussein A., *Frantz Fanon and the Psychology of Oppression* (New York: Plenum, 1985).

Burleigh, Michael, *Ethics and Extermination: Reflections on the Nazi Genocide* (Cambridge, UK: Cambridge University Press, 1997).

_____, *The Third Reich: A New History* (New York: Hill and Wang, 2000).

Burnett, Christina Duffy, and Burke Marshall, eds., *Foreign in a Domestic Sense: Puerto Rico, American Expansion, and the Constitution* (Chapel Hill, NC: Duke University Press, 2001).

Burt, Larry M., *Tribalism in Crisis: Federal Indian Policy, 1953-1961* (Albuquerque: University of New Mexico Press, 1982).

Butz, Arthur R., *The Hoax of the Twentieth Century: The Case Against the Presumed Extermination of European Jewry* (Torrance, CA: Institute of Historical Review, 1976).

Byers, Michael, *Custom, Power and the Power of Rules: International Relations and Customary International Law* (Cambridge, UK: Cambridge University Press, 1999).

Bytwerk, Randall L., *Julius Streicher: The Man Who Persuaded a Nation to Hate Jews* (New York: Dorset Press, 1983).

Cabral, Amilcar, *Revolution in Guinea: Selected Texts* (New York: Monthly Review Press, 1969).

_____, *Unity and Struggle: Speeches and Writings* (New York: Monthly Review Press, 1979).

Caldwell, George, *Indian Residential Schools: A Research Study of the Child Care Programmes for Nine Residential Schools in Saskatchewan* (Ottawa: Canadian Welfare Council, 1967).

Canadian Council of Catholic Bishops, *Let Justice Flow Like a Mighty River* (Ottawa: Catholic Church of Canada, 1995).

Carnoy, Martin, *Education as Cultural Imperialism* (New York: David McKay, 1974).

Chalk, Frank, and Kurt Jonassohn, *The History and Sociology of Genocide: Analyses and Case Studies* (New Haven, CT: Yale University Press, 1990).

Champagne, Duane, ed., *Contemporary Native American Cultural Issues* (Walnut Creek, CA: AltaMira Press, 1999).

Charny, Israel W., *How Can We Commit the Unthinkable? Genocide, the Human Cancer* (Boulder, CO, Westview Press, 1982).

_____, ed., *Towards the Understanding and Prevention of Genocide: Proceedings of the International Conference on Holocaust and Genocide* (Boulder, CO: Westview Press, 1984).

_____, ed., *Genocide: A Critical Bibliographic Review*, 2 vols. (London: Mansell, 1991).

_____, ed., *The Encyclopedia of Genocide*, 2 vols. (Santa Barbara, CA: ABC-CLIO, 1999).

Child, Brenda J., *Boarding School Seasons: American Indian Families, 1900-1940* (Lincoln: University of Nebraska Press, 1998).

Chomsky, Noam, *American Power and the New Mandarins* (New York: Pantheon, 1967).

_____, *Necessary Illusions: Thought Control in Democratic Societies* (Boston: South End Press, 1989).

Chrisjohn, Roland, and Sherri Young with Michael Maraun, *The Circle Game: Shadows and Substance in the Indian Residential School Experience in Canada* (Penticton, B.C.: Theytus Books, 1997).

Chrisman, William H., *The Opposite of Everything is True: Reflections on Denial in Alcoholic Families* (New York: William Morrow, 1991).

Churchill, Ward, *Fantasies of the Master Race: Literature, Cinema and the Colonization of American Indians* (Monroe, ME: Common Courage Press, 1992; San Francisco: City Lights, [2ⁿᵈ ed.] 1998).

_____, *Indians Are Us? Culture and Genocide in Native North America* (Monroe, ME: Common Courage Press, 1994).

_____, *From a Native Son: Selected Essays in Indigenism, 1985-1995* (Boston: South End Press, 1996).

_____, *A Little Matter of Genocide: Holocaust and Denial in the Americas, 1492 to the Present* (San Francisco: City Lights, 1997).

_____, *Fantasies of the Master Race: Literature, Cinema, and the Colonization of American Indians* (San Francisco: City Lights, [2ⁿᵈ ed.] 1998).

_____, *Perversions of Justice: Indigenous Peoples and Angloamerican Law* (San Francisco: City Lights, 2003).

_____, *Acts of Rebellion: The Ward Churchill Reader* (New York: Routledge, 2003).

_____, *On the Justice of Roosting Chickens: Reflections on the Consequences of American Conquest and Carnage* (Oakland, CA: AK Press, forthcoming in 2003).

Churchill, Ward, ed., *Marxism and Native Americans* (Boston: South End Press, 1983).

Churchill, Ward, and Jim Vander Wall, *The COINTELPRO Papers: Documents from the FBI's Secret Wars Against Dissent in the United States* (Cambridge, MA: South End Press, [Classics ed.] 2002).

Churchill, Ward, and J.J. Vander Wall, *Cages of Steel: The Politics of Imprisonment in the United States* (Washington, D.C.: Maisonneuve Press, 1992).

Churchill, Ward, and Mike Ryan, *Pacifism as Pathology: Reflections on the Role of Armed Struggle in North America* (Winnipeg: Arbiter Ring, 1998).

Clark, Blue, Lone Wolf v. Hitchcock: *Treaty Rights and Indian Law at the End of the Nineteenth Century* (Lincoln: University of Nebraska Press, 1999).

Clark, Bruce, *Native Liberty, Crown Sovereignty: The Existing Aboriginal Right of Self-Government in Canada* (Montréal: McGill-Queens University Press, 1990).

Clark, Dorothy K., *Casualties as a Measure of Effectiveness of an Infantry Battalion* (Baltimore: Operations Research Office, Johns Hopkins University, 1954).

Coates, Ken, Peter Limqueco and Peter Weiss, eds., *Prevent the Crime of Silence: Reports from the Sessions of the International War Crimes Tribunal Founded by Bertrand Russell* (London: Allen Lane/Penguin, 1971).

Cohen, Stanley, *States of Denial: Knowing About Atrocities and Suffering* (Cambridge, UK: Polity Press, 2001).

Cole, Douglas, and Ira Chaikan, *An Iron Hand Upon the People: The Law Against the Potlatch on the Northwest Coast* (Vancouver: Douglas & McIntire, 1990).

Coleman, Michael C., *American Indian Children at School, 1850-1930* (Jackson: University of Mississippi Press, 1993).

Cooper, Michael L., *Indian School: Teaching the White Man's Way* (New York: Clarion Books, 1999).

Courtois, Stéphane, et al., in *The Black Book of Communism: Crimes, Terror, Repression* (Cambridge, MA: Harvard University Press, 2000).

Dadrian, Vahakn N., *The History of the Armenian Genocide: Ethnic Conflict from the Balkans to Anatolia to the Caucasus* (Oxford, UK: Berghahn Books, [3rd ed.] 1997).

Daklugie, Asa, *Indeh: An Apache Odyssey* (Norman: University of Oklahoma Press, 1988).

Danieli, Yael, ed., *International Handbook of Multigenerational Legacies of Trauma* (New York: Plenum Press, 1998).

Davis, Robert, and Mark Zannis, *The Genocide Machine in Canada: The Pacification of the North* (Montréal: Black Rose Books, 1973).

Dawidowicz, Lucy S., *The War Against the Jews, 1933-1945* (New York: Holt, Rinehart & Winston, 1975).

_____, *The Holocaust and the Historians* (Cambridge, MA: Harvard University Press, 1981).

Deloria, Vine Jr., and Clifford M. Lytle, *American Indians, American Justice* (Austin: University of Texas Press, 1983).

_____, *The Nations Within: The Past and Future of American Indian Sovereignty* (New York: Pantheon, 1984).

Deloria, Vine Jr., and Raymond J. DeMallie, *Documents of American Indian Diplomacy: Treaties, Agreements, and Conventions, 1775-1979*, 2 vols. (Norman: University of Oklahoma Press, 1999).

Deloria, Vine Jr., and David E. Wilkins, *Tribes, Treaties, and Constitutional Tribulations* (Austin: University of Texas Press, 1999).

Dimsdale, Joel E., ed., *Survivors, Victims, and Perpetrators: Essays on the Nazi Holocaust* (New York: Hemisphere, 1980).

Dixon, Joseph K., *The Vanishing Race: The Last Great Indian Council* (Garden City, NY: Doubleday, 1913).

Dobyns, Henry F., *Their Number Become Thinned: Native American Population Dynamics in Eastern North America* (Knoxville: University of Tennessee Press, 1983).

Drinnon, Richard, *Keeper of Concentration Camps: Dillon S. Myer and American Racism* (Berkeley: University of California Press, 1987).

Drost, Pieter N., *The Crime of State* (Leyden: A.W. Sythoff, 1959).

Duran, Eduardo F., *Transforming the Soul Wound: A Theoretical/Clinical Approach to American Indian Psychology* (Berkeley, CA: Folklore Institute, 1990).

_____, and Bonnie M. Duran, *Native American Postcolonial Psychology* (Albany: State University of New York Press, 1995).

Edelstein, E.L., Donald L. Nathanson and Andrew M. Stone, eds., *Denial: A Clarification of Concepts and Research* (New York: Plenum Press, 1989).

Elbaum, Max, *Revolution in the Air: Sixties Radicals and the turn to Lenin, Mao and Che* (London: Verso, 2002).

Ellis, Clyde, *To Change Them Forever: Indian Education at the Rainy Mountain Boarding School, 1893-1920* (Norman: University of Oklahoma Press, 1996).

Ellis, Pearl Idelia, *Americanization Through Homemaking* (Los Angeles: Wetzel, 1929).

Elson, Ruth M., *Guardians of Tradition: American Schoolbooks of the Nineteenth Century* (Lincoln: University of Nebraska Press, 1964).

Epstein, Helen, *Children of the Holocaust: Conversations with Sons and Daughters of Survivors* (New York: Bantam, 1979).

Etzioni, Amitai, ed., *Complex Organizations: A Sociological Reader* (Chicago: Aldine, 1961).

Evans, Richard J., *Lying About Hitler: History, Holocaust, and the David Irving Trial* (New York: Basic Books, 2001).

Eynsenck, M.W., *The Blackwell Dictionary of Cognitive Psychology* (Oxford, UK: Blackwell, 1994).

Fanon, Frantz, Frantz Fanon, *A Dying Colonialism* (New York: Grove Press, 1965).

_____, *The Wretched of the Earth* (New York: Grove Press, 1966).

_____, *Black Skins, White Masks: The Experiences of a Black Man in a White World* (New York: Grove Press, 1967).

Finkelhor, David, and Kirsti Yllo, *License to Rape: Sexual Abuse of Wives* (New York: Holt, Rinehart & Winston, 1985).

Finkelstein, Norman G., *The Holocaust Industry: Reflections on the Exploitation of Jewish Suffering* (London: Verso, 2000).

Fixico, Donald L., *Termination and Relocation: Federal Indian Policy, 1945-1960* (Albuquerque: University of New Mexico Press, 1986).

Fleming, Gerald, *Hitler and the Final Solution* (Berkeley: University of California Press, 1982).

Foucault, Michel, *Discipline and Punish: The Birth of the Prison* (New York: Vintage Books, 1979).

Fournier, Suzanna, and Ernie Crey, *Stolen From Our Embrace: The Abduction of First Nations Children and the Restoration of Aboriginal Communities* (Vancouver: Douglas & McIntyre, 1997).

Fraenkel, Ernst, *The Dual State: A Contribution to the Theory of Dictatorship* (New York: Oxford University Press, 1941).

Friedrichs, David O., ed., *State Crime, Vol. I: Defining, Delineating and Explaining State Crime* (Aldershot, UK: Ashgate, 1998).

Friere, Paulo, *Pedagogy of the Oppressed* (New York: Herder and Herder, 1972).

Funk, Jack, and Gordon Lobe, eds., *"...and They Told Us Their Stories": A Book of Indian Stories* (Saskatoon, Sask.: Saskatoon District Tribal Council, 1991).

Furniss, Elizabeth M., *Conspiracy of Silence: The Case of the Native Students at St. Joseph's Residential School, 1891-1920* (Williams Lake, B.C.: Cariboo Tribal Council, 1991).

_____, *Victims of Benevolence: Discipline and Death at the Williams Lake Indian Residential School, 1891-1920* (Williams Lake, B.C.: Cariboo Tribal Council, 1992).

Gibson, Nigel C., *Rethinking Fanon: The Continuing Dialogue* (New York: Humanity Books, 1999).

Gladwin, Thomas, with Ahmad Saidin, *Slaves of the White Myth: The Psychology of Neocolonialism* (Atlantic Highlands, NJ: Humanities Press, 1980).

Gordon, Lewis R., *Fanon and the Crisis of European Man: An Essay on Philosophy and the Human Sciences* (New York: Routledge, 1995).

Gordon, Sarah, *Hitler, Germans, and the "Jewish Question"* (Princeton, NJ: Princeton University Press, 1984).

Gould, Steven Jay, *The Mismeasure of Man* (New York: W.W. Norton, 1981).

Gramsci, Antonio, *The Modern Prince and Other Writings* (New York: International, 1957).

Grant, Agnes, *No End of Grief: Indian Residential Schools in Canada* (Winnipeg, Man: Pemmican Press, 1996).

Greymorning, Stephen, ed., *A Will to Survive: Indigenous Essays on the Politics of Culture, Language and Identity* (Boston: McGraw-Hill, 2004).

Grounds, Richard A., George E. Tinker, and David E. Wilkins, eds., *Native Voices: American Indian Identity and Resistance* (Lawrence: University Press of Kansas, 2003).

Grunberger, Richard, *The 12-Year Reich: A Social History of Nazi Germany, 1933-1945* (New York: Holt, Rinehart and Winston, 1971).

Guttenplan, D.D., *The Holocaust on Trial* (New York: W.W. Norton, 2001).

Haebich, Anna, *For Their Own Good: Aboriginies and the Government in the Southwest of Western Australia, 1900-1940* (Nedlands: University of Western Australia Press, 1988).

Haig-Brown, Celia, *Resistance and Renewal: Surviving the Indian Residential School* (Vancouver: Tillacum Library, 1988).

Hale, Matthew, *History of the Pleas of the Crown*, 2 vols. (Philadelphia: H.R. Small, 1847).

Hall, Kermit L., ed., *The Oxford Companion to American Law* (New York: Oxford University Press, 2002).

Harring, Sidney L., *Crow Dog's Case: American Indian Sovereignty, Tribal Law, and United States Law in the Nineteenth Century* (Cambridge, UK: Cambridge University Press, 1994).

Harrison, Paul, *Inside the Third World: The Classic Account of Poverty in the Developing Countries* (New York: Penguin Books, [3ʳᵈ ed.] 1993).

Hayes, Peter, ed., *Testimony: Contemporary Writers Make the Holocaust Personal* (New York: Times Books, 1989).

Heizer, Robert F., ed., *The Destruction of California Indians* (Lincoln: University of Nebraska Press, 1993 reprint of 1974 Peregrine Smith ed.).

Hendin, Herbert, and Ann P. Haas, *Wounds of War: The Psychological Aftermath of Combat in Vietnam* (New York: Basic Books, 1984).

Herman, Judith, *Trauma and Recovery* (New York: Basic Books, [2ⁿᵈ ed.] 1997).

Hilberg, Raul, *The Destruction of European Jews*, 3 vols. (New York: Holmes and Meier, [rev. ed.] 1985).

_____, *Perpetrators, Victims, Bystanders: The Jewish Catastrophe, 1944-1945* (New York: HarperCollins, 1992).

Hill, J.L., *The Passing of the Indian and the Buffalo* (Long Beach, CA: n.p., 1917).

Hochschild, Adam, *King Leopold's Ghost: A Story of Greed, Terror, and Heroism in Colonial Africa* (Boston: Houghton Mifflin, 1998).

Hoffmann, Peter, *The History of the German Resistance, 1933-1945* (Montréal: McGill-Queens University Press, [3ʳᵈ ed.] 1996).

Höhne, Heinz, *The Order of the Death's Head: The Story of Hitler's S.S.* (New York: Coward-McCann, 1969).

Hoig, Stan, *The Sand Creek Massacre* (Norman: University of Oklahoma Press, 1961).

Holt, Marilyn, *The Orphan Trains: Placing Out in America* (Lincoln: University of Nebraska Press, 1992).

Horowitz, Irving Louis, *Genocide: State Power and Mass Murder* (New Brunswick, NJ: Transaction Books, 1976).

Hoxie, Frederick E., *A Final Promise: The Campaign to Assimilate the Indians, 1880-1920* (Lincoln: University of Nebraska Press, 1985).

Hrdlicka, Ales, *Tuberculosis Among Certain Indian Tribes of the United States* (Washington, D.C.: Smithsonian Institution, 1909).

Hutton, Paul Andrew, *Phil Sheridan and His Army* (Lincoln: University of Nebraska Press, 1985).

Jacobs, Jane, *The Question of Separatism: Quebec and the Struggle over Sovereignty* (New York: Random House, 1980).

Jaggar, Alison M., *Feminist Politics and Human Nature* (Totawa, NJ: Rowman & Littlefield, 1983).

Jaimes, M. Annette, ed., *The State of Native America: Genocide, Colonization and Resistance* (Boston: South End Press, 1992).

James, Harry C., *Pages from Hopi History* (Tucson: University of Arizona Press, 1988).

Jaspers, Karl, *The Question of German Guilt* (New York: Fordham University Press, 2002).

Johnson, Basil, *Indian School Days* (Norman: University of Oklahoma Press, 1989).

Johnson, Broderick H., ed., *Stories of Traditional Navajo Life and Culture* (Tsaile, AZ: Navajo Community College Press, 1977).

Kabotie, Fred, *Fred Kabotie, Hopi Indian Artist: An Autobiography told with Bill Belknap* (Flagstaff: Museum of Northern Arizona/Northland Press, 1977).

Katz, Steven T., *Post-Holocaust Dialogues* (New York: New York University Press, 1983).

_____, *The Holocaust in Historical Context, Vol. 1: The Holocaust and Mass Death before the Modern Age* (New York: Oxford University Press, 1994).

Katsiaficas, George, *The Imagination of the New Left: A Global Analysis of 1968* (Boston: South End Press, 1987).

Kaywaykla, James, *In the Days of Victorio: Recollections of a Warm Springs Apache* (Tucson: University of Arizona Press, 1970).

Kelly, Lawrence C., *Assault on Assimilation: John Collier and the Origins of Indian Policy Reform* (Albuquerque: University of New Mexico Press, 1983).

Kelly, Leah Renae, *In My Own Voice: Explorations in the Sociopolitical Context of Art and Cinema* (Winnipeg: Arbiter Ring, 2001).

Kendrick, Donald, and Grattan Paxton, *Gypsies Under the Swastika* (Hartfield, UK: Hertfordshire University Press, 1995).

Kennedy, Kerry, and Nan Richardson, eds., *Speak Truth to Power: Human Rights Defenders Who are Changing Our World* (New York: Crown, 2000).

King, C. Richard, and Charles Frueling Springwood, eds., *Team Spirits: The Native American Mascots Controversy* (Lincoln: University of Nebraska Press, 2001).

Kinsman, Gary, Dieter K. Buse and Mercedes Steedman, eds., *Whose National Security? Canadian State Surveillance and the Creation of Enemies* (Toronto: Between the Lines, 2000).

Kitzinger, Cecelia, and Rachel Perkins, *Changing Our Minds: Lesbian Feminism and Psychology* (New York: New York University Press, 1993).

Knockwood, Isabelle, *Out of the Depths: The Experiences of Mi'kmaw Children at the Residential School at Shubenacadie, Nova Scotia* (Lockeport, NS: Roseway, 1992).

Krausnick, Helmut, Hans Buchheim, Martin Broszat and Hans-Adolf Jacobson, *Anatomy of the SS State* (New York: Walker, 1965).

Kritz, Neil J., ed., *Transitional Justice: How Emerging Democracies Reckon with Former Regimes*, 3 vols. (Washington, D.C.: U.S. Institute for Peace Press, 1995).

Krystal, Henry, ed., *Massive Psychic Trauma* (New York: International Universities Press, 1968).

Kuper, Leo, *Genocide: Its Political Use in the Twentieth Century* (New Haven, CT: Yale University Press, 1982).

_____, *The Prevention of Genocide* (New Haven, CT: Yale University Press, 1985).

Kvasnicka, Robert M., and Herman J. Viola, eds., *The Commissioners of Indian Affairs, 1824-1977* (Lincoln: University of Nebraska Press, 1979)

La Flesche, Francis, *The Middle Five: Indian Schoolboys of the Omaha Tribe* (Madison: University Press, 1963).

Lame Deer (John Fire) and Richard Erdoes, *Lame Deer, Seeker of Visions: The Life of a Sioux Medicine Man* (New York: Simon & Schuster, 1972).

Laqueur, Walter, *The Terrible Secret: Suppression of the Truth about Hitler's "Final Solution"* (Boston: Little, Brown, 1981).

Lavan, George, ed., *Che Guevara Speaks: Selected Writings and Speeches* (New York: Merit, 1967).

Lazarus, Edward, *Black Hills, White Justice: The Sioux Nation versus the United States, 1775 to the Present* (New York: HarperCollins, 1991).

LeBlanc, Lawrence J., *The United States and the Genocide Convention* (Durham, NC: Duke University Press, 1991).

Leland, Joy. *Firewater Myths: North American Indian Drinking and Alcohol Addiction* (New Brunswick: Rutgers University Center for Alcohol Studies No. 11, 1976).

Lemkin, Raphaël, *Axis Rule in Occupied Europe: Laws of Occupation, Analysis of Government, Proposals for Redress* (Washington, D.C.: Carnegie Endowment for International Peace, 1944).

_____, Lester, David, *Suicide '92* (Denver: American Association of Suicidology, 1992).

Suicide in American Indians (New York: Nova Science, 2001).

Leupp, Francis E., *The Indian and His Problem* (New York: Scribner's, 1910).

Lewis, Helen Matthews, Linda Johnson and Don Askins, eds., *Colonialism in Modern America: The Appalachian Case* (Boone, NC: Appalachian Consortium Press, 1978).

Lewy, Guenter, *The Nazi Persecution of the Gypsies* (New York: Oxford University Press, 2000).

Lichtenstein, Alex, *Twice the Work of Free Labor: The Political Economy of Convict Labor in the New South* (London: Verso, 1996).

Lifton, Robert Jay, and Eric Markusen, *The Genocidal Mentality: Nazi Holocaust and Nuclear Threat* (New York: Basic Books, 1988).

Limerick, Patricia Nelson, *The Legacy of Conquest: The Unbroken Past of the American West* (New York: W.W. Norton, 1987).

Lipstadt, Deborah, *Denying the Holocaust: The Growing Assault on Truth and Memory* (New York: Free Press, 1993).

Littlefield, Alice, and Martha C. Knack, *Native Americans and Wage Labor: Ethnohistorical Perspectives* (Norman: University of Oklahoma Press, 1996).

Lobo, Susan, and Steve Talbot, eds., *Native American Voices: A Reader* (New York: Longman, 1998).

Lobo, Susan, and Kurt Peters, eds., *American Indians and the Urban Experience* (Walnut Creek, CA: AltaMira Press, 2001).

Lomawaima, K. Tsianina, *They Called It Prairie Light: The Story of the Chilocco Boarding School* (Lincoln: University of Nebraska Press, 1994).

Macaulay, Thomas Babington, *Macaulay: Prose and Poetry* (Cambridge, MA: Harvard University Press, 1957).

MacGregor, Roy, *Chief: The Fearless Vision of Billy Diamond* (Toronto: Penguin, 1988).

Mancini, Matthew L., *One Dies, Get Another: Convict Leasing in the American South, 1866-1928* (Columbia: University of South Carolina Press, 1996).

Mann, Barbara Alice, *Iroquoian Women: The Gantowisas* (New York: Peter Lang, 2000).

Manvell, Roger, and Heinrich Fraenkel, *Incomparable Crime: Mass Extermination in the 20th Century* (London: Hinemann, 1967).

Marable, Manning, *Speaking Truth to Power: Essays in Race, Resistance and Radicalism* (Boulder, CO: Westview Press, 1998).

Maracle, Brian, *Crazywater: Native Voices on Addiction and Recovery* (New York: Penguin, 1993).

Mayer, Arno J., *Why Did the Heavens Not Darken? The "Final Solution" in History* (New York: Pantheon, 1990).

McBeth, Sally J., *Ethnic Identity and the Boarding School Experience of West-Central Oklahoma Indians* (Washington, D.C.: University Press of America, 1983).

McCarthy, James, *Papago Traveler: The Memoirs of James McCarthy* (Tucson: Sun Tracks/University of Arizona Press, 1985).

McDonnell, Janet A., *The Dispossession of the American Indian, 1887-1934* (Bloomington: Indiana University Press, 1991).

McNair, Peter, Alan Hoover and Kevin Neary, *The Legacy: Tradition and Innovation in Northwest Coast Indian Art* (Seattle: University of Washington Press, 1984).

Memmi, Albert, *The Colonizer and the Colonized* (Boston: Beacon Press, 1965).

_____, *Dominated Man* (Boston: Beacon Press, 1976).

Meriam, Lewis, et al., *Problem of Indian Administration* (Baltimore: Johns Hopkins University Press, 1928).

Miller, Alice, *For Your Own Good: Hidden Cruelty in Child-Rearing and the Roots of Violence* (New York: Farrar, Straus, Giroux, 1983).

Miller, J.R., *Shingwauk's Vision: A History of the Indian Residential Schools* (Toronto: University of Toronto Press, 1996).

Miller, Kerby A., *Emigrants and Exiles: Ireland and the Irish Exodus to North America* (New York: Oxford University Press, 1985).

Milloy, John S., *"A National Crime": The Canadian Government and the Residential School System, 1879 to 1986* (Winnipeg: University of Manitoba Press, 1999).

Mirikitani, Janice, *Shedding Silence: Poetry and Prose* (Berkeley, CA: Celestial Arts, 1987).

Mitchell, Frank, *Navajo Blessingway Singer: The Autobiography of Frank Mitchell* (Tucson: University of Arizona Press, 1978).

Mooney, James M., *The Aboriginal Population of America North of Mexico* (Washington, D.C.: Smithsonian Misc. Collections LXXX, No. 7, 1928).

Moore-Gilbert, Bart, *Postcolonial Theory: Contexts, Practices, Politics* (London: Verso, 1997).

Mongia, Padmini *Contemporary Postcolonial Theory: A Reader* (London/New York: Arnold, 1997).

Moses, L.G., and Raymond Wilson, eds., *Indian Lives: Essays on Nineteenth- and Twentieth Century Native American Leaders* (Albuquerque: University of New Mexico Press, 1985).

Nandy, Ashis, *The Intimate Enemy: Loss and Recovery of Self Under Colonialism* (New York: Oxford University Press, 1983).

Nannum, Hurst, *Autonomy, Sovereignty and Self-Determination* (Philadelphia: University of Pennsylvania Press, 1990).

National Prison Project, *Report on the High Security Unit for Women, Federal Correctional Institution, Lexington, Kentucky* (New York: American Civil Liberties Union, Aug. 27, 1987).

Nechi Institute, Four Worlds Development Project, Native Training Institute, and New Direction Training, *Healing Is Possible: A Joint Statement on the Healing of Sexual Abuse in Native Communities* (Edmonton: Nechi Institute, 1988).

Nock, David A., *A Victorian Missionary and Canadian Indian Policy: Cultural Synthesis vs. Cultural Replacement* (Waterloo, Ont.: Wilfred Laurier University Press, 1988).

Oak, V.V., *England's Educational Policy in India* (Madras: B.G. Paul, 1925).

Obadele, Imari Abubakari I, *Foundations of the Black Nation* (Detroit, MI: House of Songhay, 1975).

Ochberg, Frank M., and David A. Soskis, *Victims of Terrorism* (Boulder, CO: Westview Press, 1982).

Ofuatey-Kodjoe, W., *The Principle of Self-Determination in International Law* (Hamden, CT: Archon Books, 1972).

Olsen, Sylvia, with Rita Morris and Ann Sam, *No Time to Say Goodbye: Children's Stories from the Kuper Island Residential School* (Victoria, BC: Sono Nis Press, 2001).

Omi, Michael, and Howard Winant, *Racial Formation in the United States: From the 1960s to the 1990s* (New York: Routledge, 1994).

Oshinsky, David M., *"Worse Than Slavery": Parchman Farm and the Ordeal of Jim Crow Justice* (New York: Free Press, 1996).

Otis, D.S., *The Dawes Act and the Allotment of Indian Land* (Norman: University of Oklahoma Press, 1973).

Pan American Scientific Congress, *Proceedings of the Second Pan American Scientific Congress, Sec. 1: Anthropology* (Washington, D.C.: Smithsonian Institution, 1909-1910).

Parenti, Christian, *Lockdown America: Police and Prisons in the Age of Crisis* (London: Verso, 1999).

Parlow, Anita, *Cry, Sacred Ground: Big Mountain, USA* (Washington, D.C.: Christic Institute, 1988).

Patterson, William L., *The Man Who Cried Genocide: An Autobiography* (New York: New World, 1971).

Pavlic, Steve, ed., *A Good Cherokee, A Good Anthropologist: Papers in Honor of Robert K. Thomas* (Los Angeles: UCLA American Indian Studies Ctr., 1998).

Perinbaum, Marie, *Holy Violence: The Revolutionary Thought of Frantz Fanon* (Washington, D.C.: Three Continents Press, 1982).

Pettitpas, Katherine, *Severing the Ties That Bind: Government Repression of Indigenous Religious Ceremonies on the Prairies* (Winnipeg: University of Manitoba Press, 1994).

Philp, Kenneth R., *John Collier's Crusade for Indian Reform, 1920-1954* (Tucson: University of Arizona Press, 1977).

Polsky, Andrew, *The Rise of the Therapeutic State* (Princeton, NJ: Princeton University Press, 1991).

Pomerance, Michla, *The Advisory Function of the International Court in the League and U.N. Eras* (The Hague: Martinus Nijhoff, 1973).

_____, *Self-Determination in Law and Practice* (The Hague: Marinus Nijhoff, 1982).

Pratt, Richard Henry, *Battlefield and Classroom: Four Decades with the American Indian, 1867-1904* (New Haven, CT: Yale University Press, 1967 reprint of 1906 original).

Price, A. Grenfell, *White Settlers and Native Peoples: An Historical Study of Racial Contacts between English-speaking Whites and Aboriginal Peoples in the United States, Canada, Australia and New Zealand* (Cambridge, UK: Cambridge University Press, 1950).

Priest, Loring Benson, *Uncle Sam's Stepchildren: The Reformation of United States Indian Policy, 1865-1887* (Lincoln: University of Nebraska Press, 1975 reprint of 1942 original).

Prucha, Francis Paul, *Americanizing the American Indian: Writings by the "Friends of the Indian," 1880-1900* (Lincoln: University of Nebraska Press, 1973).

_____, *American Indian Policy in Crisis: Christian Reformers and the Indian, 1865-1900* (Norman: University of Oklahoma Press, 1976).

_____, *The Churches and the Indian Schools, 1888-1912* (Lincoln: University of Nebraska Press, 1979).

_____, *The Great Father: The United States Government and the American Indian* (Lincoln: University of Nebraska Press, 1984).

Qoyawayma, Polingaysi (Elizabeth Q. White), as told to Vada S. Carlson, *No Turning Back: A Hopi Indian Girl's Struggle to Bridge the Gap Between the World of Her People and the World of the White Man* (Albuquerque: University of New Mexico Press, 1964).

Raferty, Mary, and Eoin O'Sullivan, *Suffer the Little Children: The Inside Story of Ireland's Industrial Schools* (New York: Continuum, 2001).

Read, Peter, *A Rape of the Soul So Profound: The Return of the Stolen Generations* (St. Leonard's: Allen & Unwin, 1999).

Richardson, Boyce, *The People of* Terra Nullius: *Betrayal and Rebirth in Aboriginal Canada* (Vancouver/Seattle: Douglas &

McIntyre/University of Washington Press, 1993).

Rigo-Sureda, Antonio, *The Evolution of the Right to Self-Determination: A Study of United Nations Practice* (Leiden, Netherlands: A.W. Sijhoff, 1973).

Robertson, Geoffrey, *Crimes Against Humanity: The Struggle for Global Justice* (New York: New Press, 2000).

Rodinson, Maxime, *Israel: A Colonial-Settler State?* (New York: Pathfinder Press, 1973).

Rosenbaum, Alan S., ed., *Is the Holocaust Unique? Perspectives on Comparative Genocide* (Boulder, CO: Westview Press, 1996).

Russell, Diana E.H., *Rape in Marriage* (New York: Macmillan, 1982).

Sakai, J., *Settlers: The Mythology of the White Proletariat* (Chicago: Morningstar Press, [2nd ed.] 1983).

Sartre, Jean-Paul, *Colonialism and Neocolonialism* (New York: Routledge, 2001).

Sartre, Jean-Paul, and Arlette El Kaïm Sartre, *On Genocide and a Summary of the Evidence and the Judgments of the International War Crimes Tribunal* (Boston: Beacon Press, 1968).

Shkilnyk, Anastasia M., *A Poison Stronger than Love: The Destruction of an Ojibwa Community* (New Haven, CT: Yale University Press, 1985).

Schmitt, Carl, *The Crisis of Parliamentary Democracy* (Cambridge, MA: MIT Press, 1985).

Scudder, Horace E., *A History of the United States of America* (Philadelphia: J.W. Butler, 1884).

Scudder, Thayer, et al., *No Place To Go: Effects of Compulsory Relocation on Navajos* (Philadelphia: Institute for the Study of Human Issues, 1982).

Sekaquaptewa, Helen, as told to Louise Udall, *Me and Mine: The Life Story of Helen Sekaquaptewa* (Tucson: University of Arizona Press, 1962). Smith, Bradley F., *Reaching Judgment at Nuremberg* (New York: Basic Books, 1977).

Shandley, Robert R., *Unwilling Germans? The Goldhagen Debate* (Minneapolis: University of Minnesota Press, 2000)

Shengold, Leonard, *Soul Murder: The Effects of Childhood Abuse and Deprivation* (New Haven: Yale University Press, 1989).

Shortt, A., and A.G. Doughty, eds., *Canada and Its Provinces* (Toronto: University of Edinburgh Press, 1913).

Simmons, Leo W., *Sun Chief: The Autobiography of a Hopi Indian* (New Haven, CT: Yale University Press, 1942).

Sinclair, Sir Ian, *The Vienna Convention on the Law of Treaties* (Manchester, UK: Manchester University Press, [2nd ed.] 1984).

Smith, Linda Tuhiwai, *Decolonizing Methodologies: Research and Indigenous Peoples* (London: Zed Books, 1999).

Smith, Paul Chaat, and Robert Allen Warrior, *Like a Hurricane: The American Indian Movement from Alcatraz to Wounded Knee* (New York: New Press, 1996).

Sorenson, M., ed., *Manual of Public International Law* (New York: St. Martin's Press, 1968).

Spindel, Carol, *Dancing at Halftime: Sports and the Controversy over American Indian Mascots* (New York: New York University Press, 2000).

Standing Bear, Luther, *My People, the Sioux* (Lincoln: University of Nebraska Press, 1975 reprint of 1928 original).

Stannard, David E., *American Holocaust: Columbus and the Conquest of the New World* (New York: Oxford University Press, 1992).

Stanton, William, *The Leopard's Spots: Scientific Attitudes Toward Race in America, 1815-59* (Chicago: University of Chicago Press, 1960).

Stearn, E. Wagner, and Allen E. Stearn, *The Effects of Smallpox on the Destiny of the Amerindian* (Boston: Bruce Humphries, 1945).

Stewart, Irene, *A Voice in Her Tribe: A Navajo Woman's Own Story* (Socorro, NM: Ballena Press, 1980).

Strickland, Rennard, *Tonto's Revenge: Reflections on American Indian Culture and Policy* (Albuquerque: University of New Mexico Press, 1997).

Svaldi, David, *Sand Creek and the Rhetoric of Extermination: A Case Study in Indian-White Relations* (Lanham, MD: University Press of America, 1989).

Switlow, Janice G.A.E., *Gustafson Lake: Under Siege* (Peachland, B.C.: TIAC Communications, 1997).

Szasz, Margaret Connell, *Indian Education in the American Colonies, 1607-1783* (Albuquerque: University of New Mexico Press, 1988).

_____, *Education and the American Indian: The Road to Self-Determination Since 1928* (Albuquerque: University of New Mexico Press, [3rd ed.] 1999).

_____, ed., *The Cultural Broker: Link Between American Indian and White Worlds, 1690s-1990s* (Norman: University of Oklahoma Press, 1994).

Szasz, Thomas, *The Therapeutic State: Psychiatry in the Mirror of Current Events* (Buffalo, NY: Prometheus Books, 1984).

Talayesva, Don, *Sun Chief: The Autobiography of a Hopi Indian* (New Haven, CT: Yale University Press, 1942).

Terr, Lenore C., *Too Scared to Cry: How Trauma Affects Children and Ultimately Us All* (New York: Basic Books, 1990).

Thompson, Edward, and Geoffrey T. Garratt, *The Rise and Fulfillment of British Rule in India* (Allahabad: Central Book Depot, 1962).

Thompson, Gerald, *The Army and the Navajo: The Bosque Redondo Reservation Experiment, 1863-1868* (Tucson: University of Arizona Press, 1982).

Thornton, Russell, *American Indian Holocaust and Survival: A Population History Since 1492* (Norman: University of Oklahoma Press, 1987).

Tinker, George E., *Spirit and Resistance: Political Theology and American Indian Resistance* (Minneapolis: Fortress Press, 2004).

Titley, E. Brian, *A Narrow Vision: Duncan Campbell Scott and the Administration of Indian Affairs in Canada* (Vancouver: University of British Columbia Press, 1986).

Tolnay, Stewart E., and E.M. Beck, *A Festival of Violence: An Analysis of Southern Lynchings, 1882-1930* (Urbana: University of Illinois Press, 1955).

Treat, James, *Around the Sacred Fire: Native Religious Activism in the Red Power Era: A Narrative Map of the Indian Ecumenical Conference* (New York: Palgrave, 2003).

Trennert, Robert A. Jr., *The Phoenix Indian School: Forced Assimilation in Arizona, 1891-1935* (Norman: University of Oklahoma Press, 1988).

Tucker, William H., *The Science and Politics of Racial Research* (Urbana: University of Illinois Press, 1994).

van der Kolk, Bessel A., ed., *Psychological Trauma* (Washington, D.C.: American Psychiatric Press, 1987).

van der Kolk, Bessel A., Alexander C. McFarlane, and Lars Weisaeth, eds., *Traumatic Stress: The Effects Overwhelming Experience on Mind, Body, and Society* (New York: Guilford Press, 1996)

Vasarhelyi, Istvan, *Restitution in International Law* (Budapest: Hungary Academy of Science, 1964).

Vidal-Naquet, Pierre, *Assassins of Memory: Essays on Denial of the Holocaust* (New York: Columbia University Press, 1992).

Viola, Herman J. , *Thomas L. McKenney: Architect of America's Early Indian Policy, 1816-1830* (Chicago: Swallow Press, 1974).

wa Thiongo, Ngugi, *Decolonizing the Mind: The Politics of Language in African Literature* (London/Nairobi/Portsmouth, NH: James Curry/EAEP/Heinemann, 1986).

Wade, Wyn Craig, *The Fiery Cross: The Ku Klux Klan in America* (New York: Simon and Schuster, 1987).

Waldram, James B., D. Ann Herring and T. Kue Young, *Aboriginal Health in Canada: Historical, Cultural, and Epidemiological Perspectives* (Toronto: University of Toronto Press, 1995).

Walker, Lenore, *The Battered Woman* (New York: Harper & Row, 1979).

Wallimann, Isidor, and Michael N. Dobkowski, eds., *Genocide and the Modern Age: Etiology and Case Studies of Mass Death* (Westport, CT: Greenwood Press, 1987).

Washburn, Wilcomb E., *The Assault on Indian Tribalism: The General Allotment Dawes Act of 1887* (Philadelphia: J.B. Lippincott, 1975).

_____, *Red Man's Land, White Man's Law* (Norman: University of Oklahoma Press, [2nd ed.] 1995).

Weston, Burns H., Richard A. Falk and Anthony D'Amato, eds., *Basic Documents in International Law and World Order* (Minneapolis: West, 1990).

Wherrett, George Jasper, *The Miracle of Empty Beds: A History of Tuberculosis in Canada* (Toronto: University of Toronto Press, 1977).

Whitewolf, Jim, *Jim Whitewolf: The Life of a Kiowa Apache Indian* (New York: Dover, 1969).

Wilkins, David E., and K. Tsianina Lomawaima, *Uneven Ground: American Indian Sovereignty and Federal Law* (Norman: University of Oklahoma Press, 2001).

Wilson, Dick, *The Long March, 1935: The Epic of Chinese Communist Survival* (New York: Viking, 1971).

Wilson, John P., Zev Harel and Boaz Kahana, eds., *Human Adaptation to Extreme Stress: From the Holocaust to Vietnam* (New York: Plenum, 1988).

Winnie, Lucille, *Sah-gan-de-oh: The Chief's Daughter* (New York: Vantage Press, 1969).

Witmer, Linda F., *The Indian School: Carlisle, Pennsylvania, 1879-1918* (Carlisle, PA: Cumberland County Historical Society, [2nd ed.] 2000).

Wittgenstein, Ludwig, *An Inquiry into Meaning and Truth* (New York: W.W. Norton, 1940).

Wilkins, David E., *American Indian Sovereignty and the Supreme Court* (Austin: University of Texas Press, 1997).

Williams, Patrick, and Laura Chrisman, eds., *Colonial Discourse and Post-Colonial Theory: A Reader* (New York: Columbia University Press, 1994).

Wolf, Patrick, *Settler State Colonialism and the Transformation of Anthropology: The Politics and Poetics of an Ethnographic Event* (London: Cassell, 1999).

Wolf, Robert Paul, Barrington Moore, Jr., and Herbert Marcuse, *A Critique of Pure Tolerance* (Boston: Beacon Press, 1965).

Woodward, C. Vann, *The Strange Career of Jim Crow* (New York: Oxford University Press, [3rd ed.] 1974).

Yava, Albert, *Big Falling Snow: A Tewa-Hopi Indian's Life and Times and the History and Traditions of His People* (Albuquerque: University of New Mexico Press, 1978).

Yllo, Kersti, and Michele Bograd, *Feminist Perspectives in Wife Abuse* (Beverly Hills, CA: Sage, 1988).

York, Geoffrey, *The Dispossessed: Life and Death in Native Canada* (Boston: Little, Brown, 1992).

York, Geoffrey, and Loreen Pindera, *People of the Pines: The Warriors and the Legacy of Oka* (Boston: Little, Brown, 1991).

Zitkala-Sa (Gertrude Bonnin), *American Indian Stories* (Lincoln: University of Nebraska Press, 1985 reprint of 1921 original).

Zündel, Ernst, *The Hitler We Love and Why* (Toronto: Samistat, 1984).

Book Chapters

Arechaga, Eduardo Jiminez de, "International Responsibility," in Sorenson, *Manual of Public International Law.*

Bistritz, Janice, "Transgenerational Pathology in Families of Holocaust Survivors," in Braham, *Psychological Perspectives on the Holocaust.*

Brooks, Roy L., "What Form Redress?" in his *When Sorry Isn't Enough.*

Buchanan, Ann, "Intergenerational Child Maltreatment," in Danieli, *Multigenerational Legacies of Trauma.*

Bulhan, Hussein A., "Revolutionary Psychiatry of Fanon," in Gibson, *Rethinking Fanon.*

Chomsky, Noam, "Objectivity and Liberal Scholarship," in his *American Power and the New Mandarins.*

Churchill, Ward, "Naming Our Destiny: Toward a Language of American Indian Liberation," in his *Indians Are Us?*

_____, "Let's Spread the 'Fun' Around: The Issue of Sports Team Names and Mascots," in his *From a Native Son.*

_____, "In the Matter of Julius Streicher: Applying Nuremberg Standards in the United States," in his *From a Native Son.*

_____, "Indians 'R' Us: Reflections on the 'Men's Movement,'" in his *From a Native Son.*

_____, "Lie for Lie: Linkages Between Holocaust Deniers and Proponents of the 'Uniqueness' of the Jewish Experience in World War II,' " in his *A Little Matter of Genocide.*

_____, "Cold War Impacts on Native North America: The Political Economy of Radioactive Colonization," in his *A Little Matter of Genocide.*

_____, "It Did Happen Here: Sand Creek, Scholarship and the American Character," in his *Fantasies of the Master Race* (2nd ed.).

_____, "A Breach of Trust: The Radioactive Colonization of Native North America," in his *Perversions of Justice.*

_____, "Charades Anyone? The Indian Claims Commission in Context," in his *Perversions of Justice.*

_____, "The Crucible of American Indian Identity: Native Tradition versus Colonial Imposition in Postconquest North America," in his *Perversions of Justice.*

_____, "Forbidding the G-Word in Canada: Holocaust Denial as Judicial Doctrine in Canada," in his *Perversions of Justice.*

_____, "Like Sand in the Wind: The Making of an American Indian Diaspora in the United States," in his *Acts of Rebellion.*

_____, "On the Intersection of Justice and History" in his *Acts of Rebellion.*

_____, "The Nullification of Native North America? An Analysis of the 1990 American Indian Arts and Crafts Act," in his *Acts of Rebellion.*

_____, "The Bloody Wake of Alcatraz: Repression of the American Indian Movement during the 1970s," in his *Acts of Rebellion.*

_____, "The Ghosts of 9-1-1: Reflections on History, Justice and Roosting Chickens," in his *On the Justice of Roosting Chickens.*

_____, "Genocide: Toward a Functional Definition," in Friedrichs, *State Crime.*

_____, "Denials of the Holocaust," in Charny, *Encyclopedia of Genocide.*

_____, "Denials of the Genocides of Non-Jewish Peoples in the Holocaust," in Charny, *Encyclopedia of Genocide.*

_____, "Genocide of South American Indians," in Charny, *Encyclopedia of Genocide.*

_____, "Genocide of Indians in the Caribbean, Mexico and Central America," in Charny, *Encyclopedia of Genocide.*

_____, "Genocide of Indians of the United States" in Charny, *Encyclopedia of Genocide.*

_____, "Genocide of Canadian Indians," in Charny, *Encyclopedia of Genocide.*

_____, "Kizhiibaabinesik: A Bright Star, She Burned Too Briefly," in Kelly, *In My Own Voice.*

Collier, John, "The Indian Bureau's Record," *The Nation,* Oct. 5, 1932.

Crow Dog, Mary, with Richard Erdoes, "Civilize Them with a Stick," in Lobo and Talbot, *Native American Voices*.

Deloria, Vine Jr., "Circling the Same Old Rock," in Churchill, *Marxism and Native Americans*.

Dimsdale, Joel E., "The Coping Behavior of Nazi Concentration Camp Survivors," in his *Survivors, Victims, Perpetrators*.

Dowker, Fay and Glenn Good, "From Alcatraz to Marion to Florence: Control Unit Prisons in the United States," in Churchill and Vander Wall, *Cages of Steel*.

Duran, Bonnie, and Eduardo Duran, "Applied Postcolonial Clinical and Research Strategies," in Battiste, *Reclaiming Indigenous Voice and Vision*.

Duran, Eduardo, Bonnie Duran, Maria Yellow Horse Brave Heart, and Susan Yellow Horse-Davis, "Healing the American Indian Soul Wound," in Danieli, *Multigenerational Legacies of Trauma*.

Elliot, C.A., "Sexually and Physically Abused Native Youth," in Lester, *Suicide '92*.

Fein, Helen, "Scenarios of Genocide: Models of Genocide and Critical Responses," in Charny, *Towards the Understanding and Prevention of Genocide*.

Fish-Murray, Caroline C., Elizabeth V. Koby and Bessel A. van der Kolk, "Evolving Ideas: The Effect of Abuse on Children's Thought," in van der Kolk, *Psychological Trauma*.

Gagné, Marie-Anik, "The Role of Dependency and Colonialism in Generating Trauma in First Nations Citizens: The James Bay Cree," in Danieli, *Multigenerational Legacies of Trauma*.

Goffman, Erving, "The Characteristics of Total Institutions," in Etzioni, *Complex Organizations*.

Goldhagen, Daniel Jonah, "*Modell Bundesrepublik*: National History, Democracy, and Internationalization in Germany," in Shandley, *Unwilling Germans?*

Graham, Dee L., Edna Rawlings and Nelly Rumini, "Survivors of Terror: Battered Women, Hostages, and the Stockholm Syndrome," in Yllo and Bograd, *Feminist Perspectives in Wife Abuse*.

Gramsci, Antonio, "The Southern Question," in his *The Modern Prince and Other Writings*.

Guevara, Ernesto (Ché), "Notes on Man and Socialism in Cuba," in Lavan, *Che Guevara Speaks*.

Hancock, Ian, "Responses to the Porrajmos: The Romani Holocaust," in Rosenbaum, *Is the Holocaust Unique?*

Harff, Barbara. "The Etiology of Genocides," in Wallimann and Dobkowski, *Genocide and the Modern Age*.

Herman, Judith L., and Bessel A. van der Kolk, "Traumatic Antecedents of Borderline Personality Disorder," in van der Kolk, *Psychological Trauma*.

Hill, Leonidas E., "The Trial of Ernst Zundel: Revisionism and the Law in Canada," *Simon Wiesenthal Annual, 1989*.

Holm, Tom, "Politics Came First: A Reflection on Robert K. Thomas and Cherokee History," in Pavlic, *A Good Cherokee, A Good Anthropologist*.

Kahana, Eva, Boaz Kahana, Zev Harel, et al., "Coping with Extreme Trauma," in Wilson, Harel and Kahana, eds., *Human Adaptation to Extreme Stress*.

Katz, Steven T., "The 'Unique' Intentionality of the Holocaust," in his *Post-Holocaust Dialogues*.

Kawash, Samira, "Terrorists and Vampires: Fanon's spectral violence of decolonization," in Alessandrini, *Frantz Fanon*.

Kelly, Lawrence C., "Charles Henry Burke," in Kvasnicka and Viola, *The Commissioners of Indian Affairs*.

Korn, Richard, "Effects of Confinement in the HSU," in National Prison Project, *Report on the High Security Unit for Women*.

Krystal, Henry, and William G. Niederman, "Clinical Observations on the Survivor Syndrome," in Krystal, *Massive Psychic Trauma*.

Larson, Janet, "And Then There Were None," *Christian Century*, Jan. 26, 1977.

Lewis, Norman, "The Camp at Cecilio Baez," in Arens, *Genocide in Paraguay*.

Lopate, Phillip, "Resistance to the Holocaust," in Hayes, *Testimony*.

Macaulay, Thomas Babington, "Minute of 2 February 1835 on Indian Education," in *Macaulay: Prose and Poetry*.

Marcuse, Herbert, "Repressive Tolerance," in Wolf, Moore, and Marcuse, *A Critique of Pure Tolerance*.

May, Philip A., "The Epidemiology of Alcohol Abuse among American Indians: The Mythical and Real Properties," in Champagne, *Contemporary Native American Cultural Issues*.

Means, Russell, "The Same Old Song," in Churchill, *Marxism and Native Americans*.

Moisa, Ray, "The BIA Relocation Program," in Lobo and Talbot, *Native American Voices*.

Mooney, James, "The Passing of the Indian," in *Proceedings of the Second Pan American Scientific Congress*.

Morris, Glenn T., "Vine Deloria, Jr., and the Development of a Decolonizing Critique of Indigenous Peoples and International Relations," in Grounds, Tinker, and Wilkins, *Native Voices*.

Moses, Rafael, "Denial in the Political Process," in Edelstein, Nathanson and Stone, *Denial*.

Nader, Kathleen Olympia, "Violence: Effects of Parents Previous Trauma on Currently Traumatized Children," in Danieli, *Multigenerational Legacies of Trauma*.

Nagata, Donna K., "Intergenerational Effects of the Japanese American Internment," in Danieli, *Multigenerational Legacies of Trauma*.

Nathanson, Donald L., "Denial, Projection and the Empathic Wall," in Edelstein, Nathanson and Stone, *Denial*.

Niederland, William G., "The Clinical Aftereffects of the Holocaust on Survivors and Their Offspring," in Braham, *Psychological Perspectives on the Holocaust*.

Pratt, Richard Henry, "The Advantages of Mingling Indians with Whites," *Proceedings and Addresses of the National Education Association, 1895* (Washington, D.C.: National Educational Association, 1895).

PeeAce, John, "We Almost Won," in Funk and Lobe, *"…and They Told Us Their Stories."*

Raphael, Beverly, Pat Swan, and Nada Martinek, "Intergenerational Aspects of Trauma for Australian Aboriginal People," in Danieli, *Multigenerational Legacies of Trauma*.

Rose, Wendy, "The Great Pretenders: Further Reflections on Whiteshamanism," in Jaimes, *State of Native America*.

Ross, William G., "RICO," in Hall, *Oxford Companion to American Law*.

Russel, Axel, "Late Effects: Influence on the Children of the Concentration Camp Survivor," in Dimsdale, *Survivors, Victims, Perpetrators*.

Ryan, Mike, "Solitude as Counterinsurgency: The U.S. Isolation Model of Political Incarceration," in Churchill and Vander Wall, *Cages of Steel*.

Sano, Fukoka, "BoP Overseer: A Glimpse of J. Michael Quinlan," in Churchill and Vander Wall, *Cages of Steel*.

Sartre, Jean-Paul, "A Victory," in his *Colonialism and Neocolonialism*.

_____, "Albert Memmi's *The Colonizer and the Colonized*," in his *Colonialism and Neocolonialism*.

_____, "Colonialism is a System," in his *Colonialism and Neocolonialism*.

_____, "Preface to *The Wretched of the Earth*," in his *Colonialism and Neocolonialism*.

_____, "Preface" to Fanon, *The Wretched of the Earth*.

_____, "On Genocide," in his and Arlette El Kaïm Sartre's, *On Genocide*.

_____, "On Genocide," in Coates, Limqueco and Weiss, *Prevent the Crime of Silence*.

Saward, Michael, *Co-optive Politics and State Legitimacy* (Hanover, NH: Dartmouth Group, 1991).

Scott, D.C., "Indian Affairs, 1867-1912," in Shortt and Doughty, *Canada and Its Provinces*.

Smith, Roger W., "Human Destructiveness and Politics: The Twentieth Century as an Age of Genocide," in Wallimann and Dobkowski, *Genocide and the Modern Age*.

Solkoff, Norman, "The Holocaust: Survivors and Their Children," in Basoglu, *Torture and Its Consequences*.

Stanley, Samuel, "Staying the Course: Action and Reflection in the Career of Robert K. Thomas," in Pavlic, *A Good Cherokee, A Good Anthropologist*.

Stannard, David E., "Uniqueness as Denial: The Politics of Holocaust Scholarship," in Rosenbaum, *Is the Holocaust Unique?*

Strentz, Thomas, "The Stockholm Syndrome: Law Enforcement Policy and Victim Behavior," in Ochberg and Soskis, *Victims of Terrorism*.

Symonds, Martin, "Victim Responses to Terror: Understanding and Treatment," in Ochberg and Soskis, *Victims of Terrorism*.

Bessel A. van der Kolk, Bessel A., "The Body Keeps Score: Approaches to the Psychobiology of Post Traumatic Stress Disorder," in van der Kolk, McFarlane, and Weisaeth, *Traumatic Stress*.

Tinker, George, "Spirituality, Native American Personhood, Sovereignty and Solidarity," in Abraham and Mbuy-Beya, *Spirituality in the Third World*.

Whitt, Laurie Anne, "Cultural Imperialism and the Marketing of Native America," in Champagne, *Contemporary Native American Cultural Issues*.

Wilson, Bill, "Aboriginal Rights: A Non-Status Indian View," in Boldt and Long, *The Quest for Justice*.

Wright, Quincy, "The Law of the Nuremberg Tribunal, Part II," in Baird, *From Nuremberg to My Lai*.

Wurmser, Léon, "Cultural Paradigms of Denial," in Edelstein, Nathanson and Stone, *Denial*.

Articles

Adams, Ian, "The Indians: An Abandoned and Dispossessed People," *Weekend Magazine*, July 31, 1965.

_____, "The Lonely Death of Charlie Wenjack," *Maclean's Magazine*, Feb. 1967.

Agger, Inger, and Soren B. Jensen, "Testimony as Ritual and Evidence in Psychotherapy for Political Refugees," *Journal of Traumatic Stress*, No. 3, 1990.

Ah-nen-la-de-ni (Daniel LaFrance), "An Indian Boy's Story," *The Independent*, July 30, 1903.

Alexander, Edward, "Stealing the Holocaust," *Midstream*, Vol. 26, No. 9, Nov. 1980. Dadrian, Vahakn N., "A Typology of Genocide," *International Review of Modern Sociology*, No. 5, Fall 1975.

Bennett, Paul W., "Turning 'Bad Boys' into 'Good Citizens': The Reforming Impulse of Toronto's Industrial Schools Movement, 1883-1920," *Ontario History*, Vol. 78, No. 3, 1986.

Brinkley, Joel, "American Indians Say Government Has Cheated Them Out of Billions," *New York Times*, Jan. 7, 2003.

Bryer, Jeffrey, et al., "Childhood Sexual and Physical Abuse as Factors in Adult Psychiatric Illness," *American Journal of Psychiatry*, No. 148, 1987.

Bryer, J.B., B.A. Nelson, J.B. Miller and P.A. Krol, "Childhood Physical and Sexual Abuse as Factors in Adult Psychiatric Illness," *American Journal of Psychiatry*, No. 144, 1987.

Bull, Linda R., "Indian Residential Schooling: The Native Perspective," *Canadian Journal of Native Education*, No. 18 (supplement), 1991.

Burgess, Ann W., and Lynda L. Holmstrom, "Rape Trauma Syndrome," *American Journal of Psychiatry*, No. 131, 1974; 1986.

Charny, Israel W., "'Innocent Denials' of Known Genocides: A Further Contribution to a Psychology of Genocide Denial (Revisionism)," *Internet on the Holocaust and Genocide*, No. 46, Sept. 1993.

Cienfuegos, A.J., and C. Monelli, "The Testimony of Political Repression as a Therapeutic Instrument," *American Journal of Orthopsychiatry*, No. 53, 1983.

Cleaver, Eldridge, "Cleaver on Cleaver," *Ramparts*, Dec. 14-28, 1969

Collier, John, "The Vanishing American," *Nation*, Jan. 11, 1928.

Connelly, Vera L., "The Cry of a Broken People," *Good Housekeeping*, Feb. 1929.

Chrisjohn, Roland, et al., "Faith Misplaced: The Lasting Effects of Abuse on a First Nations Community," *Canadian Journal of Native Education*, No. 18, 1991.

Churchill, Ward, "American Indian Lands: The Native Ethic and Resource Development," *Environment*, Vol. 28, No. 6, July-Aug. 1986.

_____, "Genocide: Toward a Functional Definition," *Alternatives*, Vol. XI, No. 3, July 1986.

_____, "Forbidding the 'G-Word': Holocaust Denial as Judicial Doctrine in Canada," *Other Voices*, Feb. 2000.

Churchill, Ward, and Winona LaDuke, "Native America: The Political Economy of Radioactive Colonization," *Journal of Ethnic Studies*, Vol. 13, No. 3, Fall 1985.

Curtis, E.S., "Vanishing Indian Types: The Tribes of the Northwest Plains," *Scribner's*, June 1906.

Davies, Alan T., "The Queen Versus James Keegstra: Reflections on Christian Antisemitism in Canada," *American Journal of Theology and Philosophy*, Vol. 9, Nos. 1-2, 1988.

_____, "A Tale of Two Trials: Antisemitism in Canada," *Holocaust and Genocide Studies*, Vol. 4, 1989.

Dillingham, Brint, "Indian Women and IHS Sterilization Practices," *American Indian Journal*, Vol. 3, No. 1, Jan. 1977.

Draper, William R., "The Last of the Red Race," *Cosmopolitan*, Jan. 1902.

Eaton, W.W., J.J. Sigal, and M. Weinfeld, "Impairment in Holocaust Survivors After 33 Years: Data from an Unbiased Community Sample," *American Journal of Psychiatry*, No. 139, 1982.

Elliot, Stanton, "The End of the Trail," *Overland Monthly*, July 1915.

Fein, Helen, "Genocide: A Sociological Perspective," *Current Sociology*, Vol. 38, No. 1, 1990.

Flower, B.O., "An Interesting Representative of a Vanishing Race," *Arena*, July 1896.

Green, A.H., "Dimensions of Psychological Trauma in Abused Children," *Journal of the American Association of Child Psychiatry*, No. 22, 1983.

Green, Rayna, "The Pocahontas Perplex: The Image of Indian Women in American Culture," *Massachusetts Review*, Vol. 16, No. 4, 1975.

Greenawalt, Alexander K.A., "Rethinking Genocidal Intent: The Case for a Knowledge-Based Interpretation," *Columbia Law Review*, Dec. 1999.

Grinstead, E.P., "The Value of Military Drills," *Native American*, Mar. 21, 1914.

Guevara, Ernest (Ché), "El socialismo y el hombre en Cuba," *Marcha*, Mar. 12, 1965.

Gundlach, James H., Nelson P. Reid and Alden E. Roberts, "Native American Migration and Relocation," *Pacific Sociological Review*, No. 21, 1978.

Haley, Sarah, "The Vietnam Veteran and His Preschool Child: Child-Rearing as a Delayed Stress in Combat Veterans," *Journal of Psychotherapy*, No. 4, 1983.

Harff, Barbara, and Ted Gurr, "Toward an Empirical Theory of Genocide and Politicide: Identification and Measurement of Cases Since 1945," *International Studies Quarterly*, Vol. 32, No. 3, Sept. 1988.

Harper, Allan G., "Canada's Indian Administration: Basic Concepts and Objectives," *American Indigena*, Vol. 5, No. 2, 1945.

Harvey, Charles M., "The Last Race Rally of Indians," *World's Work*, May 1904.

Hauptman, Laurence, "Mythologizing Westward Expansion: Schoolbooks and the Image of the American Frontier Before Turner," *Western Historical Quarterly*, No. 8, July 1977.

_____, "Westward Course of Expansion: Geography Schoolbooks and Manifest Destiny," *Historian*, No. 40, May 1978.

Havighurst, Robert J., "The Extent and Significance of Suicide among American Indians Today," *Mental Health*, No. 55, 1971.

Hayner, Priscilla B., "Fifteen Truth Commissions—1974-1994: A Comparative Study," *Human Rights Quarterly*, No. 16, 1994.

Herman, Judith L., Diana E.H. Russell and Karen Trocki, "Long-Term Effects of Incestuous Abuse in Childhood," *American Journal of Psychiatry*, No. 143, 1986.

Higginson, Ella, "The Vanishing Race," *Red Man*, Feb. 1916.

Hormack, Vicki, "Residential schools planted seed of violence, instructor says," *Opasquia Times*, Nov. 23, 1990.

Hrdlicka, Ales, "The Vanishing Indian," *Science*, No. 46, 1917.

Huttenbach, Henry, "Locating the Holocaust on the Genocide Spectrum: Towards a Methodology of Definition and Categorization," *Holocaust and Genocide Studies*, Vol. 3, No. 3, 1988.

Ing, N. Roselyn, "The Effects of Boarding Schools on Native Child-Rearing Practices," *Canadian Journal of Native Education*, No. 18 (supplement), 1991.

Jaffe, Ruth, "Dissociative Phenomena in Former Concentration Camp Inmates," *International Journal of Psycho-Analysis*, No. 49, 1968.

Kaufman, Arthur, "Gasoline Sniffing among Children in a Pueblo Village," *Pediatrics*, No. 51, 1973.

Kaye, Mike, "The Role of Truth Commissions in the Search for Justice, Reconciliation and Democratization: The Salvadoran and Honduran Cases," *Journal of Latin American Studies*, No. 29, Oct. 1997.

Kennedy, J. Michael, "Truth and Consequences on the Reservation," *Los Angeles Times Magazine*, July 7, 2002.

Kinzie, J.D., R.H. Frederickson, R. Ben, et al., "PTSD Among Survivors of Cambodian Concentration Camps," *American Journal of Psychiatry*, No. 141, 1984.

Kluznik, J.C., N. Speed, C. Van Valkenberg, et al., "Forty Year Follow Up of U.S. Prisoners of War," *American Journal of Psychiatry*, No. 143, 1986.

LaDuke, Winona, and Ward Churchill, "Radioactive Colonization and Native Americans," *Socialist Review*, No. 81, May 1985.

LaFarge, Oliver, "Revolution with Reservations," *New Republic*, Oct. 9, 1935.

Laufer, R.S., E. Brett and M.S. Gallops, "Symptom Patterns Associated with Post-Traumatic Stress Disorder among Vietnam War Veterans Exposed to War Trauma," *American Journal of Psychiatry*, No. 142, 1985.

Lippman, M., "The Drafting of the 1948 Convention on the Prevention and Punishment of Genocide," *Boston University International Law Journal*, No. 3, 1984.

Lister, Eric, "Forced Silence: A Neglected Dimension of Trauma," *American Journal of Psychiatry*, No. 139, 1982.

Lupton, L.F.S., "The Extermination of the Beothuks of Newfoundland," *Canadian Historical Review*, Vol. 58, No. 2, 1977.

Marcus, Andrew, "Genocide in Australia," *Aboriginal History*, Vol. 25, 2001.

Marks-Jarvis, Gail, "The Fate of the Indian," *National Catholic Reporter*, May 27, 1977.

May, Frederick A., "The Epidemiology of Alcohol Abuse among American Indians: Mythical and Real Properties," *American Indian Culture and Research Journal*, Vol. 18, No. 2, 1994.

McCall, Cheryl, "Life on Pine Ridge Bleak," *Colorado Daily*, May 16, 1975.

Morris, B., and R. Groves, "Canada's Forgotten Peoples: The Aboriginal Rights of Metis and Non-Status Peoples," *Law & Anthropology*, No. 2, 1987.

Moshman, David, "Conceptual Restraints on Thinking About Genocide," *Journal of Genocide Research*, Vol. 3, No. 3, 2001.

Murphy, Joseph, "Health Problems of the Indians," *Annals of the Academy of Political Science*, No. 37, Mar. 1911.

Niederman, William G., "Clinical Observations on the 'Survivor Syndrome,'" *International Journal of Psycho-Analysis*, No. 49, 1968.

Nicolosi, Michelle, "'Code of Silence' Among Priests Shields Abusers: Hundreds of Clergy Victims as Children, Many Experts Believe," *Seattle Post Intelligencer*, Sept. 23, 2004.

O'Nell, T.D., "Feeling Worthless," *Culture, Medicine and Psychiatry*, No. 16, 1993.

Papazian, Pierre, "A 'Unique Uniqueness'?" *Midstream*, Vol. 30, No. 4, 1984.

Pollack, V.E., J. Briere and L. Schneider, et al., "Childhood Antecedents of Antisocial Behavior: Parental Alcoholism and Physical Abuse," *American Journal of Psychiatry*, No. 147, 1990.

Remington, Gary, and Brian Hoffman, "Gas Sniffing as Substance Abuse," *Canadian Journal of Psychiatry*, No. 29, 1984.

Rogan, Mary, "Please Take Our Children Away," *New York Times Magazine*, Mar. 4, 2001.

Salmon, Roberto Mario, "The Disease Complaint at Bosque Redondo (1864-1868)," *Indian Historian*, No. 9, 1976.

Schulte-Tenckhoff, Isabelle, "The Irresistible Ascension of the UN Declaration of the Rights of Indigenous Peoples: Stopped Dead in Its Tracks?" *European Review of Native American Studies*, Vol. 9, No. 2, 1995.

Schurz, Carl, "Present Aspects of the Indian Problem," *North American Review*, cxxxiii (July 1881).

Segal, J., E.J. Hunter and Z. Segal, "Universal Consequences of Captivity: Stress Reactions Among Divergent Populations of Prisoners of War and Their Families," *International Journal of Social Science*, No. 28, 1976.

Smith, Roger W., Eric Markusen, and Robert Jay Lifton, "Professional Ethics and the Denial of the Armenian Genocide," *Holocaust and Genocide Studies*, No. 9, 1995.

Snell, J.E., R.J. Rosenwald, and A. Robey, "The Wife-Beater's Wife," *Archives of General Psychiatry*, No. 11, 1964.

Sorkin, Alan L., "The Economic and Social Status of the American Indian, 1940-1970," *Nebraska Journal of Economics*, No. 22, Spring 1974.

Stephon, Richard J., "Richard Henry Pratt and His Indians," *Journal of Ethnic Studies*, No. 15, Summer 1987.

Strickland, Rennard, "Indian Law and the Miner's Canary: The Signs of Poison Gas," *Cleveland State Law Review*, No. 39, 1991.

Terr, Lenore C., "Childhood Traumas: An Overview and Outline," *American Journal of Psychiatry*, No. 148, 1991.

Thomas, Robert K., "Colonialism: Classic and Internal," *New University Thought*, Vol. 4, No. 4, Winter 1966-67.

Thornton, Russell, "American Indian Historical Demography: A Review Essay with Suggestions for the Future," *American Indian Culture and Research Journal*, No. 3, 1979.

Trennert, Robert A. Jr., "Educating Indian Girls at Nonreservation Boarding Schools, 1878-1920," *Western Historical Quarterly*, Vol. 13, No. 3, 1982.

_____, "Corporal Punishment and the Politics of Indian Reform," *History of Education Quarterly*, Vol. 29, No. 4, 1989.

Ward, J.A., and Joseph Fox, "A Suicide Epidemic on an Indian Reserve," *Canadian Psychiatric Association Journal*, Mo. 22, 1977.

Westermeyer, Joseph, "The Drunken Indian: Myths and Realities," *Psychiatric Annals*, No. 4, 1974.

Williams, Ethel J., "Too Little Land, Too Many Heirs: The Indian Heirship Land Problem," *Washington Law Review*, No. 46, 1971.

Official Documents (Canada)

Bryce, P.H., *Report on the Indian Schools of Manitoba and the Northwest Territories* (Ottawa: Government Printing Bureau, 1907).

Canadian Civil Liberties Association, *Brief to the Senate Standing Committee on Civil and Constitutional Affairs on Hate Propaganda* (Ottawa: Supplies and Services, Apr. 22, 1952).

Davin, Nicholas F., *Report on Industrial Schools for Indians and Halfbreeds* (Ottawa: Dept. of Indian Affairs, Mar. 14, 1879).

Dept. of External Affairs, Canada, *Canada and the United Nations* (Ottawa: Supplies and Services, 1948).

Dept. of Indian Affairs, Canada, *Annual Report* (Ottawa: Supplies and Services, 1889).

_____, *Canada: Indian Treaties and Surrenders from 1680 to 1890*, 3 vols. (Ottawa: Queen's Printer, 1891).

_____, *Annual Report* (Ottawa: Supplies and Services, 1895).

_____, "Report of the Deputy Superintendent General," in *Canada, Sessional Papers (No. 27), 1901: Report of the Department of Indian Affairs for 1900* (Ottawa: Supplies and Services, 1901).

_____, Dept. of Indian Affairs, *Annual Reports* (Ottawa: Supplies and Services, 1915).

Dept. of Indian and Northern Affairs, Canada, *Indian Acts and Amendments, 1868-1950* (Ottawa: Treaties and Historical Research Center, 1981).

House of Commons, Canada, *Report of the Special Committee on Hate Propaganda in Canada* (Ottawa: Supplies and Services, 1952).

_____, *Report of the Special Committee of the House of Commons on Indian Self-Government* (Ottawa: Supplies and Services, 1983).

Royal Commission on Aboriginal Peoples, *Looking Forward, Looking Back: Report of the Royal Commission on Aboriginal Peoples, Vol. 1* (Ottawa: Canada Communications Group, 1996).

_____, *Restructuring the Relationship: Report of the Royal Commission on Aboriginal Peoples, Vol. 2* (Ottawa: Canada Communications Group, 1996).

_____, *Bridging the Cultural Divide: Aboriginal People and Criminal Justice in Canada: Report of the Royal Commission on Aboriginal Peoples, Vol. 3* (Ottawa: Canada Communications Group, 1996).

_____, *Perspectives on Realities: Report of the Royal Commission on Aboriginal Peoples, Vol. 4* (Ottawa: Canada Communications Group, 1996).

_____, *Renewal: A Twenty Year Commitment: Report of the Royal Commission on Aboriginal Peoples, Vol. 5* (Ottawa: Canada Communications Group, 1996).

Stewart, Jane, *Gathering Strength: Canada's Aboriginal Action Plan* (Ottawa: Dept. of Indian and Northern Affairs, 1998).

Official Documents (Organization of American States)

OAS Assembly, American Declaration on the Rights and Duties of Man (O.A.S. Off. Rec. OEA/Ser. L/V/L4 Rev. (1965)).

_____, American Declaration on Human Rights (O.A.S. Treaty Ser. No. 36, O.A.S. Off. Rec. OEA/Ser. L/V/II.23 doc. 21 rev. 6 (1979), *reprinted in* 9 I.L.M. 673 (1970)).

Official Documents (United Nations)

International Court of Justice, "Reservations to the Convention on Punishment and Prevention of Genocide," *ICJ Reports of Judgments, Advisory Opinions and Orders* (The Hague: ICJ, 1951).

U.N. General Assembly, United Nations Charter (59 Stat. 1031; T.S. No. 993, 3 Bevans 1153, 1976 Y.B.U.N. 1043 (1945)).

_____, Statute of the International Court of Justice (59 Stat. 1031, T.S. No. 993, 3 Bevans 1153, 1976 Y.B.U.N. 1052 (1945).

_____, Convention on Punishment and Prevention of the Crime of Genocide (U.N. GAOR Res. 260A(III), (1948)).

_____, Universal Declaration of Human Rights (U.N.G.A. Res. 217 A (III), U.N. Doc. A/810, at 71 (1949)).

_____, Declaration on the Granting of Independence to Colonial Countries and Peoples (U.N.G.A. Res. 1514 (XV), 15 U.N. GAOR, Supp. (No. 16) 66, U.N. Doc. A/4684 (1961)).

_____, International Convention on the Elimination of All Forms of Racial Discrimination (660 U.N.T.S. 195, *reprinted in* 5 I.L.M. 352 (1966)).

_____, International Covenant on Economic, Social and Cultural Rights (U.N.G.A. Res. 2200 (XXI), 21 U.N. GAOR, Supp. (No. 16) 49, U.N. Doc. A/6316 (1967), *reprinted in* 6 I.L.M. 360 (1967)).

_____, Vienna Convention on the Law of Treaties (U.N. Doc. A/CONF.39/27 at 289 (1969), 1155 U.N.T.S. 331, *reprinted in* 8 I.L.M. 679 (1969)).

_____, Universal Declaration on the Eradication of Hunger and Malnutrition (U.N. Doc. E/Conf. 65/20, Ch. IV (1974)).

_____, Declaration on the Elimination of All Forms of Intolerance and of Discrimination Based on Religion or Belief (U.N.G.A. Res. 36/55, 36 U.N. GAOR, Supp. (No. 51) 171, U.N. Doc. A/36/684 (1981), *reprinted in* 21 I.L.M. 205 (1982)).

_____, Convention Against Torture and Other Cruel or Degrading Treatment or Punishment (U.N.G.A. Res. 39/46 Annex, 39 U.N. GAOR, Supp. (No. 51) 197, U.N. Doc. E/CN.4/1984/72, Annex (1984), *reprinted in* I.L.M. 1027 (1984)).

_____, the International Covenant on Civil and Political Rights (U.N.G.A. Res. 2200 (XXI), 21 U.N. GAOR, Supp. (No. 16) 52, U.N. Doc. A/6316 (1967), *reprinted in* 6 I.L.M. 368 (1967)).

_____, Declaration on the Right to Development (U.N.G.A. Res. 41/128, 41 U.N. GAOR, Supp. (No. 53) U.N. Doc. A/41/925 (1986)).

_____, Declaration on the Right to Development (U.N.G.A. Res. 41/128, 41 U.N. GAOR, Supp. (No. 53) U.N. Doc. A/41/925 (1986)).

_____, Convention on the Rights of the Child (U.N.G.A. Res. 44/25, Annex, 44 U.N. GAOR, Supp. (No.49) at 167, U.N. Doc. A/RES/44/25 (1989), *reprinted in* 28 I.L.M. 1457 (1989)).

U.N. Secretariat, *Multilateral Treaties Deposited with the Secretary General: Status as of 31 December 1989* (St/Leg/Ser. E/8 97-98 (1990)).

Official Documents (United States)

Commission on Wartime Relocation and Internment of Civilians, *Personal Justice Denied: Report of the Commission on Wartime Relocation and Internment of Civilians* (Seattle: University of Washington Press, 1982).

Groves, Edna, "Report on the Flandreau Indian School" (Washington, D.C.: Bureau of Indian Affairs [NA, RG 75], May 12, 1925).

National Institute of Education, *Conference on the Educational and Occupational Needs of American Indian Women, October 1976* (Washington, D.C.: U.S. Dept. of Education, Off. of Educational Research and Improvement, 1980).

U.S. Bureau of the Census, *Fifteenth Census of the United States, 1930: The Indian Population of the United States and Alaska* (Washington, D.C.: U.S. Government Printing Office, 1937).

U.S. Dept. of Health and Human Services, Indian Health Service, *A Roundtable Conference on Dysfunctional Behavior and Its Impact on Indian Health* (Albuquerque & Washington, D.C.: Kauffman/Public Health Service, 1991).

_____, *Trends in Indian Health* (Washington, D.C.: Public Health Service, 1995).

U.S. Dept. of Health, Education and Welfare, *A Study of Selected Socio-Economic Characteristics of Ethnic Minorities Based on the 1970 Census, Vol. 3: American Indians* (Washington, D.C.: U.S. Government Printing Office, 1974).

U.S. Dept. of Interior, Bureau of Indian Affairs, *Annual Report of the Commissioner of Indian Affairs* (Washington, D.C. 34th Cong., 1st Sess., 1856).

_____, *Annual Report of the Commissioner of Indian Affairs* (Washington, D.C.: 43rd Cong., 1st Sess., 1873).

_____, *Annual Report of the Commissioner of Indian Affairs* (Washington, D.C.: 49th Cong., 2nd Sess., 1886).

_____, *Annual Report of the Commissioner of Indian Affairs* (Washington, D.C.: 50th Cong., 1st Sess., 1888).

_____, *Annual Report of the Commissioner of Indian Affairs* (Washington, D.C.: 51st Cong., 2nd Sess., 1891).

_____, *Annual Report of the Commissioner of Indian Affairs* (Washington, D.C.: 52nd Cong., 1st Sess., 1892).

_____, *Annual Report of the Commissioner of Indian Affairs* (Washington, D.C.: 54th Cong., 2nd Sess., 1897).

_____, *Annual Report of the Commissioner of Indian Affairs* (Washington, D.C.: 55th Cong., 2nd Sess., 1898).

_____, *Education Circular No. 130* (Washington, D.C.: Office of Indian Affairs, Jan. 15, 1906).

_____, *Rules for the Indian School Service* (Washington, D.C.: U.S. Dept. of Interior, 1898).

U.S. Dept. of State, *Restatement (Third) of the Foreign Relations Law of the United States* (Washington, D.C.: U.S. Dept. of State, 1987).

U.S. Dept. of War, Bureau of Indian Affairs, *Annual Report of the Commissioner of Indian Affairs* (Washington, D.C.: 37th Cong., 3rd Sess., 1863).

U.S. Public Health Service, *Contagious and Infectious Diseases Among the Indians* (Washington, D.C.: 63rd Cong., 1st Sess., [Senate Doc. 1038] 1913).

U.S. Senate, Committee on Indian Affairs, *Survey of Conditions of the Indian in the United States* (Washington, D.C.: 71st Cong., 1st Sess., 1929).

Wilbur, Ray Lyman, and William A. DuPuy, *Conservation in the Department of Interior* (Washington, D.C.: U.S. Dept. of Interior, 1931).

Official Documents (Other)

Foreign Office of Belgium, *The Sacred Mission of Civilization: To Which Peoples Should the Benefit be Extended?* (New York: Belgian Government Information Center, 1953).

Theses and Dissertations

Bonnell, Sonciray, *Chemawa Indian Boarding School: The First One Hundred Years, 1880-1980* (Hanover, NH: MA thesis, Dartmouth College, 1997).

Jerrill, Robin, "Women and Children First: The Forced Sterilization of American Indian Women" (Wellesley, MA: undergraduate honors thesis, Wellesley College, 1988).

Kizer, William, "History of the Flandreau Indian School, Flandreau, South Dakota" (Vermillion: MA thesis, University of South Dakota, 1940).

Oestreicher, Pamela Holco, *On the White Man's Road? Acculturation and the Fort Marion Southern Plains Prisoners* (Lansing: Ph.D. dissertation, Michigan State University, 1981).

Putney, Diane, *Fighting the Scourge: American Indian Morbidity and Federal Policy, 1897-1928* (Marquette, MI: Ph.D. dissertation, Marquette University, 1980).

Index

Darlington (Cheyenne): 72*p*
Dole, William P.: 21
Dougherty, Glen: 64, 107*n*443
Douglas, William Gareth: 107*n*445
Drost, Pieter N.: 85*n*39
Dunn, Willie: ix
Duran, Jacob: 103*n*350
Dutch (Netherlands; Holland): 5; reject purported U.S. ratification of the Genocide Convention: 9

E

ECOSOC, *see* United Nations
Eichmann, Adolf: 83*n*2
Encyclopedia of Genocide: xliv
England/English: inculcation of epidemics among Indians by: 34; *also see* Britain/British; United Kingdom (U.K.)
ethnocide: as synonym for genocide: 7; coinage of term: 7; distortive use of term: xlv, xviii*n*13, 7, 85*n*39
extermination centers: Auschwitz: 5, 97*n*233; distinguished from concentration camps: 97*n*233

F

Fairclaugh, Ellen: 33
Fanon, Frantz: 77; *Wretched of the Earth* authored by: 77
Favel, Blaine: 66
Federation of Saskatchewan Indians: 66
Finland/Fins: rejects purported U.S. ratification of the Genocide Convention: 9
Fort Hall Reservation: 17
Fort Marion (FL): 15*p*; army prison at: 14
Fort Peck Reservation: 17
Fraenkel, Ernst: 86*n*56
France/French: Holocaust denial statute of: 2; rejects purported U.S. ratification of the Genocide Convention: 9

G

Genocide Convention, *see* Convention on Punishment and Prevention of the Crime of Genocide
genocide: as "denationalization": 4; as "human cancer": 3; as "incomparable crime": 1; biological construction of ("biological genocide"): 4, 6, 7; Canada and: 8-9, 78; coinage of term: xlv, 2; concept of: xliii, 1-8; cultural construction of ("cultural genocide"):xix*n*18, 3-4, 6, 7; definition of:

xlv, 3-8; definitional distortions of: xlv, xviii*n*13, 1-2; denials of: xlvi, xlviii-xix*n*17, xix*n*18, xix*n*19, xix*n*20, 78, 113*n*514; ethnocide as synonym for: xlv, 7; equated to colonialism by Sartre: 77-8; Klan lynchings as: 10; legal definition of: 8; Lemkin's definition of: 3-8; nonhierarchical nature of: 6-7; nonlethal dimensions of: 3-8; neonanazi denials and: 74-5; of American Indians: xlvi, xlviii-xix*n*17, xix*n*18; of Armenians: 2; of Gypsies: 2; of Jews (judeocide): xlvi, xix*n*20, 1; physical construction of ("physical genocide"): 5-6, 7; relationship to killing of: 1, 3, 5-6; scholarship on: xliii-xliv, xlv, 1-3, 78; U.S. and: 9-10, 78; *also see* Convention on Punishment and Prevention of the Crime of Genocide (1948); Lemkin, Raphaël
Germans/Germany: 2, 5, 67; and legacy of concentration camps: 67; "ethnic Germans" and: 5; "genocidal mentality" of: 100*n*293; postwar suicide rate of: 110*n*478; question of collective guilt and: 80, 100*n*292, 116*n*535
Gould, Canon S.: 55
Graham, W.H.: 47, 57, 106*n*410
Gramsci, Antonio: 108*n*457
Grant, Pres. Ulysses S.: 94*n*178
Grant-John, Wendy: 44-5
Gypsies (Sinti and Romani): nazi genocide of: 2; suicide rate of, under nazis: 110*n*478

H

Hailman, Warren: 50
Harper, Allan: 18
Harvard University: 74
Havighurst, Robert: 60
Hearst, Patty: 109*n*472
Hébert, Yves: 50
Herman, Dr. Judith: 74
Hines, Charlie: 58
Hitler, Adolf: xlvi, 2, 92*n*134; and extermination of European Jews; 106*n*418
Hogarth, Judge Douglas: 62
Holland, *see* Dutch
Horowitz, Irving Louis: 3
Hugonard, Fr.: 37

I

imperialism: xix*n*21; anti-imperialism and: 79-82; *also see* colonialism/colonization
India/(East) Indians: 76

individual schools (U.S.): Albuquerque Indian School: 25, 48, 54; Anadarko ndian Boarding School: 59; Carlisle Indian Industrial School: 13, 24, 26*p*, 34-5, 44, 45*p*, 46, 53*p*, 59, 72; Chemewa Indian School: 35, 98*n*250; Cheyenne River Indian Boarding School: 59; Chilocco Indian Agricultural School: 24, 47, 48, 59, 101*n*316; Crow Creek Indian School: 35, 101*n*310; Flandreau Indian School: 31, 46, 51, 98*n*250; Fort Lewis Indian School: 24; Fort Shaw Indian School: 24; Fort Sill Indian School: 52; Fort Stevenson Indian Boarding School: 49, 102*n*327, 105*n*378; Genoa Indian Industrial School: 35, 47, 48; Grand Junction Indian Boarding School: 59; Haskell Institute (Haskell Indian School): 25, 32, 35, 36, 45, 47, 51*p*, 56*p*, 96*n*214; Phoenix Indian Industrial School: xixn18, 25, 26*p*, 28*p*, 37, 54, 59, 61, 103*n*350, 104*n*358, 108*n*460; Rice Indian School: 95*n*198; Riverside Indian School: 98*n*250; Santa Fe Indian School: 25, 98*n*250; Santee Indian Boarding School: 35; Sequoia Indian Boarding School: 98*n*250; Sherman Institute: 25*p*, 26, 46*p*, 47, 98*n*250; St. Francis Indian Boarding School: 54; Walker River Agency Indian School: 52; Wittenberg Indian Boarding School: 59

Indonesia/Indonesians: 83*n*2

Ing, N. Roselyn: 110*n*476

International Court of Justice ("World Court"): 80

International Criminal Court: 80, 85-6*n*44

International League for the Rights of Man: 84*n*11

Iraq/Iraqis: 86*n*44

Ireland/Irish: compulsory education imposed upon: 76; rejects purported U.S. ratification of the Genocide Convention: 9

Israel/Israelis: 2; refuses International Criminal Court jurisdiction: 86*n*44

Italy/Italians: rejects purported U.S. ratification of the Genocide Convention: 9

J

Jaspers, Karl: 116*n*535; *The Question of German Guilt* authored by: 80

Jews/Judaism: 44, 94*n*176; denial of genocide against: xlvi, xixn20; effects of "ghettoization" upon: 102*n*329; exclusivist scholarship of: 1-2; "Good Germans" and: 100*n*292; 100*n*293; Holocaust scholarship

of: xliii; judeocide committed against: xlvi, xixn20, 1, 84*n*14, 102*n*329, 105*n*405, 106*n*418; neonazi Holocaust denial and: 74-5; suicide rate of, under nazis: 110*n*478

Jones, William A.: 14, 18

Justin, Maurice: 58

K

Kansas State Militia: 25

Khmer Rouge: 83*n*2

Kissiti, Richard: 53*p*

Korn, Dr. Richard: 70

Ku Klux Klan: as criminal organization: 10; lynchings of African Americans by: 10

Kuper, Leo: xlvi, 2

L

LaFarge, Oliver: 44

La Fleshe, Francis: 103*n*351

Laird, David: 99*n*271

Lemkin, Raphaël: 12, 78; coins term "ethnocide": 7; coins term "genocide": xlv, 2; defines term "genocide": 3-8; International Criminal Court proposal of: 85*n*44; retained by UN to draft Genocide Convention: 5, 85*n*31; "Secretariat's Draft" produced by: 5-6; *also see* Convention on Punishment and Prevention of the Crime of Genocide (1948)

Leonard, Mary ("Wikew"; "the ogre"): 55

Leupp, Francis: 12

Libya/Libyans: 86*n*44

Lifton, Robert J.: 2

Little bear, Pius: 59

Luxemburg: 5

M

MacPherson, Judge J.T.: *Daishowa* opinion of: xixn19

Maczynski, Jerzy: 64

Malcolm X: 81

Marcuse, Herbert: 91*n*108

Markusen, Eric: 2

Martin falls Reserve: 58

McCaskill, D.: 50

McConnell, William: 36, 39

McGougall, John: 94*n*181

McIntee, Harold: 64

Meighan, Arthur: 43

Meriam Report: 30

Methodist Church: 94*n*181

Michael, Johnny: 58

Ward Churchill and Coyote ji Jaga, photo by Natsu Taylor Saito.

Ward Churchill (Keetoowah Band Cherokee) is Professor of American Indian Studies and Chair of the Department of Ethnic Studies at the University of Colorado/Boulder. A member of the Leadership Council of the American Indian Movement of Colorado, he is a past National Spokesperson for the Leonard Peltier Defense Committee, delegate to the United Nations Working Group on Indigenous Populations and member of the People's International Tribunal, Hawai'i (1993). An acclaimed public speaker and prolific author, his books are listed at the front of this volume.